Agricola in Scotland

Also by Simon Elliott

Sea Eagles of Empire
Empire State: How the Roman Military Built an Empire
Septimius Severus in Scotland
Roman Legionaries
Ragstone to Riches
Julius Caesar: Rome's Greatest Warlord
Old Testament Warriors
Pertinax: The Son of a Slave Who Became Roman Emperor
Romans at War
Roman Britain's Missing Legion: What Really Happened to IX Hispana?
Roman Conquests: Britain
Alexander vs Caesar: Who Was the Greatest Commander in the Ancient World?
Ancient Greeks at War
Roman Britain's Pirate King
The Legacy of Rome
Great Battles of the Early Roman Empire
Roman Special Forces and Special Ops
Vandal Heaven: Reinterpreting Post-Roman North Africa

Agricola in Scotland

The Northern Campaigns of Roman Britain's Great Warrior Governor

Simon Elliott

Pen & Sword
MILITARY

First published in Great Britain in 2025 by
Pen & Sword Military
An imprint of Pen & Sword Books Limited
Yorkshire – Philadelphia

Copyright © Simon Elliott 2025

ISBN 978 1 39906 828 4

The right of Simon Elliott to be identified as
Author of this Work has been asserted by him in accordance
with the Copyright, Designs and Patents Act 1988.

A CIP catalogue record for this book is
available from the British Library.

All rights reserved. No part of this book may be reproduced, transmitted, downloaded, decompiled or reverse engineered in any form or by any means, electronic or mechanical including photocopying, recording or by any information storage and retrieval system, without permission from the Publisher in writing. NO AI TRAINING: Without in any way limiting the Author's and Publisher's exclusive rights under copyright, any use of this publication to "train" generative artificial intelligence (AI) technologies to generate text is expressly prohibited. The Author and Publisher reserve all rights to license uses of this work for generative AI training and development of machine learning language models.

Typeset by Mac Style
Printed in the UK by CPI Group (UK) Ltd, Croydon, CR0 4YY.

The Publisher's authorised representative in the EU for product safety is Authorised Rep Compliance Ltd., Ground Floor, 71 Lower Baggot Street, Dublin D02 P593, Ireland.
www.arccompliance.com

For a complete list of Pen & Sword titles please contact

PEN & SWORD BOOKS LIMITED
47 Church Street, Barnsley, South Yorkshire, S70 2AS, England
E-mail: enquiries@pen-and-sword.co.uk
Website: www.pen-and-sword.co.uk
or
PEN AND SWORD BOOKS
1950 Lawrence Road, Havertown, PA 19083, USA
E-mail: uspen-and-sword@casematepublishers.com
Website: www.penandswordbooks.com

To my wife Sara, with thanks for everything. Love, support, advice, guidance, kindness, and proofreading! All my love, always!

Contents

List of Maps		viii
List of Illustrations		ix
Introduction		xi
Chapter 1	Early Imperial Rome	1
Chapter 2	Agricola's Army	21
Chapter 3	Roman Britain in the Later First Century AD	35
Chapter 4	Early Life and Career	61
Chapter 5	Return to Britannia	93
Chapter 6	Campaigns in the Far North: AD 79/80	113
Chapter 7	Campaigns in the Far North: AD 81/82	132
Chapter 8	Campaigns in the Far North: AD 83 and Mons Graupius	147
Conclusion		171
Bibliography		182
Index		188

List of Maps

1. Agricola's Campaigns, AD 78–83   xix
2. The Battle of Watling Street   75
3. The Battle of Mons Graupius   151

List of Illustrations

1. Agricola as governor in Britannia. (© *Graham Sumner*)
2. Marcus Favonius Facilis, *legio* XX *Valeria Victrix* centurion based in Colchester, wearing finely decorated *lorica hamata* chainmail. (© *Graham Sumner*)
3. Veteran legionary of *legio* II *Augusta* wearing *lorica segmentata* and imperial Gallic helmet. (© *Graham Sumner*)
4. Auxiliary *eques* on campaign in Britain. (© *Graham Sumner*)
5. Agricola and Tacitus on the Great Hall frieze of Roman generals and emperors in National Galleries of Scotland. (*Public domain*)
6. Statue of Agricola in his birthplace in Fréjus (Roman *Forum Julii*) in modern France. (*Rafał Klisowski via Wikimedia Commons/CC BY-SA 3.0*)
7. Domitian, third, last and least successful of the Flavian emperors. Assassinated in AD 96. (*Castro Pretorio via Wikimedia Commons/CC BY-SA 4.0*)
8. Vespasian, founder of the Flavian dynasty. (*Carole Raddato via Wikimedia Commons/CC BY-SA 2.0*)
9. Fragments of a dedicatory inscription found near the *forum* of *Verulamium*, modern St Albans. (*Carole Raddato via Wikimedia Commons/CC BY-SA 2.0*)
10. *Mamucium*, the Flavian vexillation fort founded by Agricola. Together with its *vicus*, today it has grown into mighty Manchester. (*Author's copyright*)
11. Fine tombstone of a Roman cavalry *eques* from Corbridge (Roman *Coria*), now in the Tullie House Museum and Art Gallery, Carlisle. (*Author's copyright*)
12. A full legion on the march, with senior officers and standard-bearers to the fore. Recreated in Lincoln Museum. (*Author's copyright*)

13. The Colosseum. The ultimate monument to the Flavian dynasty in Rome. (*Author's copyright*)
14. *Forum*, Pompeii. Looking north towards mighty Vesuvius. (*Author's copyright*)
15. Statue of Mars, legionary fortress, York (Roman *Eboracum*). Founded by the IXth legion under the governor Cerialis in his conquest of Brigantian territory. (*Author's copyright*)
16. Principate legionary, resplendent in *lorica segmentata*, imperial Gallic helmet and *scutum*, wielding a *gladius hispaniensis*. (*Painted by the author*)
17. Principate legionary, with *singulum* military belt with *baltea* straps covering the groin area. (*Painted by the author*)
18. Highly decorated Roman centurion. (*Painted by the author*)
19. Legionary *scorpio* bolt-shooter, used to great effect by Agricola in his campaigns in the far north of Britain. (*Painted by the author*)
20. Three veteran Roman legionaries carrying much of their kit, depicted in a commemorative slab found at the Roman Antonine Wall fort at Croy Hill. (*Author's copyright*)
21. The price of imperial failure in the AD 69 'Year of the Four Emperors'. Vandalised silver bust of Galba. (*Author's copyright*)
22. An incredible survival from the classical world. An intact Roman legionary *scutum*, found at Dura-Europus on the eastern frontier. (*Author's copyright*)
23. An almost complete Roman legionary's *lorica segmentata* cuirass. Found at the site of the AD 9 Varian Disaster in the Teutoburg Forest, Germany. (*Author's copyright*)
24. The *forum Romanum*, centre of political life in ancient Rome. (*Author's copyright*)
25. The Cramond Lioness, found at the Roman fort and military harbour on the Forth. (*Author's copyright*)
26. Statue of Gnaeus Julius Agricola, on the terrace above the Great Bath in the Roman Baths, Bath, Somerset. (*Author's copyright*)
27. Fine example of an imperial Gallic legionary helmet. (*Author's copyright*)

Introduction

Famous men have from time immemorial had their life stories told, and even our generation, with all its indifference to the present, has not quite abandoned the practice; outstanding personalities still win occasional triumph over that fault common to small and great states alike, ignorant hostility to merit.

Here we are first introduced to Gnaeus Julius Agricola, greatest of the warrior governors of Roman Britain, in a passage written by his son-in-law Publius Cornelius Tacitus (*The Agricola*, 1.1).

Agricola was a Roman military leader *par excellence*, with a career defined by superlatives. First, and most importantly, he was the only Roman who could claim to have conquered the whole main island of Britain, if only briefly. As I will set out, this was the most fantastical of achievements, accomplished against enormous odds at the far northwestern extremity of the European landmass. Other Romans tried, notably Septimius Severus in his AD 209 and AD 210 campaigns, but all ultimately failed. Thus, Agricola's achievement here is truly unique, and a standout event in British history.

Second, he is the only Roman senator known to have served all three military ranks on the *cursus honorum* Roman aristocratic career path in the same province, this being Britain. Thus, at various times there, he was a military tribune, a *legatus legionis* in charge of a legion, and the governor. Further, the seven years he served as governor in Britain was longer than any other Roman governor in the province.

Third, while in Britain he fought at two of the most important battles in British history. The first was in the final defeat of Boudicca in AD 60/61 as a junior officer, this under another superlative warrior governor, Gaius Suetonius Paulinus. The second was as governor when leading the Roman forces that defeated Calgacus and the Caledonians at Mons Graupius in AD 83.

Agricola is one of the better-known figures in the history of Roman Britain, largely through the writings of Tacitus. We can still see him across the country today, largely through the cultural appropriation of the Roman world by Victorian elites keen to promote their own imperial project. Thus, visitors to Bath will see Agricola's 1.5m high statue on the walkway overlooking the Great Bath, alongside those of other notable Romans in Britain's history including Caesar, Claudius, Constantine, Hadrian and Paulinus. The originals were all created by sculptor G.A. Lawson for the grand public opening of the baths in 1897. Meanwhile, in Manchester Town Hall can be found another statue of Agricola, this above the main entrance to this magnificent Neo-Gothic celebration of the city's growing importance, built between 1868 and 1877. Inside, in the Great Hall, the warrior governor appears as one of twelve magnificent murals painted by Ford Maddox Brown. Completed in 1893, these show defining moments in Manchester's history. Both representations of Agricola commemorate the founding of the Roman fort and *vicus* of *Mamucium* in the mid-Flavian period while he was campaigning in the region against the native Brigantes. Additionally, visitors to National Galleries Scotland will see in the Great Hall a frieze of Roman generals and emperors with relevance to Britain created by William Brassey Hole in 1897. Here, Agricola, Tacitus and Calgacus are prominent to the right of Hadrian, the latter synonymous with the division of the south and north of Britain through the building of his wall in the AD 120s.

In terms of chapter flow, after this short introduction I first set out the history of early imperial Rome in Chapter 1. My aim here is to provide context for Agricola's life and times. In Chapter 2, I then discuss Agricola's army, given this is a story defined by relentless military campaigning. Next, Chapter 3 moves the focus to Britain in the Julio-Claudian period, setting the scene for Agricola's later arrival. My biographical narrative then begins in Chapter 4, where I cover his family, upbringing and early career. This includes his first posting to Britain as a military tribune on the staff of Paulinus in the campaign against Boudicca, his marriage to Domitia Decidiana, and his role in the AD 69 'Year of the Four Emperors'. In Chapter 5, I then narrate Agricola's return to Britannia as the *legatus legionis* in command of *legio* XX *Valeria Victrix*, and in particular his role in the governor Quintus Petillius Cerialis' campaign against the Brigantes. After an interlude back in the imperial centre, the chapter closes with Agricola's final return to Britain as governor, and his AD 77 Welsh campaign and AD 78 Brigantian campaign. Chapter 6 moves on to Agricola's first two campaigns in the far north in AD 79 and AD 80, with Chapter 7 then covering those in AD 81 and AD 82, including his abortive plan to invade Ireland. Finally, in Chapter 8, I detail his final campaign against Calgacus, which culminated in the major engagement at Mons Graupius. The book closes with my conclusion, where I set out the story of Agricola and Domitian's later years, and discuss Agricola's legacy today, particularly the impact the endgame of his campaigns have had on the political settlement of modern Britain.

With contemporary sources, the story of Agricola was a true rarity, a full biography of a non-imperial leading Roman. This is Tacitus' *De vita et moribus Iulii Agricolae*, today known as *The Agricola*. As noted, Tacitus was Agricola's son-in-law, born around AD 56 and long outliving Agricola, eventually dying around AD 120. Of an equestrian family, he had a long career in imperial service, including with Agricola. He is one of the best-received classical historians, with his major works being *The Agricola*, *The Germania*, *The Histories* and *The Annals*. The first was his earliest work, written around AD 98, five years after his father-in-law's death. As always, any primary source from the ancient world comes with a historiography health warning regarding accuracy given the various motivations and literary practices of each writer, and the way each individual text survived through to our day. That is particularly the case with Tacitus, given his obvious pro-Agricolan bias and his overt antipathy to Domitian (well founded in my opinion, as the reader will see). Nevertheless, Tacitus is by some way our best source regarding Agricola, and I use him extensively while providing literary balance for the modern reader.

Another key source is Gaius Suetonius Tranquillus with his *De vita Caesarum*, known today as *The Twelve Caesars*. Written in the Hadrianic period, this provides pen portrait chapters of the Julio-Claudian and Flavian emperors, with his narratives on Vespasian, Titus and Domitian particularly important. Other contemporary writers have also proved useful, particularly Claudius Ptolemy with his *Geography*, which was written in the Antonine period, and Cassius Dio with his *Roman History*, written in the later Severan period.

In terms of modern sources, there are many available to the reader wishing to examine various specific aspects of Agricola's life, times and campaigns. Two of the most useful are Anthony Birley's 2005 *The Roman Government of Britain*, and more recently, Simon Turney's 2022 *Agricola: Architect of Roman Britain*. The first provides an excellent overview of Agricola's progress along the *cursus honorum*, while the second has a very useful discussion regarding the exact location of the battle at Mons Graupius.

Next, some general background. The story of the Roman world featured three phases – the Roman Republic, and the Principate and Dominate phases of empire. The former began with the overthrow of the last Etrusco-Roman king, Tarquin the Proud, in 509 BC and ended with the Senate acknowledging Augustus as the first emperor in 27 BC. Next, the Principate was the early phase of the empire, dating from Augustus' accession to that of Diocletian in AD 284 at the end of the 'Crisis of the Third Century'. The name Principate is derived from the term *princeps*, meaning chief or master in the context of first among equals. Then, given the major structural changes required to the nature of the Roman Empire as it exited the third-century crisis, the period that followed is called the Dominate. This was a new, far more overtly imperial system, the title based on the word *dominus*, which referenced lord, with the emperor now the equivalent of an eastern potentate. Traditionally it ends with the fall of the western Roman Empire in AD 476, the surviving Roman east then often called the Byzantine Empire. The campaigns of Agricola in the far north of Britain took place in the Principate as the empire grew to maturity.

The Roman world at the time of Agricola was divided into provinces, their structure across the broad expanse of the imperium detailed in Chapter 1. The word province itself provides interesting insight into the Roman attitude to its empire, the Latin *provincia* referencing land 'for conquering'. There were two kinds of province in the late Republic and Principate. These were senatorial provinces left to the Senate to administer, whose governors were officially called proconsuls and remained in post for a year, and imperial provinces retained under the supervision of the emperor. The emperor personally chose the governors for these, they often being styled *legati Augusti pro praetor* to mark them out officially as deputies of the emperor. Senatorial provinces tended to be those deep within the empire where less trouble was expected. Clearly, that was not the case with Britannia when Agricola conquered the far north, which was an imperial province. Both proconsuls and governors held full imperium on behalf of the emperor in their provinces, in particular regarding military and legal matters. They were assisted in the running of the province by another senior official called a procurator. These were akin to a modern chancellor and had responsibility for making the province pay, and ensuring it was *pretium victoria* – worth the conquest.

Meanwhile, military installations played a key role in the Roman campaigns of conquest in Britain. In that regard, I have used the current size-based hierarchy as a means of describing their size as they occur in the narrative. Starting with the largest, these are 20ha-plus legionary fortresses for one or more legions, then 12ha-plus vexillation forts holding a mixed force of legionary cohorts and auxiliaries, next 1ha-plus forts for outpost garrisons, and finally, fortlets for part of an auxiliary unit. Military settlements associated with such fortifications are called a *canaba* when connected with a legionary fortress, and a *vicus* elsewhere.

In terms of the built environment, this again features heavily in the story of the Roman campaigns of conquest in Britain. Here, larger towns are referenced as one of three types. These are *coloniae* chartered towns for military veterans (in Britain, for example Colchester), *municipia* chartered towns of mercantile origin (in Britain, for example St Albans) and *civitas* capitals, these last the Roman equivalent of a modern county town featuring the local government of a region (in Britain, for example Canterbury). Settlement below this level is referenced as either a small town (defined as a variety of diverse settlements that often had an association with a specific activity such as religion, administration or industry), villa estates or non-villa estates.

An understanding of the social structure of Roman society is also very useful when considering the campaigns of conquest in Britain. In terms of ranking within the aristocracy, at the very top was the senatorial class, said to be endowed with wealth, high birth and 'moral excellence'. There were around 600 senators in the late first century AD. Those of this class were patricians, a social political rank, with all those below including other aristocrats being plebeians. Next was the equestrian class, lesser aristocrats with slightly less wealth but usually with a reputable lineage. They numbered some 30,000 across the empire in the late first century AD. Finally, in terms of aristocracy there was the curial class, with the bar set slightly lower again. The latter were usually merchants and mid-level landowners, making up a large percentage of the town councillors in the Principate empire. Below this were freemen, who were free in the sense that they had never been slaves. They included the majority of smaller-scale merchants, artisans and professionals in Roman society. All of the above classes were also full *cives Romani* citizens of the empire if they came from Italy. They enjoyed the widest range of protections and privileges as defined by the Roman state, and as such could travel the breadth of the empire pursuing their professional ambitions. Free Roman women had a limited type of citizenship and were not allowed to vote or stand for public or civil office. Freemen born outside of Italy in the imperial provinces were called *peregrini* (in Latin meaning 'one from abroad') until Caracalla's AD 212 *constitutio Antoniniana* edict, which made all freemen of the empire citizens. As such, in the first and second centuries AD, *peregrini* made up the vast majority of the empire's inhabitants.

Further down the social ladder one then had freedmen – former slaves who had been manumitted by their masters either through earning enough money to buy their freedom or for good service. Once free, these former slaves often remained with the wider family of their former owner, frequently taking their name in some way. Providing the correct process of manumission was followed, freedmen could become citizens/*peregrini*, though with fewer civic rights than a freeman, including not being able to stand for the vast majority of public offices. Their children were freemen. Meanwhile, at the bottom of society were slaves.

Next, an understanding of some key words used in the book are useful from the beginning, especially for those new to the Roman military. These are:

- *Battlespace*. The wider region of conflict in which a given campaign took place, for example the far north of Britain in Agricola's case.

- *Symmetric and Asymmetric Warfare*. In the first instance, war between fairly evenly matched belligerents. In the second, conflict where one is so dominant that the other is forced to use unconventional strategies and tactics, for example guerrilla warfare. By way of example, in the Roman world their many conflicts with the Sassanid Persians can be described as symmetrical given both sides were so evenly matched, while their campaigns against the natives in the far north of Britain often forced the latter to respond asymmetrically.
- *Legionaries and Auxiliaries*. For the majority of the Roman Republic, and the Principate phase of empire, the premier Roman warrior was the legionary, a heavily armed and armoured infantryman who often formed the main line of battle. From the time of Augustus, supporting troops were then organised into formal units known as auxiliaries, often lesser in quality to legionaries but still a match for most opponents the Romans faced. Auxiliaries provided both foot troops and most of the cavalry in Principate Roman armies, and played a key role in Agricola's campaigns in the far north of Britain.
- *Romanisation*. From the onset of the Roman occupation of a new province, many economic and social changes unfolded. Romanisation is a term often used to describe this process. The word has proved controversial academically, given it is often associated with modern concepts of imperialism. However, if taken at face value, it is a useful term given the broad appreciation it gives showing how conquered territory became 'Roman', and so I use it here.
- *Briton*. Given the complex nature of the geographical make-up of pre-Roman and Roman Britain, I use the term Briton to detail any native of the main island of the archipelago. When necessary, I add a geographical descriptor, for example in Agricola's case, the Britons of the far north.
- *Littoral*. A maritime region alongside the shore of a sea, river, canal or lake. Important here, given the extensive use by the Romans of their fleets close inshore to support military operations on land. Agricola's use of the *Classis Britannica* British regional fleet in his campaigns in the far north is an excellent example.

Lastly, here I would like to thank the many people who have helped make this work on Agricola's campaigns in the far north of Britain possible. This includes Professor Andrew Lambert of the War Studies Department at KCL, Dr Andrew Gardner at UCL's Institute of Archaeology and Dr Steve Willis at the University of Kent. Next, my publisher Phil Sidnell. Also, Professor Sir Barry Cunliffe of the School of Archaeology at Oxford University and Professor Martin Millett at the Faculty of Classics, Cambridge University for their encouragement. Next, my patient proofreader and lovely wife Sara, and my dad John Elliott and friends Pete Savin, Stuart Thomas and Hunter Hope, all companions in my various escapades to research this book. As with all of my literary work, all have contributed greatly and freely, enabling this book on Agricola to reach fruition. Finally, I would like to thank my family, especially my tolerant wife Sara once again, and children Alex (a teacher of history) and Lizzie.

Thank you all.

Simon Elliott
June 2024

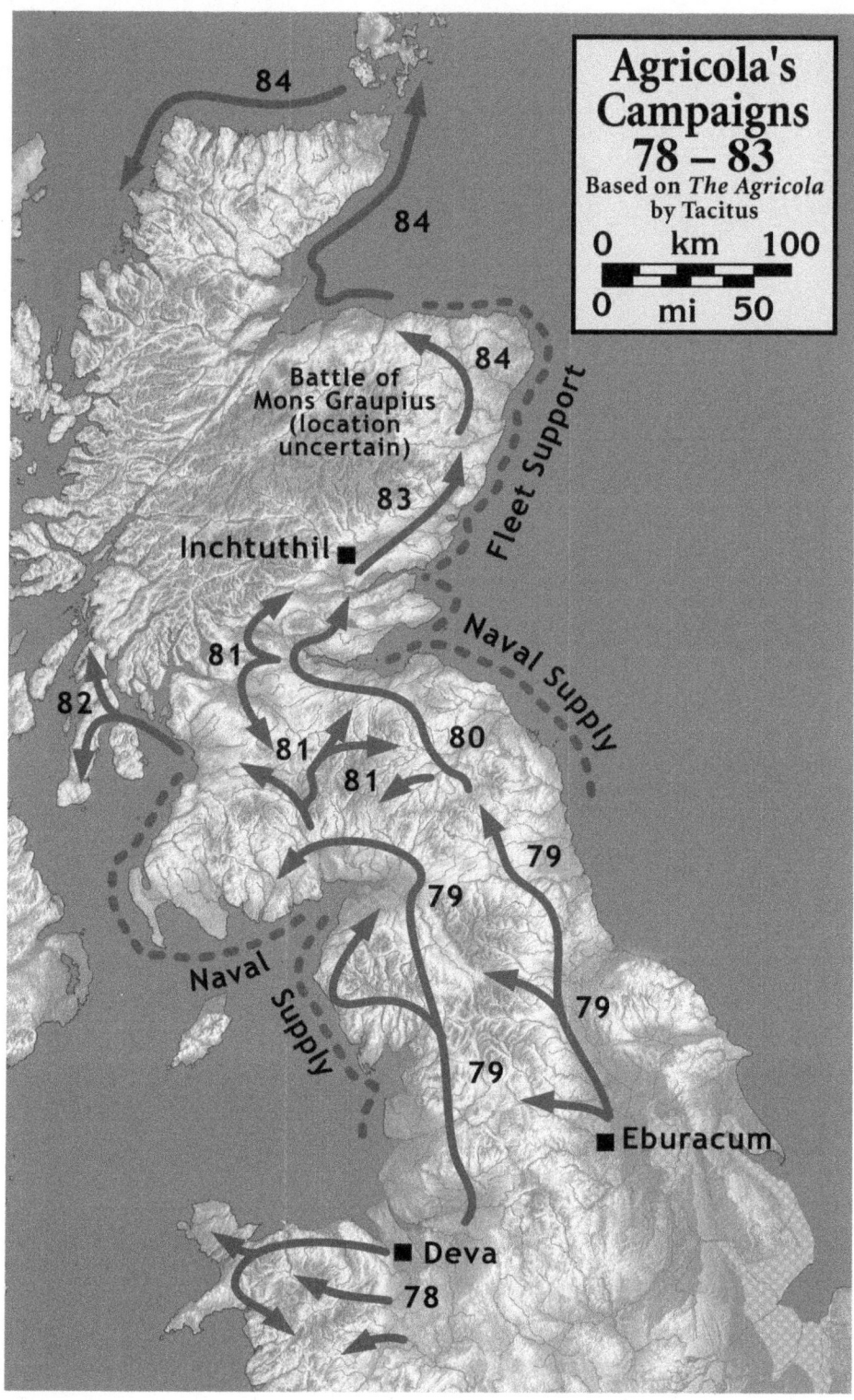

Map 1.

Chapter 1

Early Imperial Rome

The Flavian conquest campaigns of Gnaeus Julius Agricola in Britain took place towards the end of the first century AD as the Principate Roman Empire matured. Rome's rise to this point of greatness had been a painstaking process, featuring long periods of civil war, conquest and consolidation. Within these were many setbacks, though here Rome showed one of its greatest strengths. This was its ability to assimilate many of the ideas, both cultural and practical, of its opponents. This, together with true Roman grit, and an enviable ability to withstand adversity and always come back fighting, ensured the longevity of both Republic and Empire.

Here I set out a detailed background history of the Roman Republic and early Roman Empire, both essential to fully understand Agricola's story. In the first instance, it is important to remember that Agricola's campaigns in the far north of Britain took place only a century after the end of the Republic. Thus, the mindset of his generation of patricians was shaped by the key events of the Republic, particularly late on. Gaius Marius, Lucius Cornelius Sulla and Gaius Julius Caesar were still as relevant in his day as they were in their own. Further, the army that Agricola led to mighty victory in the far north of Britain was the direct result of centuries of military evolution as the Roman Republic grew to dominate the Mediterranean and northwestern Europe. Meanwhile, the recent turmoil of the Julio-Claudian/Flavian transition was also at the forefront of Agricola's thinking. This was not only because his orders in Britain reflected the Flavian desire for martial success to boost the new dynasty's legitimacy, but also because his own father had been executed by Nero. Thus, understanding the early Principate empire is also crucial here.

The Roman Republic

The origins of Rome are shrouded in myth. The most familiar founding story is that concerning the twins Romulus and Remus. In this tale, they were born in the Latin town of Alba Longa to the Vestal Virgin Rhea Silvia. She was the daughter of a former king, Numitor, who had been usurped and imprisoned by his brother Amulius. It was the latter who forced Rhea Silvia to become a Vestal after taking the crown. She conceived the twins when visited by Mars in a sacred grove dedicated to the God of War. Amulius ordered the twins killed and so their mother abandoned them on the banks of the river Tiber. There they were saved by the river god Tiberinus. The story then says the twins were suckled by a she-wolf in a cave later called the Lupercal. They were eventually adopted by a shepherd called Faustulus, growing to manhood unaware of their aristocratic origins. However, their natural leadership qualities came to the fore and through a series of escapades, they eventually became aware of their own identities, later helping restore their grandfather to his throne. They then decided to build their own settlement on the banks of the Tiber and chose the site that later became Rome. The twins then fell out over which of the seven hills there they should build the new town on, Romulus preferring the Palatine Hill and Remus the Aventine Hill. When Romulus claimed divine support for his choice, violence broke out and Romulus killed Remus. The former then founded Rome on the Palatine Hill, the date for this event set by Roman annalists as 21 April 753 BC.

This dramatic legend had to be reconciled with another great founding myth of Rome. This was set much earlier, in the context of the Trojan War. Here, the Trojan refugee Aeneas escaped to Italy following the fall of Troy, landing near Anzio, south of Rome, with his followers after a series of adventures across the Mediterranean. After defeating local opposition, his son Iulus, namesake of the later Julio-Claudian family, founded Alba Longa and established the line of kings that bridged the gap between the Trojan Wars in the later second millennium BC and Rome's ultimate founding. The Roman poet Virgil later merged both stories in his first-century BC epic *The Aeneid*, one of Rome's greatest literary works.

However the original settlement was founded, Rome's location was crucial to its subsequent rise to global dominance. It was one of a number built on hilltops on the left bank of the river Tiber in central Italy at its lowest crossing point. The river is one of two major waterways that rise in the central Apennine Mountains bisecting Italy, the Tiber flowing south into the Tyrrhenian Sea. The other is the river Arno, which flows west into the same sea. The region between the two, from Pisa in the north to Ostia (the port of Rome) in the south, was called Etruria and was originally home to a Villanovan Iron Age culture that began around 900 BC.

This had evolved by the early seventh century BC into the Etruscan culture, with the growing villages of rich Etruria coalescing into powerful city-states such as Caere, Veii and Tarquinii. Etruscan influence spread rapidly, largely through their seafaring skills, with a mercantile empire soon established in the western Mediterranean. Through this, they soon came into contact with the Greek colonies in southern Italy and eastern Sicily, and the Phoenicians who were establishing the Punic Empire in North Africa. From the former they adopted the Greek hoplite phalanx as the principal formation of their better-armed troops. This gave them a distinct edge as they looked south to the settlements above the eastern bank of the Tiber, including Rome, and the region to its south called Latium. Soon these were all under their control, with Rome being governed by an Etrusco-Roman king. The second of these, Servius Tullius (579 BC to 535 BC), was particularly important given he formalised the military systems of Rome for the first time, following Etruscan tradition by introducing the hoplite phalanx for the best Etrusco-Roman troops (see detail in Chapter 2).

Etruscan power reached its height in the mid-sixth century BC when they conquered much of Campania below Latium, including many of the Greek settlements of Magna Graecia. However, crucially they failed to capture the key city of Cumae there. This formed the centre of regional resistance to Etruscan rule, defeating the latter in battle in 524 BC. The event emboldened the other conquered settlements and those in Latium formed the Latin League, which, together with the Greek settlements of Magna Graecia, began to drive the Etruscans back north into Etruria. Rome's first rise to regional dominance occurred at this time when it became the principal town of the league during the reign of Tarquin the Proud (534 BC to 509 BC). He was still nevertheless Etrusco-Roman, and in 509 BC, the Roman aristocracy expelled him and the Republic was born. It was in the context of the latter event that we have the story of Horatio and his two companions holding the last bridge over the river Tiber from Etruscans returning to try to help Tarquin. As the legend goes, their sacrifice proved worthwhile, with Tarquin the last Roman king.

After the fall of the monarchy, the new Roman Republic came under the control of the patrician Senate, where the most important members of the nobility enacted legislation under the aegis of two annually elected consuls. The remaining citizens had no political authority, even though many were as wealthy, if not more so, than many of the senators. Tensions between the two classes grew rapidly, particularly as the poorer residents provided the bulk of the army. In 494 BC, matters came to a head when the plebeians went on strike. They gathered outside Rome and refused to move until they were granted representation, this event called the first *secessio plebis*. Against the odds, the dramatic move worked and the plebeians were rewarded with their own assembly called the *Concillium Plebis* (Council of the Plebs). This body had a degree of oversight on the legislation proposed by the consuls and enacted by the Senate. Thus, while the government of the Roman Republic was by no means democratic (also excluding women from any public office), it was more so than the preceding monarchy. This became an important part of the Roman psyche.

During the early Republic, Roman foreign policy and military activity was often far from successful. Much of the fifth century BC was spent struggling against external threats from near and far. In the first instance, Rome fought the Latin War with its erstwhile Latin League partners from 498 BC to 493 BC. Even though Rome was victorious in the main engagement at the Battle of Regillus in 496 BC, the city had to acknowledge her Latin neighbours as equals in the subsequent Cassian Treaty.

As Etruscan power waned, the Latin League then spent much of the next fifty years fending off repeated raiding in force by the various hill tribes of the Apennines, for example the Aequi, Umbri, Sabini and Volsci. These found themselves increasingly squeezed out of their own lands and onto the plains of Latium by the expansion of the Samnites to the south and east. By the mid-fifth century BC, these tribes, driving all before them, burst into southern Italy and conquered Campania, Apulia and Lucania. The Latin towns led the fightback, with the Aequi defeated in 431 BC and the Volsci then driven back into the hills. The Latin League then consolidated their control over central western Italy, with comparative peace descending on the region for a short time.

However, this was not to last as the Etruscans to the north remained a threat. They again drew the attention of Rome, which, in 404 BC, began an eight-year siege of the Etruscan city of Veii. This finally fell in 396 BC and proved to be the high point for Roman foreign policy in the first half of the fourth century BC. This was because their next opponents were the Senones Gauls from northern Italy. Here, Celts from central Europe had been settling in the Po Valley for some time, challenging the Etruscans who had established Bologna (later Roman *Bononia*) as their principle city there. The riches to the south proved too strong a draw and, after bursting through Etruria, a Gallic army under the chieftain Brennus found itself on the borders of Latium. Rome deployed its legions, expecting a swift victory, but was shocked when they were annihilated at the Battle of Allia in 390 BC. This was only 17km to the north of Rome, which was promptly sacked. This traumatic event prompted the building of the first defensive circuit of the city in the form of the 11km long Servian Walls.

In the midst of these events, an appointment occurred in Rome that was to have a profound effect on the development of the Roman military system, leading to the appearance of the legionary for the first time. This was the election of Marcus Furius Camillus as consular tribune to command the army in 401 BC. A patrician with extensive experience of campaigning against the Aequi and Volsci, he realised Rome's incessant campaigning, which came to a head with the long siege of Veii, was proving financially unsustainable. He therefore raised taxation to a level where it could support the army on long campaigns, helping rebalance the books of the Roman treasury. Then, with his Camillan reform of the military, he introduced the manipular system into the legions of Rome, a revolutionary development.

The new system was quickly tested, once more against the Etruscans to the north. In the mid-fourth century BC, Rome and her Latin League partners fought a series of increasingly vicious wars against the Etrurian city-states. A final assault in 351 BC broke Etruscan resistance, who then lost Bologna to the Gauls in 350 BC. The absence of an opponent to the north now left the towns of Latium free to look inwards once more, and a final struggle for dominance of the Latin League began. Rome emerged as the victor and now controlled all of western Italy from southern Etruria to northern Campania.

By now city-sized, its next opponents were the Samnites of Samnium, an Oscan-speaking people of south central Italy used to fighting in the rough terrain of their homelands. Initially an ally of the Latin League against the Volsci, war broke out with Rome in 343 BC. This lasted for fifty years through the First, Second and Third Samnite Wars and included the famous Roman defeat at the Caudian Forks in 321 BC. Rome never forgave the Samnites for this humiliation and within five years, the 'Caudine Peace' had broken down, with hostilities renewed. The Samnites were for the most part victorious, but typically, the Romans refused to accept defeat and tenaciously fought back. The Samnites eventually sued for peace in 304 BC. This was again short-lived, lasting only six years. The Samnites then launched a full-out assault on Rome in 296 BC, gathering together a coalition of allies including the Gauls, the remaining Etruscan city-states and Umbrians, aiming to curb the growing of Rome once and for all. Again they were initially successful, but ultimately lost the key battle at Sentinum in 295 BC when only the Gauls turned up to fight alongside them. This marked the end of Samnite resistance to Roman expansion southwards, and of Etruscan independence. It was also a remarkable example of Roman grit, they never cowing to adversity and always coming back until victorious – a lesson that echoed through to Agricola's day.

Rome next turned its attention to northern Italy, where the Gauls still dominated. In the early 280s BC, a large-scale migration took place of the Gallic peoples of central Europe and northern Italy, caused by population pressure. Huge tribal groupings began to head eastwards and south. Soon the Senones tribe were once more on the borders of Etruria, now under Roman control. In 284 BC, a Roman army, 13,000 strong, marched north to intercept them but was massacred at the Battle of Arretium. The Romans responded with more grit, launching a massive counterstrike into the heart of Senonian territory in the Po Valley. After a brief struggle, they evicted the whole tribe out of Italy. Another Gallic tribe, the Boii, then raided south but were fought to a standstill and sued for peace. This ended effective Gallic resistance in the north.

Rome now controlled most of the Italian peninsula excepting the Greek cities to the south, which became the next object of its attention. The Republic tried to force them into an alliance, but was quickly rebuffed. Taranto, the leading naval power on the peninsula, then appealed for help from Pyrrhus of Epirus on the western coast of the Balkans. The Epirot king, a relation of Alexander the Great, responded positively and in 280 BC crossed the Adriatic with an army 25,000 strong. These crack troops fought in the Hellenistic military tradition with pikemen, lance-armed shock cavalry and war elephants. A Roman army quickly marched south when word reached the city that Pyrrhus was gathering allies from Rome's enemies across Italy, of which by this time there were many, all holding grudges after earlier defeats. A major battle ensued at Heraclea. This was the first time the Romans, with their maniples of legionaries, fought a Macedonian-style phalanx. It was to prove a bruising experience, with Pyrrhus winning narrowly. Two further battles occurred at Asculum in 279 BC, another narrow Epirot victory, and Beneventum in 275 BC, when the Romans were finally victorious. The war had been a close-run thing, though, and made a lasting impression on the Romans. One result was the evolution of the Camillan manipular system into a more streamlined form known as the Polybian system, after the second-century Greek historian. It also marked the beginning of Roman interest in that most tantalising of ancient warfare troop types, the war elephant.

Roman expansion continued and now began to take on an international flavour. By 272 BC, Taranto had been captured, providing Rome with an effective maritime capability for the first time. This caused an inevitable clash with Carthage, the regional superpower of the western Mediterranean, and the First Punic War broke out in 264 BC over control over the key Sicilian city of Messina. This lasted until 241 BC and included the Battle of Agrigentum on the south coast of Sicily in 261 BC, where the legions of Rome defeated the Carthaginians for the first time in a set-piece battle. After this, the conflict was largely naval, with the Romans copying Carthaginian maritime technology and tactics and ending the war the victor. Carthage evacuated Sicily and paid a huge indemnity.

However, it was the Second Punic War that truly tested the power and resilience of Rome to breaking point. This broke out in 218 BC and lasted seventeen years, with the Roman fleet at the outset cutting off the

Carthaginian North African homeland from its colonies in Spain. The Carthaginian leader Hannibal responded with his audacious plan to invade Italy through southern Gaul and the Alps, defeating the legions of Rome and their allies three times at the Trebia in 218 BC, Lake Trasimene in 217 BC and Cannae in 216 BC. The last of these was a battle of titanic scale, with 50,000 Carthaginians facing 86,000 Romans. Hannibal here completed his famous double envelopment of the legions. A massacre followed, with 50,000 Romans killed. Such losses would bring most opponents to their knees, but not Rome. Soon new legions were raised, including two of freed slaves. Even though most of southern Italy now defected to Hannibal, he failed to capture Rome itself given his lack of a viable siege train, and was ultimately pinned down in southern Italy. Attempts to resupply him from North Africa and Spain failed due to Roman naval power, and in 204 BC, Rome went on the offensive. This featured the consul Publius Cornelius Scipio (later Africanus) landing a sizeable force of 25,000 in the Carthaginian heartland near Tunis. The legions, joined by Numidian allies including their famous light cavalry, had their revenge for Cannae in 202 BC when Scipio finally defeated Hannibal at Zama. Peace quickly followed, under the most onerous terms for the Carthaginians.

The Third Punic War broke out in 146 BC with Carthage backed into a corner by the escalating demands of Rome. This was a very one-sided affair, with Carthage itself destroyed and 50,000 of its citizens sold into slavery. The event marked the beginning of Rome's mastery of the western Mediterranean, with Sicily, Sardinia, Corsica, the Balearic Islands, Spain and North Africa gradually coming under direct Roman control.

Meanwhile, an additional outcome of the Second Punic War was that Roman attention also turned to the eastern Mediterranean and the remaining Hellenistic kingdoms there. Here, the Macedonian king Philip V had been caught trying unwisely to agree a treaty with Hannibal when the latter was still in Italy. Soon the First Macedonian War began, followed by three more that finally saw Macedonia become a Roman province in 146 BC. Rome was also victorious fighting the over-confident Seleucid monarch Antiochus III in the Seleucid–Rome War. The final resistance to Roman hegemony in Greece came in 146 BC when the Achaean League in the northern and central Peloponnese declared war on Rome. The ensuing Achaean War was a short-lived affair, the Achaeans being totally defeated and its leading city Corinth sacked and razed to the ground.

Rome was now the undoubted superpower in the Mediterranean, its legions triumphant across the region. One result of its spectacular success against the Hellenistic kingdoms was that fabulous amounts of loot and plunder now began making their way to Rome, enriching senatorial army commanders and troops alike. This is what fell into Rome's lap, dwarfing the riches amassed after the defeat of Carthage. The aristocracy back in Rome could now see fortunes were to be made in the east through military conquest, which from this point proved an enormous draw. Soon, civil war loomed on the horizon.

As the Republic matured, victorious and rich Rome turned on itself. First, in 133 BC, the tribune Tiberius Sempronius Gracchus proposed to distribute stretches of state-owned land in Italy, illegally occupied by the rich, to the poor. However, instead of following the usual practice of first consulting the Senate, he presented his idea directly to an assembly of the people. In so doing, he deposed from office another tribune opposing the distribution, arguing that his reforms should be funded from the money that came from the riches now pouring into Rome from the eastern Mediterranean. His land bill passed but, when he tried to stand for election for another term, he was assassinated by a group of senators. This set the tone for all that followed in the next century.

In 123 BC, Tiberius' brother Gaius was elected as a tribune, introducing a whole package of radical legislation. By far his most controversial reform was regularisation of the *cura annonae* grain supply in Rome. Due to the city's rapid growth, it was increasingly reliant on grain imports from Sicily, North Africa and Egypt. The price of this grain could fluctuate wildly, influenced by factors as diverse as slave revolts, plagues of locusts or simply the size of the annual harvest each year. This fluctuation exposed the citizens of Rome to occasional food shortages when the price was too high or the amount of grain available too low. Gaius therefore stabilised the price of grain at a sustainable level, and introduced a state subsidy to pay for it. To raise the funds for the subsidy he introduced a system of tax farming in Rome's newly conquered territories in the eastern Mediterranean, where huge corporations publicly bid for the right to collect the taxes for a percentage of profit. Despite the system being open to huge levels of corruption, which in some cases beggared the new provinces, the people of Rome didn't care. They now had their cheap grain, with the system lasting into the late Republic.

Gaius was now getting into his stride, but realised he would need another term as tribune to complete his ambitious reforms. He didn't want to stand for election again himself, but put forward his closest supporter, Fulvius Flaccus, to take his place. However, such was Gaius' popularity that he was re-elected anyway, alongside his friend. Their manifesto was even more radical than that for Gaius' first term of office. It included a plan to enfranchise all Italian citizens, and for a major Roman colony to be built on the site of Carthage, the Punic capital laid waste by Rome at the end of the Third Punic War. Gaius himself travelled to North Africa to see the latter founded. Both policies caused even more friction with the Senate and their supporters, and when Gaius and Flaccus failed to be re-elected in 121 BC, they knew they were exposed to retribution. An attempt to drag them before the Senate failed when they refused to attend, Flaccus convincing Gaius that it was a trap, and so it proved. Bloodshed soon followed, with Gaius fleeing and eventually taking his own life with the help of a servant in a sacred grove. Some 250 of his supporters also died, fighting a rearguard action to buy him time to escape, ironically on the same bridge held by Horatio and his companions 400 years earlier.

Next, towards the end of the century, a new figure rose to pre-eminence in Rome, one who would come to dominate Roman politics for the first decades of the first century BC. This was the highly successful statesman and soldier Gaius Marius, who eventually served as consul an unprecedented seven times. The context for his rise to the top was the next great external threat to the Republic, in the form of the sanguineous Cimbrian Wars.

The Cimbri were a Germanic people who originated from Jutland in modern Denmark. In the later second century BC, they, along with neighbouring tribes such as the Teutons and Ambrones, migrated south into Gaul, where they fought a series of wars with the Gallic tribes. In 113 BC, they invaded the lands of the Taurisci, a confederation of Gallic tribes in Noricum (modern Austria and part of Slovenia). These were

Roman allies and the Senate decided to send an army to their aid. This marked the beginning of the Cimbrian War, which lasted until 101 BC. Here, time and again, the manipular legions were defeated by the Cimbri across southern Gaul as the Romans tried and failed to get to grips with the fierce Germans. Soon panic gripped Rome, with the phrase *terror cimbricus* used to describe the mood of the people. However, Roman grit showed through again, this time in the form of Marius. He was born in 157 BC, though not to an aristocratic family. Through sheer hard work and ambition, he rose to become a *quaestor* in 123 BC, then tribune of the plebs in 119 BC and *praetor* in 115 BC. He proved a supreme soldier, first in Spain, where he earned fame by defeating a bandit uprising, and then setting Rome's silver mining interests there on a firm footing. Then in 109 BC, he travelled to Numidia to serve as the *legate* under the consul Quintus Metellus Numidicus. Here the Romans were engaged in the Jugurthine War against the rogue Numidian king, Jugurtha. This had broken out in 112 BC and was proving difficult for Rome to conclude satisfactorily. Marius and Metellus soon fell out, especially when the latter's troops began supporting Marius' own claim to take over complete command of the legions there. Marius then returned to Rome in 107 BC to stand for consul, succeeding and then initiating a new series of reforms of the Roman military, which crucially replaced the manipular system of the Polybian legions with a brand-new system based on cohorts (see Chapter 2 for full detail). Marius was then granted Numidia as his own province, where he returned with fresh troops, officially taking control of the campaign from Metellus.

His first act there was to send his *quaestor* and future enemy Sulla to nearby Mauretania to negotiate the kingdom withdrawing its support for Jugurtha. Then, with the help of the Mauritanian king Bocchus I, Sulla captured Jugurtha and the war ended. Marius was wildly popular among the plebeian classes in Rome and despite Sulla's key role in Jugurtha's demise, he was acclaimed the hero of the hour, being granted a triumph by the Senate. Then, after another shattering defeat of the legions at the hands of the Cimbri, the Roman people turned to Marius for salvation. He was elected consul again in 104 BC, even though he was still in Numidia concluding matters there. Arriving back in Rome for his triumph, he took up his consulship immediately.

Marius now gathered together an army to counter any Cimbri invasion, basing it in southern Gaul. There he waited, training new legions and being elected consul again in 103 BC and 102 BC. In the latter year, he finally confronted the Cimbris' allies who had started to move south. At the Battle of Aquae Sextiae in Aix-en-Provence, he destroyed a combined force of Teutons and Ambrones, inflicting 90,000 casualties on the Germans and capturing 20,000, including the Teuton king, Teutobod.

Marius was elected consul again in 101 BC and in that year was able to tackle the Cimbri head-on. The enormous tribe had begun to move south and for the first time penetrated the Alpine passes, entering Cisalpine Gaul in northern Italy. The Roman force there of 20,000 troops withdrew behind the Po River, allowing the Cimbri to devastate the fertile countryside to its north. This gave Marius time to arrive with his legions from southern Gaul, his army now totalling 32,000 men. He then led the combined Roman force to an immense victory at the Battle of Vercellae, near the confluence of the Po and Sesia rivers. Defeat for the Cimbri was total, they losing up to 160,000 men with 60,000 captured, including a large number of camp followers. Soon the slave markets of Rome were overflowing. Marius was once again the hero of the hour, though the successful conclusion of the Cimbrian War marked the beginning of the long enmity between Marius and Sulla as the latter felt that, certainly in the Jugurthine War, the consul hadn't given him the credit for his actions.

Marius' success had one unforeseen circumstance that in retrospect hastened the collapse of the Republic. This was the appearance of a new phenomenon at the top of Roman society, a class of political leaders who were effectively independent warlords, each with their own armies. The term warlord might seem anachronistic given the structured nature of Roman society, but is very appropriate for the likes of Marius, Sulla, Gnaeus Pompey, Marcus Licinius Crassus, Caesar, Mark Antony and Gaius Octavian. Crucially, the new Marian legions included all the specialists needed to enable them to operate independently in the field, free from long lines of supply. This made them very mobile. Further, Marius removed the property requirement to serve in the legions, opening their ranks to the lower end of Roman society. With little money of their own, such troops proved very loyal to their leaders. Thus, at a stroke, Marius allowed the very rich to raise their own highly manoeuverable, ultra-loyal legions in large numbers. A particular driver here was the vast wealth of the former Hellenistic kingdoms in the eastern Mediterranean detailed above, forever drawing these warlords to the region, ever desirous of enriching themselves, their soldiers and their supporters back in Rome.

The appearance of the first of these warlords was the catalyst behind the emergence for the first time of two specific political 'parties' in Rome. These were the reactionary pro-Senate *optimates* (the 'best ones') and the radical, reforming *populares* ('favouring the people'). From this point onwards, the late Republican warlords had to pick a side if they wanted political support, with Sulla soon the darling of the *optimates* and Marius the *populares*.

These disagreements were set aside for a short period in the early 90s BC when Rome was rocked by a conflict that caught many by surprise. This was the Social War, a vicious affair when some of Rome's erstwhile Italian *socii* allies in the Apennines rose in revolt. Troops from the Italian legions, armed in the Roman fashion, had frequently fought alongside Rome's own legions. Indeed, they had proved so valuable to Marius that he granted Roman citizenship to his own Italian troops. However, this gave a newfound sense of power to the Italian political classes, who now demanded a greater say in Roman foreign policy. After all, it was their soldiers who were fighting and dying alongside those of Rome. With trouble brewing, in 91 BC the tribune Marcus Livius Drusus proposed new legislation in Rome to try to avert a crisis developing. This would have admitted all Italians to citizenship, but provoked a huge backlash in the Senate, with Drusus soon assassinated. This was the last straw for the Italians and many now rose in revolt.

The rebels were initially successful, with the Marsi in the northern Apennines inflicting defeats on Roman armies in the north, and the Samnites bursting onto Campanian coastal plains in the south. There, the rich cities along the Bay of Naples, for example Surrentum, Stabiae, Herculaneum and Nola, fell one by one. Pompeii was spared a siege given it supported the rebellion from early on, though paid the price for this later.

Marius was in charge of the Roman forces in the northern sector. Now 67, he was less energetic than previously and viewed as slower on campaign by the *optimates* than his rival Sulla. The Senate accused him of indecision, though when he did attack the Marsi he won two great victories. He then waited to be appointed supreme commander of all the Roman forces in the field, but when this did not happen he retired to Rome, taking no further part in the war.

The Senate realised this revolt needed to be brought to a halt as quickly as possible and decided to offer the rebels concessions, with the consul Lucius Julius Caesar helping pass a law granting Roman citizenship to any Italians who hadn't participated in the uprising. The move proved decisive and soon the rebellion faltered. The Senate then appointed new military commanders tasked with bringing the war to a conclusion. Here, the consul Gnaeus Pompeius Strabo was placed in charge of the three legions in the north, while Sulla was given command of those in the south. Victory followed victory for the Romans, and the war was over by 89 BC.

All now seemed set for a period of peace after the dramas of the Jugurthine, Cimbrian and Social Wars. However, this proved a false hope because in 88 BC a full-scale civil war broke out. The protagonists were none other than Rome's two leading warlords, Marius and Sulla.

Sulla's First Civil War lasted from 88 BC to 87 BC and occurred in the context of the First Mithridatic War, Rome's first conflict with Mithridates VI of Pontus. This began in 89 BC, with Sulla being given command of the army in his capacity as one of the two consuls. This was a plum command for the ambitious warlord, as he knew there was fabulous wealth to be gained by conquering Mithridates' empire in Anatolia, around the Black Sea and in Greece. Some of this territory comprised Roman provinces seized by the Pontic king, so there was also glory to be had restoring Roman rule. However, Marius also wanted the post. Having encountered Mithridates on an earlier tour to the east, when he had warned the king not to fight with Rome, he thought himself to be the expert on the region. Relations between Sulla and Marius, already poor, became increasingly strained and in 88 BC, conflict broke out.

The flashpoint occurred when one of the tribunes of the plebs, Sulpicius, suggested that the votes of the recently enfranchised Italians be evenly split among the existing Roman voting tribes. The Senate blocked the move, so he turned to Marius for support, then putting forward a long list of proposals to the popular assembly designed to bypass the Senate. One of his suggestions was to take command of the army away from Sulla, the *optimates*' champion. This was a real threat to the consul and he played for time by retiring to his private quarters to examine the heavens for omens. This was one of his rights as a consul and meant that all public business in Rome had to cease until Sulla had completed his task. Sulpicius now overreacted, bringing his *populares* supporters onto the streets of the capital. Violence between the *optimates* and *populares* ensued, with Sulla having to flee and seek shelter with Marius. The latter saw his opportunity and made a number of demands of the consul, who agreed to allow public business to return to normal. In short order, he was stripped of his command, with Marius now put in charge of the army to fight Mithridates.

Sulla knew his days would be numbered if he stayed in Rome and fled. He headed south, reaching an army of six veteran legions at Nola in Campania whom he'd commanded in the Social War. He convinced them to support him before Marius' own tribunes arrived, who were then killed when they tried to take control of the force. The importance of this cannot be underestimated, it being the first time the legions had chosen to side with a warlord against the Republic itself. Sulla now marched on Rome, joined by his fellow consul Quintus Pompeius Rufus. The pair fought their way into the city and a pitched battle ensued in the *Esquiline forum* between the *optimates* and *populares*. There, after a promising start, Marius and Sulpicius suffered a resounding defeat. The latter was betrayed and executed, with Marius fleeing to Africa.

Sulla now took control of the city, posting troops throughout the capital to ensure order. He then addressed the popular assemblies to defend his own actions, before taking away their powers to legislate unless on a law already passed by the Senate. He then added 300 new members to the chamber to ensure its support. The power of the various public tribunes was also reduced. With peace restored in Rome, at least for now, he then sent his army back to Campania and resumed his post as consul.

However, all was not well. Another Roman army was at large in Italy under Gnaeus Pompeius Strabo, the father of Caesar's later rival Pompey. Sulla gave command of the force to his own ally Rufus, but when the latter arrived to take command, he was killed by Pompey Strabo's loyal legionnaires. This was only the first of a number of setbacks for Sulla, the most important being the failure of his candidates to replace him and Rufus as consuls for 87 BC. The winners were Lucius Cornelius Cinna and Gnaeus Octavius, the former a well-known opponent of his. To counter this, Sulla forced Cinna to vow to support him. However, once in office, Cinna immediately broke the oath. He tried to impeach Sulla, but the warlord ignored him. He took command of the army once more and marched east to fight Mithridates.

With Sulla gone, Cinna tried to revive Sulpicius' voting plans for the Italians, with his fellow consul Octavius leading the opposition. On the day of the vote, the tribunes vetoed the law and rioting ensued in the *forum Romanum*, with Octavius' supporters chasing Cinna's men away. Cinna fled the pandemonium and headed for Capua in Campania, where he won over the loyalty of a Roman force (Sulla's troops there had already left), additionally recruiting Italians to swell his numbers. The old warrior Marius now returned from Africa to join him and together they besieged Octavius in Rome. The latter secured the backing of Pompey Strabo and his troops, but he died soon after helping repel a Marian assault on the city. Marius then cut off the food supply to the capital.

The armies of the two factions now confronted each other near the Alban Hills southeast of Rome, but before an engagement could occur, the Senate turned on Octavius and entered into negotiations with Marius and Cinna. The pair then took control of Rome without a fight, with Octavius beheaded. In a sign of things to come, his head was then displayed in the *forum Romanum*. A massacre followed of Marius and Cinna's opponents, with Sulla declared a public enemy. His house was burnt down and property confiscated, his laws repealed, and Marius (for the seventh time) and Cinna became the consuls for 86 BC.

The middle years of the first century BC were dominated by two further individuals of great significance to the story of Rome. The first was Pompey, the other arguably the greatest Roman of all, Caesar. Though originally allies (Pompey married Caesar's daughter Julia in 59 BC), they later became the bitterest of enemies. Both had seen great military success, Pompey in Spain and the east, Caesar in Gaul, where he famously defeated the Gallic leader Vercingetorix at the siege of Alesia in 52 BC, this the culmination of his conquest in Gaul. His campaigns there included his two incursions to Britain in 55 BC and 54 BC, which put the future province on the Roman map for the first time. It was here

Agricola was later able to claim to be the first Roman to conquer the whole main island of Britain.

Pompey and Caesar differed principally in their political powerbases, the former relying on the support of the *optimates* in the Senate while the latter chose a populist route championing the *populares'* cause. Their rivalry was well recorded, particularly in the surviving letters of another contemporary politician, Marcus Tullius Cicero. Caesar himself also knew the power of a good press and made sure he recorded his victories for posterity, for example in his *Conquest of Gaul*, the latter a collection of his annual reports back to Rome while on campaign there.

Pompey and Caesar were kept in check through most of the 50s BC by the First Triumvirate, where Rome's richest man, Marcus Licinius Crassus, joined them to dominate public life. However, Julia died in 54 BC and then, when Crassus himself was killed campaigning against the Parthians at the Battle of Carrhae in 53 BC, war between the two protagonists became inevitable. First blows were struck in January 49 BC when Caesar famously crossed the Rubicon River with his *legio* XIII *Gemina* against the expressed orders of the *optimates*-dominated Senate. This waterway, to the south of Ravenna in northeastern Italy, marked the division between Italy proper and Cisalpine Gaul to the north. Caesar's move was a direct challenge to the Republic's authority, but instead of confronting him as he approached Rome, Pompey fled to Greece, where, after a lengthy campaign, Caesar finally defeated him at the crucial Battle of Pharsalus in 48 BC. Pompey was beheaded soon afterwards after fleeing to Egypt, and within two years, Caesar was the sole master of the Roman world after campaigning in Egypt, Asia Minor, North Africa and Spain. When back in Rome, he was declared dictator and embarked on a major programme of reform, including of the calendar. He also settled thousands of landless veteran soldiers, whose debts he cancelled, on publicly owned land. Such actions set him aloof from his noble peers, both *optimates* and *populares*, leading to friction with the Senate. This soon grew to breaking point. Matters came to a head with his assassination aged 55 on the Ides of March in 44 BC in the Senate House *curia*, then temporarily housed in the Theatre of Pompey in the *Campus Martius* (Fields of Mars). The Liberators, as the assassins dubbed themselves, were a posse of senators keen to turn the clock back to the 'great' days of the earlier Republic.

However, their actions totally failed, given the event martyred Caesar in the eyes of his contemporaries and started the final vicious round of civil wars that destroyed the Republic and created the empire. In the decade after his death, Caesar's supporters, led by his general Mark Antony, first fought and defeated his assassins, and then turned on themselves. A brief attempt to restore peace occurred with the Second Triumvirate, but again this failed. War broke out once more and by 31 BC there was only one man left standing – Caesar's great-nephew and adopted son Octavian – this after he and his general Marcus Agrippa defeated Mark Antony and Cleopatra VII Philopator at the naval battle of Actium in northern Greece.

Octavian was keenly aware that the Roman political classes and wider population were exhausted after nearly a century of civil war, especially the recent brutal campaigns following the death of Caesar. A shrewd political operator, instead of announcing himself a 'dictator', he quietly started to gather the reins of power within Rome. Then, in 27 BC, when it was obvious to all where the power in Rome now lay, the Senate declared him Augustus (from the Latin *augere*, meaning 'illustrious one') and *princeps* (meaning 'master'). Thus was born the Roman Empire, initially in the form of his Principate. The title *princeps* was then assumed by each subsequent emperor on their accession, though in reality was a conceit, allowing the empire to be explained away as a simple continuance of the Republic when in reality it was a true dictatorship.

The Principate Empire

The Principate featured eight distinct dynasties and periods, within which sat a number of major military campaigns. Those relevant to the story of Agricola are:

- The Julio-Claudian dynasty, lasting from the accession of Augustus in 27 BC to the death of Nero in AD 68. This period included the Cantabrian Wars in the late first century BC, the loss of Varus' three legions in Teutoburg Forest in AD 9, and the initial campaigns of conquest in Britain from the Claudian invasion of AD 43 onwards (these fully detailed in Chapter 2).

- The 'Year of the Four Emperors' in AD 69, with Vespasian the ultimate victor.
- The Flavian dynasty, from Vespasian's accession to the death of his younger son Domitian in AD 96. This included the defeat of the Batavian revolt of Gaius Julius Civilis in AD 70, the later campaigns of conquest in Britain (including Agricola's campaigns in the far north), and the First 'Great' Jewish Revolt, which lasted from AD 66 to AD 73.

The subsequent dynasties and periods of the Principate, after Agricola's time, were the Nervo-Trajanic dynasty, the Antonine dynasty, the 'Year of the Five Emperors' in AD 193, the Severan dynasty, and the 'Crisis of the Third Century'.

Thanks to Augustus and his stealthy gathering of the levers of imperial power, future emperors had few checks and balances on their authority. Their powers included:

- Regulating the Senate, including convening its sessions and setting the agenda for all its meetings. The emperor also had total control over who was appointed a senator.
- Controlling the Roman calendar.
- The authority to consecrate temples and oversee religious ceremonies as the *Pontifex Maximus* leader of the College of Priests.
- Being the supreme commander of the Roman military.
- Assuming the powers of *tribunicia potestas* (the power of coercion) and *sacrosanctity* (legal inviolability through sacred law).
- Exercising regional authority through the appointment of governors in imperial provinces, approving the appointment of proconsuls in senatorial provinces, and appointing the procurator in all provinces.

Using these powers, each emperor exercised imperial authority through three main bodies, which remained in place throughout the Principate. The first was the *Consilium Principis* main council, created to be the central imperial advisory body. This was effectively always in session, providing the emperor with advice on military, legal and diplomatic matters. Next came the *fiscus* imperial treasury, controlled by an *a rationibus* financial officer (later replaced by one styled an *a rationalis*). This was the magnet for the wealth generated by each province and was used to fund all the emperor's activities, including the use of the Roman military. The word *fiscus* is very specific and refers to the personal treasury of the emperor, literally translating as 'basket' or 'purse'. Finally came the Praetorian Guard, founded by Augustus and later institutionalised by Tiberius (emperor AD 14 to AD 37).

By the time Agricola became governor in Britain the empire had grown to cover a vast geographic area. This encompassed the entire Mediterranean basin, English Channel and much of the North Sea, stretching all the way from the far north of Britain to distant Arabia. This was a distance of 4,200km as the crow flies. The empire's population at this time was around 65 million people, some 21 per cent of the entire world's then population. It was divided into forty-four provinces, both senatorial and imperial. These broadly broke down into seven regions, namely Britannia, Gaul and Germany, Spain, the Danube and Italy, Greece and Asia Minor, the East, and North Africa. The northern frontier along the Rhine was protected by the *limes Germanicus* and Rhaetian *limes*, while that on the Danube featured the Noric *limes*, Pannonian *limes* and Moesian *limes*. In the east, the frontier featured the Cappadocian *limes* and the *limes Arabicus*, while in North Africa, the Saharan frontier was protected by the *limes Tripolitanus* in the east and *Fossatum Africae* in the west.

Chapter 2

Agricola's Army

The Roman military at the time Agricola conquered the far north of Britain was pre-eminent in a world where to that date it lacked a true symmetrical threat. Most often on campaign and in battle, whether set piece or skirmish, it won. When it did lose to Britons, Germans or Parthians, it always learned from its mistakes and came back the better for it. This was the military most associated with the Principate. Think of legionaries resplendent in torso-covering *scutum* shields, fine *lorica segmentata* banded iron armour and bright-crested imperial Gallic helmets.

Given its importance to the story of Agricola and his campaigns in Britain, an understanding of this military establishment is essential to appreciate the wider narrative. Thus, here in this chapter, I consider the legions, auxilia and regional fleets that all, at various times, played such an important role in his conquest of the far north.

The Legions

The Roman legionary in the mid- to late first century AD was the result of nearly 600 years of military evolution in terms of tactics and equipment. This progression included five distinct phases:

- The Tullian system of Servius Tullius. This was based on an Etruscan-style hoplite phalanx of armoured spearman, *equites* who were wealthy citizen cavalry, and four classes of supporting troops.
- The Camillan system introduced by Camillus with its new manipular legion of 3,000 (later up to 5,000) men. This featured three classes of legionary, these *triarii* veterans, *principes* older warriors and *hastati* 'flower of the young men'.

- The Polybian system introduced after Rome's conflict with Pyrrhus of Epirus. This was an evolution of the Camillan system, introducing other troop types including *velite* skirmishing javelinmen.
- The Marian system introduced by Marius at the height of the Cimbrian Wars in 107 BC. His revolutionary changes introduced the 6,000-man legion, based on centuries rather than maniples, with 4,800 legionaries now all armed in the same way and the remaining 1,200 specialists and support staff. The Marian legion set the template for those of the Principate, with each a self-contained fighting force highly mobile on campaign and in battle.
- The Augustan system introduced by the first emperor after his elevation by the Senate in 27 BC. As Octavian, he had inherited sixty legions from the last, vicious round of Roman civil wars in the late first century BC. His main contribution to the evolution of the legion was to rationalise the number down to twenty-eight, this falling to twenty-five after Varus' loss of three in Germany in AD 9. The total would then hover around thirty for the next 200 years, for example twenty-nine at the time Agricola was campaigning in the far north of Britain.

The numbering and naming of the legions can seem confusing to a modern audience. This reflects their being raised by many different Roman leaders, and at different times. Some shared the same legion number but had different names. For example, there were five third legions. Others shared the same name but with different numbering, for example, *legio* I, *legio* II, *legio* III and *legio* IV *Italica*. The longevity of this numbering and naming suggests there was a strong sense of identity within these legions. As Goldsworthy says, 'legionaries were proud of their unit and contemptuous of others' (2003, 50).

Roman legions in the Principate were stationed on or near the frontiers of the empire in legionary fortresses. By this time, after the Augustan reforms, they numbered 5,500 men, organised into 10 cohorts. The first of these had 5 centuries of 160 men, with the rest 6 centuries of 80 men each. Each normal century was then broken down into ten eight-man sections called *contubernia* whose men shared a tent when on campaign and a barrack block in their home fortress. Additionally, each legion also featured 120 auxiliary cavalry who acted as dispatch riders and scouts.

Principate legions were led by a senatorial-level *legatus legionis*. His second-in-command was a *tribunus laticlavius*. This was a younger man, also of senatorial rank, gaining the experience to command his own legion in the future. Third in command was the *praefectus castrorum* camp prefect. This was a seasoned former centurion responsible for logistics and administration. Below this were five younger equestrian-level tribunes, called the *tribuni angusticlavii*. These were allocated responsibilities as required.

Control of each cohort in the legion was the responsibility of centurions, six to a normal cohort. Each had a specific title that reflected their seniority based on the old manipular legions of Camillus. In ascending order, these were *hastatus posterior, hastatus prior, princeps posterior, princeps prior, pilus posterior* and *pilus prior*. In addition, the most senior *pilus prior* in the legion through length of service also had the title *primus pilus*.

Officers controlled the legions with standards and musical instruments. Each legion had a variety of types of standard. First and foremost was the gold *aquila* eagle carried by the *aquilifer*. This only left camp when the entire legion was on campaign. Next was the *imago* standard, which featured an image of the emperor, either a bust or a portrait within a large *phalera* medallion, carried by an *imaginifer*. Then came the *signa* standards allocated to each individual century and carried by a *signifer*. Additionally, flag-based standards were used. These were called *vexilla*. One showed the name of the legion and was carried alongside the *aquila* and *imago*, while others were allocated to legionary detachments, giving them their name *vexillations*. Each *vexilla* was carried by a *vexillarius*. The standard-bearers were joined in their signalling role by a *cornicen* musician who played the *cornu* horn. These always marched at the head of the centuries with the *signifer*.

Legionaries of the Principate could be volunteers or conscripted, the latter under a levy called the *dilectus*. By the time Agricola campaigned in the far north of Britain many were increasingly enrolled as conscripts. This was because of the number of conflicts the empire was engaged in during the later first century AD, and a result of the civil wars during the 'Year of the Four Emperors' in AD 69.

Throughout the Principate, the minimum height requirement for a legionary was 1.8m. By Agricola's day their term of service was twenty-five years, with the final five served as a veteran excused guard duties. Each legionary was paid 300 *denarii* a year, from which deductions were made annually to cover the cost of clothing, equipment and food. Legionary pay was often increased through donatives by the emperor, for example the 75 *denarii* left by Augustus to all his legionaries in his will. On retirement, the legionaries were also awarded a *praemia* retirement gratuity, either in the form of a cash payment of 5,000 *denarii* or land. The latter could be a parcel of *centuriated* farmland, or a plot in a *colonia* veteran settlement.

Like all armies, the legions of Rome marched on their stomachs. In his later military manual from the fourth century AD, Vegetius said troops should never be without corn and wheat, wine, salt and vinegar (*De Re Militari*, 3.3). Roman troops of all periods used these to make bread and porridge, and added beans, eggs and vegetables. Meat would be eaten on feast days, with the wider diet being supplemented by local produce and hunting. On campaign, the daily staples were hard tack and wholewheat biscuits, with bread baked at the end of the day's march after the marching camp had been built and armour and weapons cleaned.

In terms of equipment, the principal missile weapon of the legionary in Agricola's day was still the famous *pilum* weighted javelin. Two were carried, one heavy and one light (Cowan, 2003a, 30). Originally a Spanish design adopted by the Romans, these featured barbed heads on long, tapering soft iron tangs attached to a lead-weighted socket fixed to a wooden shaft. The weighted socket provided the driving force needed to hammer the weapon through enemy shields, armour and helmets. The lighter weapon was used as the legionaries approached the enemy, while the heavier one was used immediately prior to impact. The iron shaft was designed to bend after impact to disable the use of an opponent's shield. The heavier *pila*, which could easily go through both shield and the man holding it, also doubled as a makeshift spear when needed to help repel enemy shock cavalry.

However, the principal weapon of the Principate legionary was the *gladius hispaniensis* sword. This was also originally Spanish, adopted by the Polybian legions after the Romans fought the Iberian mercenaries of Hannibal in the Second Punic War. Rather than the short stabbing sword of popular legend, it was originally a cut and thrust weapon of medium length, up to 69cm long and 5cm in width, with a tapering sharp stabbing point. Those originally used by legionaries inflicted gaping injuries that shocked their opponents in the Second Macedonian War because, as it lacked any blood runnels to let air into the wound, the sword had to be viciously twisted to release it (Matyszak, 2009, 64). This weapon developed at the beginning of the Principate into the Mainz type *gladius*. This was broader and shorter in shape, with a longer stabbing point. By the time of Agricola, this had developed further into the Pompeii-type *gladius* of the later first century AD. This was shorter again, with a shorter, triangular stabbing point. All were worn on the right-hand side if a legionary, and left if a centurion as a mark of differentiation. Many have questioned how a legionary could draw the weapon smoothly into the en garde position from the right-hand side, especially as the pommel sat just below the armpit. In his detailed analysis of the weapon, Bishop (2016, 46) explains:

> In fact, the *gladius* can be easily drawn by inverting the right hand, thumb downwards, then grasping the handgrip and pulling straight upwards. It is a quiet natural progression to continue this movement forwards to bring the sword down to the side, point forward, in the characteristic 'at the ready' position depicted on relief sculpture.

To complete his offensive weaponry, the legionary also carried a *pugio* dagger on the opposite hip to the *gladius*.

In terms of defensive panoply, the Principate legionary was equipped with the curved, rectangular *scutum*. This was a development of the more oval Republican example in use since the reforms of Camillus. The Principate version was some 83cm wide and 102cm long (Cowan, 2003a, 26). It was constructed from planed wooden strips laminated together in three layers. The shield was very heavy, weighing up to 10kg, and held by a left-handed horizontal grip using a straightened arm. It was used in close conjunction with the *gladius* in a very specific fencing technique, often taking the blow of an enemy weapon while the legionary was in the crouch, the *gladius* then driven up into the opponent's midriff or down into the upper thorax. The *scutum* could also be used as an offensive weapon in its own right to smash into an opponent and push them off balance, again exposing them to a lethal blow from the *gladius*.

For armour, legionaries of the Principate were better armoured than most regular foot troops until the later medieval period. They wore a wide variety of types of full body armour. The most commonly depicted in contemporary imagery, and also most frequently found in the archaeological record, is *lorica segmentata* banded iron armour. This was a highly effective armour made from articulated iron plates and hoops, though it was complicated to make and, especially, maintain. Fine examples of such armour can be found as sculpture on Trajan's Column, the Column of Marcus Aurelius and on the reused panels from a lost Arch of Marcus Aurelius found on the Arch of Constantine, all in Rome.

First appearing in the late first century BC, *lorica segmentata* became the standard legionary through to the mid-third century AD. The origins of this armour are unclear, though it may have originally been a form of gladiator armour. From that point, it evolved through three specific versions, these being (all named after the locations where examples were found):

- The Dangestetten-Kalkriese-Vindonissa type, those found dating to between 9 BC and AD 43.
- The Corbridge-Carnuntum type, those found dating to between AD 69 and AD 100. This would have been the most common defensive cuirass worn by Agricola's legionaries.
- The Newstead type, those found dating to between AD 164 and AD 180.

Each successive version was less complicated than that which preceded it, for example that found in the *principia* of the vexillation fort at Newstead (Roman *Trimontium*) in the Scottish Borders in 1905 featuring rivets to replace earlier bronze hinges, a single large girdle plate to replace the two previous ones, and hooks to replace earlier and more complicated belt-buckle fastenings.

Principate legionaries also wore other types of armour, for example the *lorica hamata* long chainmail hauberk. This was the principal suit of armour of the mid-late Republican legionary, a design adopted from that worn by elite Gallic warriors. It weighed around 15kg and, going full circle chronologically, replaced *lorica segmentata* as the principle legionary armour from the mid-third century AD when the latter fell out of use, largely due to its cost. Another type of body amour was the *lorica squamata* scale mail hauberk. Further, extra armour could also be fitted. This included articulated iron *manicae* arm guards, thigh guards and greaves. These are all visible on Trajan's Column in Rome. Certain troop types within the legions were also often differentially equipped with armour, with for example officers frequently shown wearing iron and bronze muscled cuirasses resplendent with medusa images on the breast plate, and centurions and *aquilifer* standard-bearers wearing chainmail throughout the Principate.

Meanwhile, the helmet of the legionary had also evolved by the time of Agricola from the various styles of the late Republic. At the beginning of the Principate, two types predominated. These were:

- The Coolus type with a round cap of bronze and small neck guard, which disappeared by the middle of the first century AD.
- The iron Port type, which featured a deep neck guard, this named after the site-type location of Port bei Nidau in Switzerland.

The latter soon developed into the classic imperial Gallic helmet often associated with the Roman legionary of the first and second centuries AD. This ubiquitous design featured an even larger neck guard, and was the most common type worn by Agricola's legionaries. All of these helmets had prominent cheek guards and a reinforcing brow ridge on the front of the cap to deflect downward sword cuts. Ear guards were added from the AD 50s.

In terms of non-military kit, a Principate legionary carried his equipment on a T-shaped pole that rested on his shoulders. This included his engineering equipment, comprising a sickle, saw, basket, pickaxe, chain, two stakes and a leather strap. These enabled him to carry out any engineering activities, for example building a marching camp at the end of every day's march in enemy territory. Also carried on the pole were a *patera* bronze mess tin, a water skin in a net bag, a cooking pot, and canvas bags for grain rations and spare clothing. His shield was held in place on his back, while helmets were usually strung from the neck across the chest. The legionary's personal marching kit also included a *paenula* hooded woollen bad weather cloak, with officers wearing the shorter rectangular *sagum*. However, the most important piece of kit when on the march was the *caligae* hobnailed sandal or the *calcei* enclosed, hobnailed boot. Overall, the marching load of the average legionary was an impressive 30kg; they were nicknamed *muli mariani* Marius' mules after the great reforming warrior consul.

Finally, Roman legionaries also provided the battlefield and siege artillery component of Roman armies when on campaign. These proved particularly valuable during Agricola's campaigns in the far north of Britain. Such weapons included light *scorpio* dart-throwers and the larger *ballista*, the latter firing large bolts and shaped stones. When at full strength each cohort fielded one of the latter and each century one of the former. This gave an impressive total of ten *ballistae* and fifty-nine *scorpiones* per legion.

The Auxilia

Legionaries were not the only soldiers in the Roman military at the time of Agricola. Before the advent of the empire, Republican Roman armies had always used allied auxiliary troops to support the legions, for example the Gallic and German cavalry often referenced by Caesar during his campaigns in Gaul. Such troops fought in their own formations and under their own commanders. All such supporting troops were then professionalised as a regular component of the Roman armed forces when Augustus became emperor, part of his much wider reforms of the Roman military. From that point, they became known as auxilia. These troops were mostly recruited from *peregrini* non-Italian freemen. Tacitus reports that by AD 25 there were as many auxilia in the Roman army as legionaries, the latter number at that time around 175,000 (*The Annals*, 4.5). Auxilia were to play a key role in Agricola's northern campaigns in Britain.

By the later first century AD, auxilia were paid 100 *denarii* per year if infantry and 200 *denarii* if cavalry, with elite cavalry based on the wing of a battle formation paid 333 *denarii*. Their term of service was twenty-five years, as with the legionaries. On retirement, the trooper was given a diploma which granted full Roman citizenship to himself and his heirs. It also gave them the legal right to marry a non-citizen woman.

The auxilia provided most of the cavalry and much of the foot complement of Roman armies. In the first instance, many of the cavalry units were among the most feared in the Roman military, specifically recruited from regions famous at the time for their formidable mounted warriors. A good example were Gallic auxiliary cavalry, descendants of Caesar's mounted troops referenced above, who were best known for their penchant for head-hunting (Perring, 2017, 46).

Auxiliary cavalry were organised into *quingenary alae* of 512 men, or *milliary alae* of 768. Each was commanded by a *praefectus alae*. The standard cavalryman at the time of Agricola was called an *equite*. Each was equipped with a *hasta* spear that could be thrown or used as a short lance, and a *spatha* long sword. Their defensive panoply included flat hexagonal or oval shields, short *lorica hamata* chainmail hauberks and a variety of types of iron and bronze helmets, often with neck and cheek guards. In the early Principate, the *equites* were supported by a variety of different types of light cavalry fighting in the style of their native region. Examples included Moorish *symmachiarii* javelin-armed skirmishers, and eastern horse archers.

In terms of auxilia foot troops, although these were the junior partners to their legionary counterparts, they were still among the best soldiers of the ancient world. There were many occasions when the fighting was done by the auxilia alone, for example under Agricola at Mons Graupius when he finally defeated the Caledonii and their allies (Tacitus, *The Agricola*, 36.1-2).

Auxilia infantry formations in the Principate were based on a single *quingenary* cohort of 480 troops, or a double-sized *milliary* cohort of 800 troops. These cohorts (both the small and large) were divided into centuries of between 80 and 100 men, these under the command of a centurion, replicating the similar structure in a legionary formation. However, the centurions, unlike the auxiliary troopers, were sometimes Roman citizens appointed from the legions. Others were drawn direct from the rank and file of the auxiliary unit. Above this level the foot cohort was commanded by an equestrian, a *praefectus* for a *quingenary* unit and a tribune for a *milliary* unit.

Auxilia foot fought in both close and loose formation, the latter making them especially useful in difficult terrain. As with the cavalry, they often retained the skills associated with their place of origin, for example the river crossing Batavian auxilia used by Aulus Plautius when fighting his way over the Medway in Kent during the AD 43 Claudian invasion of Britain (Dio, *Roman History*, 60.19).

The majority of auxiliary foot were line of battle troops who fought in a similar manner to the legionaries. They were armed with short, throwable spears called *lancea* rather than *pila* and a sword similar to the legionary *gladius*, this later replaced by the longer cavalry-style *spatha*. The auxiliary shield at the time of Agricola was usually an elongated oval plank design covering the torso with a central iron or bronze boss. Auxilia are most frequently shown wearing *lorica hamata* chainmail or *lorica squamata* scalemail hauberks, these shorter and less sophisticated than the equivalent worn by their legionary counterparts. Auxilia helmets were also less sophisticated, often cheaper bronze versions of those worn by the legionaries. The auxilia also provided most of the specialist warriors in Roman foot formations, for example archers, slingers, staff slingers and javelinmen.

Auxilia units could also be fielded in combined formations that featured both infantry and mounted troops, their organisation being less well understood. Such infantry cohorts, cavalry *alae* and combined units were very flexible and could easily be moved around the empire as needed in the same manner as vexillations of legionaries.

The Regional Fleets

The regional navies of the Roman Empire were also the result of the military reforms of Augustus, with the *Classis Britannica* British fleet playing a key role in Agricola's northern campaigns. Before the Augustan reforms, the fleets of the Republic were ad hoc in nature, designed to fight symmetrical engagements against opponents including Carthage, the Hellenistic kingdoms and in Roman civil wars in the Mediterranean. Augustus rationalised this expensive system, instead transforming the various fleets he inherited into regional navies that reflected the empire's expanding geographical reach. By the later first century AD, there were ten such fleets, each with a specific area of territorial responsibility. These are detailed in the table below, which also shows the annual stipend of each fleet's *praefectus classis* admiral, reflecting their status.

Regional Fleets of the Roman Principate.

Fleet	Annual Stipend
Classis Ravenna	300,000 sesterces
Classis Misenensis	200,000 sesterces
Classis Britannica	100,000 sesterces
Classis Germanica	100,000 sesterces
Classis Flavia Pannonica	60,000 sesterces
Classis Flavia Moesica	60,000 sesterces
Classis Pontica	60,000 sesterces
Classis Syriaca	60,000 sesterces
Classis Nova Lybica	60,000 sesterces
Classis Alexandrina	60,000 sesterces

(Ellis Jones, 2012, 61)

The *Classis Britannica* is a good example of one of the larger Principate regional fleets. This featured 900 ships and 7,000 crew, including sailors, marines and support personnel (Elliott, 2016, 63). Each regional fleet had an origin specific to its region of operations, with that in Britain dating to the original 900 vessels built by Caligula for his abortive AD 40 invasion (see Chapter 3). These were later used by Claudius for his AD 43 invasion. Though this fleet took part in every aspect of the campaigns of conquest in Britain from that point, it was actually first called the *Classis Britannica* by Tacitus in the context of the Batavian uprising in Germania Inferior in AD 70 (*The Histories*, 4.79.3).

All regional fleets performed both military and civilian roles. In the former context, the *Classis Britannica* had responsibility for the North Sea, English Channel, Atlantic approaches, Bristol Channel and Irish Sea, the east and west coasts of the main island of Britain, the river systems of Britain, and the continental coast up to the Rhine Delta. The latter is reflected in the fact that the *Classis Britannica*'s headquarters was in Boulogne-sur-Mer (Roman *Gesoriacum*) in northwestern Gaul, with additional key bases in Britain including Dover (Roman *Dubris*),

Richborough (Roman *Rutupiae*), Lympne (Roman *Lemanis*) and Pevensey (Roman *Anderitum*). Its military responsibilities included controlling the open ocean, supporting land-based military operations in the littoral zone along the coast and downriver systems, scouting and reconnaissance, and also policing and transport.

Meanwhile, in its civilian activities the *Classis Britannica* was used in a variety of roles. This included administration, engineering and construction, and running industry and agriculture. As Parfitt (2013, 45) explains: 'The *Classis Britannica* seems to have functioned as some kind of army service corps, supporting the government and provincial army, rather than [just] as a navy in the modern sense.'

The principal warship of the *Classis Britannica* (as with all regional fleets) was the small and mobile *liburnian bireme* galley equipped with ram and *ballista*. These had replaced the large polyreme galleys of the Republican civil wars by the end of the first century BC. The fleet also used a variety of *myoparo* cutters and *scapha* skiffs, and transport vessels based on Romano-Celtic designs with high freeboards and shallow drafts designed for operation in northern waters.

An equestrian-level *praefectus classis* appointed directly by the emperor commanded each regional fleet. He reported to a province's procurator rather than governor given each fleet's civilian activities, though its control fell under the latter's command when on military duty. Individuals we know of in Britain holding the role include Q. Baienus Blassianus, named in the role in an inscription from Ostia, Lucius Aufidius Pantera, who is named on an alter found at Lympne, and Marcus Maenius Agrippa, who appears on an inscription from *Camerinum* in Umbria. As part of his headquarters operation, the *praefectus classis* had a specialist staff. This included a *subpraefectus* executive officer and aide-de-camp, *cornicularius* chief of staff, *actuarii* clerks, *scribae* scribes and seconded *dupliarii* ratings attached from the fleet.

Below the headquarters staff, the fleets relied heavily on Hellenistic nomenclature in terms of command structure. The commander of a squadron of ships was called a *navarchus* (the most senior the *navarchus principes*), and the captain of an individual vessel a *trierarchus*. Aboard ship, the *trierarchus'* executive team included a *gubernator* senior officer responsible for the steering oars, a *proretus* second lieutenant and the *pausarius* rowing master. Other junior officers included the *secutor* master-at-arms, *nauphylax* officers of the watch and specialists including the *velarii* with responsibility for the sails and the *fabri* ship's carpenter.

Below this level, the ship's company was based on the military organisation of their land-based counterparts, with the basic unit called a century. This reflected the preference for close action when engaged in naval combat. The century was commanded by a centurion, he assisted by an *optio* second-in-command, a *suboptio* junior assistant, a *bucinator* bugler or *cornicen* horn player, and finally an *armorum custos* armourer. The rest of the ship's complement was comprised of marines (*ballistarii* artillery crew, *sagittarii* archers and *propugnatores* deck soldiers), *velarius* sailors, and plenty of *remiges* oarsmen. The latter were always professional rather than the slaves often depicted in popular culture, the whole company being styled *milites* (soldiers, the singular being *miles*) as opposed to *nautae* sailors. This again reflected the Roman preference for maritime close action.

In the Principate, service as a naval *miles* was similar to serving in the auxilia. Those in the *Classis Britannica* were often recruited from the former tribes of the coastal regions in northwestern Gaul. Terms of service for all ranks was twenty-six years – a year longer than their auxiliary counterparts – the reward on completion, again Roman citizenship. We have unique insight into this in the form of a recent archaeological discovery. This was the finding of the copper alloy military diploma of one Tigernos, a sailor of the *Classis Germanica*, granting him citizenship after completing his service. Interestingly, he may prove to be Britain's first known sailor as, despite his service on the Rhine, the diploma was found broken into eight pieces at the Roman fort in Lanchester (Roman *Longuvicium*), County Durham.

Each naval *miles* received three gold pieces or 75 *denarii* on enlistment. Their basic annual pay at the beginning of the Principate for the lower ranks was 100 *denarii* per year, with crewmembers with greater responsibilities being paid an additional amount on top.

Clothing for the naval *milites* differed between the regional fleets. This reflected differing climatic and operational conditions. Again using the *Classis Britannica* as an example, an essential item of clothing in northern waters would have been the *birrus* rain-proofed hooded cloak. Other key items of clothing for the *milites* of this regional fleet included the *pilos* conical felt hat, belted tunic with trousers, and sandals or felt stockings with low-cut *calcei*.

For weaponry, the marines of the regional fleets were armed in a similar manner to their land-based auxilia counterparts. Principal missile weapons, in addition to artillery, included bows, slings, javelins and darts. For hand-to-hand work, the marines also carried boarding pikes, the *hasta navalis* naval spear, various types of sword and the *dolabra* boarding axe.

Chapter 3

Roman Britain in the Later First Century AD

Prior to their first contact with the world of Rome, the indigenous peoples of the British Isles had a rich cultural history, dating back almost 10,000 years to a time when reoccupation began here after the end of the last Ice Age. Throughout this lengthy period, they maintained strong links with their continental neighbours, sharing each societal and technological development. This reached its height with the La Tène culture that dominated much of Britain at the time of Rome's first serious engagement here, Julius Caesar's two invasions in 55 BC and 54 BC. While Caesar didn't overwinter in Britain during either of his incursions, his two campaigns did put the archipelago firmly on the Roman map. It was then left to the most unlikely of Roman emperors to actually invade in strength and stay, this the ill-starred Claudius. His arrival in AD 43 established the Roman province on the main island of Britain. From that point onwards through to Agricola's time as governor, the story of Roman Britain was one of hard, often slow conquest.

In this chapter, I first detail Late Iron Age (LIA) Britain to provide context for the Roman story that follows. I then sequentially cover Caesar's two invasions, the Claudian conquest in AD 43, and the subsequent breakout campaigns through to the early AD 60s and the defeat of the Boudiccan revolt, the latter covered in the next chapter.

Late Iron Age Britain

The British Isles are the most northwesterly archipelago of the European landmass. Repopulation of what was then a peninsula began around 9600 BC after the end of the 1,200-year-long Younger Dryas cold spell that interrupted the gradual warming of northern Europe after the end of the last Ice Age. Those arriving back were hunter-gatherers, originally from the Upper Paleolithic Ahrensburgian culture, whose influence stretched from the Atlantic coast to Poland (Cunliffe, 2013, 102). These were later replaced by various Mesolithic cultures.

Then, around 5500 BC, an event occurred that has defined Britain geographically ever since. This was the final submergence of Doggerland, the North Sea land bridge linking Britain to the continent (Gaffney, Fitch and Smith, 2009, 31). However, this didn't stop the islands here remaining culturally connected to the continent. Britain continued to fully participate in each new wave of social and technological advancement originating there, with the usual vector of transmission through the southeastern region, from where new ideas and practices gradually spread throughout the rest of the British Isles. A key development in this regard was the arrival of farming at the onset of the Neolithic period around 4200 BC.

The next cultural development was the advent of the Chalcolithic period, better known as the Copper Age. In Britain, this happened from 3000 BC, followed by the Bronze Age from 2500 BC. The latter coincided with the arrival of the Bell Beaker culture, which culturally linked the islands of Britain to every corner of the European landmass, including the Mediterranean.

The British Iron Age began around 800 BC. This featured five phases, these being:

- The Earliest Iron Age from 800 BC to 600 BC. In this phase, much of Britain was part of the Hallstatt culture that predominated in western and central Europe.
- The Early Iron Age from 600 BC to 400 BC. During this period, much of Britain continued to be part of the Hallstatt culture, and was later part of its La Tène evolution.
- The Middle Iron Age from 400 BC to 100 BC, where La Tène culture continued to predominate.
- The Late Iron Age from 100 BC to 50 BC, once more La Tène in nature.
- The Latest Iron Age from 50 BC to the creation of the Roman Province of Britannia in AD 43. Again, La Tène culture featured strongly, with parts of Britain (particularly the south and east) the culture's last redoubt in northwestern Europe after Caesar's conquest of Gaul from 58 BC.

Up to the invasions of Caesar, it is clear from all preceding cultural developments in Britain that the islands were intrinsically linked with their continental neighbours through thousands of years of engagement. To those living here the physical maritime barrier of the English Channel and North Sea was actually a means of connectivity (as it was later for the Romans), rather than the obstacle we see it as today through the prism of the past 400 years of military conflict (Elliott, 2016, 82). Immediately prior to Caesar's Gallic campaigns, these links were manifest in many ways, for example the export of goods from Britain to the continent. These were well known to contemporary audiences, for example iron, as detailed by the Greek geographer Strabo (*The Geography*, 4.5) and Caesar himself (*The Conquest of Gaul*, 5.135), and many other metals too. Other exports at the time included woollen goods, hunting dogs and slaves (Elliott, 2016, 113). This connectivity was then brutally dislocated by Caesar's conquest of Gaul. From that time, Britain became a place of refuge for those on the continent fleeing his sanguineous campaigns there. Plutarch later calculated that these cost the lives of 1 million Gauls and the enslavement of another million (*Life of Caesar*, 15.5). To contextualise the scale of this loss, the entire population of LIA Britain at this time was around 2 million. Suddenly, Britain's connections with continental neighbours of like mind and culture had been shut off. The tribes here now had to deal with Romans casting an avaricious eye across the English Channel.

By the first century BC the main island of Britain, where Rome later carved its province, featured a dense network of tribes who were often at war with each other. The second-century AD polymath Claudius Ptolemy's *Geography* is our key source here (2.150). Beginning in modern Kent and heading roughly clockwise, they included the Cantiaci, the Trinovantes to their north in eastern Essex, the Catuvellauni in western Essex through to Oxfordshire, the Atrebates in the Thames Valley and the Regni and Belgae on the south coast. In the South West, one then had the Durotriges and Dumnonii, with the Dubonni and Cornovii to their north reaching into the Welsh Marches. Into Wales proper were the Silures, Demetae, Ordovices and Deceangli ranging south to north, with the Brigantes in the north of modern England, the Carvetii in the North West, the Parisi north of the Humber, the Corieltauvi (or Coritani) south of the Humber through to the East Midlands, and the Iceni in modern north Norfolk.

Heading into modern Scotland, the battlespace for Agricola's campaigns in the far north, the tribes detailed by Ptolemy there included the Votadini in the eastern Scottish Borders, the Selgovae in the central Borders, the Novantae in the western Borders, the Dumnonii around the Clyde, and the Epidii in the Mull of Kintyre. Then above the Clyde on the west coast, going south to north, were the Creones, the Carnonacae and (at the far northwestern tip of Scotland) the Caereni. On the east coast around the river Tay were the Venicones, and above them in Aberdeenshire the Vacomagi and Taexali. Broadly, throughout the Grampians were located the Caledonii, then around the Moray Firth, again going south to north, the Decantae, Lugi, Smertae and finally the Cornacii. Additionally, the Romans also interacted with the various Scots peoples of modern Ireland across the Irish Sea.

For completeness, by the reign of Commodus in the AD 180s, Dio says most of the tribes in modern Scotland had amalgamated into two huge confederations, the Maeatae and Caledonians. He says that 'the Maeatae live next to the cross-wall which cuts the island in half, and the Caledonians are beyond them' (*Roman History*, 77.12). Most modern commentators interpret this fortification as the Antonine Wall on the Clyde–Forth line, placing the Maeatae in the Scottish Borders, Fife and the lower Midland Valley, and the Caledonians in the upper Midland Valley and Scottish Highlands. The causal event behind this merging of the various native peoples living in the region during the earlier Flavian 'tribal' period was interaction with the Roman province to the south. Here, the Roman administration was able to influence political, economic and societal developments in the unconquered far north by favouring certain elites and groups through the judicious distribution of wealth and power. This enabled some to dominate others. Sadly for Rome, as will be seen in later chapters, this diplomatic strategy didn't take into account the long-term animosity of those living in the region to the Roman world. Thus, while it did facilitate the creation of much larger political groupings there, it didn't lead to Roman conquest (and indeed may have prevented it). I mention this post-Flavian development here for two reasons. First, later Principate historians including Dio and Herodian provide much detail of the natives in the far north, which in their day were the Maeatae and Caledonians. Analogously, this is directly relevant to the earlier 'Flavian' tribal period. Second, and confusingly, we have the use of Caledonians in both phases. Ptolemy details the Caledonii as the main tribe living in the Grampians, while later we have the Caledonian confederation from the late second century AD onwards. These are clearly different entities, the latter much larger than the former though likely taking their name from the original core tribe in the Grampians. In this work, I will be explicit about which I am discussing.

The economy of LIA Britain was dominated by agriculture. This was at its most advanced in the lowlands of LIA Britain, with all members of society except the upper elite levels of the aristocracy involved. In general, in the lowlands mixed agriculture was practised with both livestock and crops farmed (Jones and Mattingly, 1990, 5). Most of the farming was subsistence in nature, with any agricultural surplus supplied to tribal leaders for storage. This helped mitigate against any harvest shocks, and also underpinned trade for manufactured goods both regionally and with the continent. Based on the archaeological record, the main animals farmed included pigs, goats, cattle and sheep, the balance depending on where in Britain the farming was taking place. In terms of crops, native Britons used rectangular fields for the most part, and may also have used a field rotation system whereby a given field would be left fallow for a year, with livestock grazing on it. This helped keep weeds in check, and also fertilised the land with manure. LIA Britons used an ard type light plough drawn by oxen, this a simple design that lacked a mud board. Sometimes called a scratch plough, this could only cut a shallow and narrow furrow. However, as the LIA progressed the Britons did make some advances in agricultural practice, for example digging drainage ditches to drain waterlogged land (and thus open it up to agriculture) and to water their fields. The most common arable crops were spelt, emmer and einkhorn wheat, and barley. Oats, rye and millet were also grown.

Industry also existed in LIA Britain, though not on the scale of agricultural activity. For example, coins were minted (mostly copies of Mediterranean issues), pottery produced, mill and quern stones manufactured, and mining and metal production carried out. Technological innovation also occurred, for example with the adoption of the potter's wheel, the rotary quern and the lathe.

In terms of settlement, there was no Mediterranean-style stone-built urban environment in LIA Britain, with the largest communities gathered in *oppida* proto-towns. These were the central administrative centres for the larger tribes, defined by their well-designed ditch and bank defensive linear earthworks. Jones and Mattingly say that some of these settlements were huge, with vast areas of land contained within massive systems of dykes (1990, 47). A prime example was Camulodunum (later, Roman *Colonia Claudia Victricensis*), capital of the Catuvellauni at the time of the Claudian invasion in AD 43. Such settlements appear to have been an innovation of the early first century BC, with Haywood arguing they had evolved from hill forts, long a key feature of the British rural landscape (2009, 78). Below this level, the majority of the population lived in farming villages of varying sizes and types, or in isolated farmsteads.

The military system of the native Britons fought first by Caesar, and later by the Principate empire in its various campaigns of conquest in Britain (including those of Agricola in the far north), remained the same for most of the Roman occupation, and was rooted in the LIA La Tène traditions of the continent. This featured a chariot-riding aristocracy, skirmishing cavalry riding ponies, line of battle troops armed with short spears, and sling or javelin-armed skirmishing foot. In terms of army size, given few native British troops were professional, various sized gatherings are reported in contemporary history. For example, when Cassivellaunus (likely the tribal leader of the Catuvellauni in the mid-first century BC) fought Caesar he fielded a large force of chariots manned by 4,000 charioteers late in the 54 BC campaign, having sent the rest of his army home. However, given he was the leader of all resistance to Caesar in the southeast of Britain, it has been estimated he could have led up to 80,000 men if needed. Meanwhile, as fully detailed in Chapter 4, Boudicca could have led a force of 230,000 (Dio's figure, *Roman History*, 62.8), including 100,000 warriors, in her incendiary insurrection against the Roman occupation in AD 60/61. However, at the other end of the scale the Caledonii and their allies who fought Agricola at Mons Graupius in AD 83 only numbered 30,000, and as detailed in Chapter 8, were easily defeated by the Roman auxilia alone.

The elite troops in native British armies were the chariot-riding nobility. They were most popular among the tribes in the southeast and east of Britain at the time of the Caesar's 55 BC and 54 BC incursions, but were used throughout the British Isles given the status they bestowed on the chariot rider. Native British chariots featured two ponies harnessed with a yoke and breast straps to a draft pole, a wooden fighting platform with wicker sides, and two wheels on a centrally mounted axle (Allen, 2001, 47). They featured two crewmembers, these being an unarmed driver and the noble. The latter carried a large Gallic shield that was either oval, sometimes with the upper and lower ends removed, or round. Both types featured a central boss. All were of plank construction, often covered in a thin sheet of bronze or with a leather hide. The noble also wore various kinds of Gallic helmet and a chainmail hauberk. He was armed with javelins and the long iron Gallic slashing sword.

Caesar, Dio and Tacitus all describe these native chariots in action, with all reporting how manoeuverable they were and saying the Britons deliberately rode them across the front of an enemy battleline, which they showered with javelins and insults. The noble then often jumped down to fight on foot, leading his own war band.

Meanwhile, British cavalry were much lighter than their Gallic counterparts. They acted in a supporting role to the chariots. Specifically, they skirmished with javelins, attacked flanks and pursued routers. When used in conjunction with the chariots they proved a particular nuisance for Caesar in his two incursions to Britain, and later the Claudian invasion.

By far the biggest component of native British armies was their line of battle spearmen. These were mostly farmers called up in a mass levy when needed who were armed in a similar manner to the warriors faced by Caesar in his conquest of Gaul. The main defensive equipment was the Gallic shield as used by the chariot-riding nobility, or a simpler wicker and hide design, the latter more common in the far north. Few wore helmets and fewer any form of armour. The main weapon was a light spear or javelin, with some troops also armed with the long Gallic sword or a dagger. In Britain these warriors formed a spear wall if required, usually in a strong defensive position as with those opposing the Claudian invasion in the river crossing battle in Kent in AD 43 (Elliott, 2016, 115), and the Caledonii and their allies who deployed on the steep slopes of

Mons Graupius in AD 83. However, the preferred tactic was the use of natural terrain to ambush their opponents, often as part of a guerrilla campaign. The native Britons who later fought Septimius Severus in the far north in AD 209 and AD 210 provide a good example of this.

Meanwhile, in Britain the favoured missile weapon used by skirmishers was the sling, particularly in the southwest. The Durotriges and Dumnonii tribes who fought Vespasian are a good example of this. Javelin-armed skirmishers are also reported, though no bowmen, at least until later in the Roman occupation.

Finally, regarding LIA Britain, all the Roman campaigns here (including those of Agricola) were heavily influenced by geology and geography. Jones and Mattingly highlight that broadly there are two geological zones here (1990, 1). These are the western and northern region, featuring many older and harder rock formations (both igneous and metamorphic), and the southern and eastern region (including much of the Midlands) where many of the rocks are softer and sedimentary in nature. Though by no means uniform, the former zone features much of the highlands of Britain where military campaigning was difficult, while the latter zone features much of the more fertile lowlands.

Focusing specifically on modern Scotland given this was the Agricolan battlespace, its geology and geography as part of Jones and Mattingly's western and northern region is unusually varied, featuring often complicated drift geology. The three main geological subdivisions there are:

- The Southern Uplands, lying to the south of the Southern Uplands Fault (and largely composed of Silurian deposits).
- The Central Lowlands, a rift valley mainly comprising Paleozoic formations.
- The Highlands and Islands, a diverse area lying to the north and west of the Highland Boundary Fault.

It is this latter Highland Boundary Fault (or Highland line) that played the key geological role in the campaigns in Scotland of both Agricola and Septimius Severus given it runs southwest to northeast from the Isle of Arran to Stonehaven, delineating the Scottish Highlands from the more fertile Midland Valley (including Fife) and Scottish Borders to its south and east. Here, for simplicity, I will use the terms highlands for land north of the Highland line, and lowlands for that to its south. More specific detail is given about the differences between the Agricolan battlespace in the far north and the Roman province of Britannia to its south in Chapter 5.

Further key features of the geography of the main island of Britain are its rivers and waterways. These were widely used in all of Rome's military campaigns here, including those of Agricola. Indeed, it is no coincidence that nearly all Roman fortresses, forts and stone-built settlements in Britain are sited on navigable rivers.

In terms of the specific weather conditions during the Agricolan campaigns in the far north, modern scientific research provides useful detail. This shows that the weather in the region at the time was not far removed from that we experience today, except it was perhaps slightly warmer and wetter earlier in the Roman occupation (Grainge, 2005, 37). The principal type of system dominating weather patterns in the islands of Britain during the occupation were Atlantic lows, just as they are today, with the prevailing winds usually originating from the westerly quadrant. These winds are created by North Atlantic depressions moving east or northeast across the open ocean before meeting the northwestern European landmass, usually hitting Ireland and Britain first. Such weather systems are then modified as they interact with high-pressure systems when they approach the continental land mass. It is this set of interactions that leads to what we today call Britain's unpredictable weather, and which the Romans simply called wet and cold.

Specifically regarding the Agricolan battlespace in the far north, both Dio (76.5) and Herodian (2.15) say the weather there during the Roman occupation was even grimmer than the Romans detail for the provincial south. In a detailed analysis looking at this differential today, Ottaway uses data taken between 1971 and 2000 to show that on the south coast of Britain there was an average of 1,750 hours of sunshine per year, compared to 1,149 in Malham Tarn in North Yorkshire (2013, 16). This differential is even more pronounced as one heads into the far north. Meanwhile, again using Yorkshire as an example in the same time period, Ottaway shows that in terms of rainfall there is a very pronounced difference in the amount experienced in the upland Pennines when compared to the lowlands, with 1,518mm per annum at Malham Tarn compared to 600mm in York itself, this a useful analogy for the rest of Britain. Thus, the overall picture is one where the north of the islands of Britain receives less sunlight than the south, and with more rain in the upland regions, including much of modern Scotland.

Caesar in Britain

Britain was known in the Mediterranean world prior to Caesar's engagements here, though not well. The earliest reference to its existence appears in the sixth century BC *Massaliot Periplus* merchant's handbook, now lost but referenced in the *Ora maritima* poem written by the Roman poet Avienus in the late fourth century AD.

The original sixth-century BC work is also the first to attribute a name for the inhabitants of the archipelago, calling the Britons the *Albiones* for the Irish *Iverni*. Herodotus is the next to reference islands in northwestern Europe in the fifth century BC, he describing the Cassiterides in his *Histories*. These have often been associated with Britain, given the name translates as 'tin islands', this important metal a key export from Britain from prehistoric times. More clarity then comes in the form of the fourth century BC Greek geographer Pytheas. From Marseille (the Greek colony of *Massilia*, also home of the *Massaliot Periplus* detailed above), his definitive work is similarly lost to us, but key sections have been preserved by ancient authors including Strabo, Pliny the Elder and Diodorus. Pytheas was the first person to record a circumnavigation of Britain during his maritime exploration of northwestern Europe. This also took in a visit to modern Denmark and seemingly an extraordinary visit to Iceland. His reports on the British Isles set a template for most of what followed in the classical world, highlighting their triangular shape and describing Kent, Land's End in Cornwall and the Orkneys. He also notes for the first time the name from which our current 'Britain' is derived, he reporting that the natives were called the *pretani*. This translates as painted ones, referencing the native practice (at least where he visited) of their painting themselves in woad designs, and wearing tattoos.

Roman Britain in the Later First Century AD

Both Strabo and Pliny made extensive use of Pytheas in their much later descriptions of Britain, the latter going into an immense amount of detail, for instance describing the forty islands of the Orkneys, the seven of the Shetlands, the thirty of the Hebrides, and also describing the Isle of Anglesey. Pytheas' work is also evident in the physical descriptions of Britain by others, for example Caesar himself. His *Conquest of Gaul* gives us our first detailed insight into LIA Britain through the descriptions of his two campaigns there.

Caesar's landings in Britain were in effect large-scale armed reconnaissances. They took place as part of his campaigns to conquer Gaul, which had begun in 58 BC and were now almost complete. He was keenly aware of the support being given to any remaining Gallic resistance from Britain, and knew it was here that the Gallic elites who refused to bow to the might of Rome were fleeing. He also knew there was huge political kudos to be made by visiting this most fantastical of lands across terrifying *Oceanus*, as the Romans then knew the English Channel. Always aware of his reputation and legacy back in Rome, he decided to act, and decisively.

For his first attempt in 55 BC, Caesar marched his legionaries from *legio* VII and *legio* X (around 12,000 men) north to the territory of the Morini opposite Kent. Here he gathered eighty transports and eighteen additional vessels modified to carry horses, together with war galleys from the Mediterranean. Knowing the value of scouting, he then sent his tribune Caius Volusenus in a *trireme* to identify a safe landing area on the east Kent coast. Caesar then waited for favourable conditions before crossing the Channel, arriving in late August off Dover, though his cavalry transports missed the tide and were never to arrive. Here he found native British troops massed on the coast awaiting his arrival, no doubt bolstered by Gallic refugees, and so he headed north. His fleet eventually weighed anchor between Walmer and Pegwell Bay, below Ramsgate. However, the Britons had tracked his fleet and were once again arrayed along the shore. He therefore carried out an amphibious assault, with the fleet and the legions working closely together. Caesar ordered his war galleys driven hard ashore to the north of his chosen landing area, the aim being to turn the Britons' left flank. From this position the *quinqeremes*, *quadiremes* and *triremes* were able to enfilade the landing area using *ballistae* and hand-held missile weapons. However, even then the legionaries were reluctant to land as the Britons held their ground.

Here the *aquilifer* of *legio* X rescued the day. Sensing the reticence of his colleagues to disembark, he leapt into the shallows and declared, 'Leap, fellow soldiers, unless you wish to betray your eagle to the enemy. I, for my part, will perform my duty to the Republic and to my general' (Julius Caesar, *The Conquest of Gaul*, 4.25). This worked, the shamed legionaries swarming ashore. Once engaged in hand-to-hand combat they were quickly successful, and the defeated leaders of the Britons sued for peace. However, bad weather later damaged many of Caesar's ships and, after some localised campaigning, the Romans returned to the continent using the remaining serviceable ships.

Showing typical Roman grit, Caesar determined the next year to return once more, and in much greater force. Thus, in 54 BC he gathered 5 legions and 2,000 cavalry. Learning from his experiences the previous year regarding the type of vessel best suited for amphibious operations in Britain, he also ordered the construction of 600 specially built ships. These featured lower freeboards than his Mediterranean-style vessels, enabling easier disembarkation, and had wider beams to carry bulkier loads. To these vessels Caesar added 200 locally chartered transports, a further 80 ships that had survived the previous year's incursion, and 28 war galleys (again a mix of *quinqeremes*, *quadiremes* and *triremes* from the Mediterranean).

The size of Caesar's force clearly intimidated the Britons as the landing on the east coast of Kent was this time unopposed. However, just as in 55 BC, bad weather intervened again. While Caesar was campaigning inland against a large British force, a storm badly damaged many of his transports anchored off the coast of Kent. Realising the vulnerability to his rear, he quickly returned to the landing area and initiated an urgent repair operation. The legions then renewed their campaign against the Britons, quickly forcing a crossing of the Thames and capturing the main base of the British leader Cassivellaunus, who then sued for peace. Terms were quickly agreed, including the Britons supplying hostages and agreeing to pay an annual tribute to Rome. Honour satisfied, Caesar returned to the landing area in Kent and re-embarked his forces for the return journey to northeastern Gaul, this taking place in two waves given the scale of ship losses in the earlier storm. Both arrived back safely towards the end of September. Thus ended his engagement with Britain.

The Claudian Invasion of Britain

While Caesar can be credited with the first and second Roman invasions of Britain, it was the third that successfully set up the province of Britannia, changing the history of the islands forever. This was that of Claudius in AD 43.

Though Augustus had planned three invasions of Britain in 34 BC, 27 BC and 24 BC, all were cancelled. The next emperor to plan a crossing to Britain was Caligula, though his attempt in AD 40 proved farcical and never left the Gallic coast. However, he did set in place a vast logistical operation, which, though unused in his case, three years later allowed Claudius to mount his successful invasion. This included building a lighthouse, extensive harbour works, wharfing and a large number of fully stocked warehouses at the key regional port of Boulogne-sur-Mer, and constructing 900 brand-new ships.

Claudius' reason for invading Britain was simple. After becoming emperor in AD 41, he desperately needed martial success to secure his position in Rome, given the unlikely nature of his ascent to the throne. He found it in far-off Britain, with Suetonius providing the detail. He says, 'he decided Britain was the country where a real triumph could most readily be earned' (*The Twelve Caesars*, 17.1).

Opportunity was provided by the death of Cunobelinus, king of the Catuvellauni. He was succeeded by Caratacus and Togodumnus, his two sons, who launched an offensive against their Atrebates neighbours in the Thames Valley. At the time, these were Roman allies. The Catuvellauni were victorious, with the Atrebatian king Verica fleeing to Rome. Here he sought an audience with Claudius. Caratacus and Togodumnus then overplayed their hand, demanding Verica's extradition. Claudius rebuffed them, with disturbances following in Britain against Roman merchants already embedded in the future province, a legacy of the earlier Caesarian invasions. With the means already available thanks to Caligula, and now the opportunity, Claudius decided to invade. The scene was set for one of the greatest amphibious operations in the pre-modern world.

Claudius took no chances. He gathered his army of conquest under the highly experienced Pannonian governor, Aulus Plautius, with another seasoned warrior in the future emperor Vespasian appointed as one of the legionary *legates*. The invasion force comprised four legions (*legio* II *Augusta*, *legio* IX *Hispana*, *legio* XIV *Gemina* and *legio* XX *Valeria Victrix*) together with auxiliaries, totalling 40,000 men. The 900 ships were also loaded with 3,000 tonnes of grain to feed the invasion force for at least three months after arrival.

A controversy now occurred. The legionaries, superstitious of *Oceanus* and mysterious Britain, refused to board their ships. At the last minute, the day was saved by Claudius' freedmen Narcissus, who boarded a vessel and shamed the soldiery into following him. The huge force then set sail in three divisions, arriving unopposed in mid to late summer, the British warriors having dispersed to gather the harvest.

There is much debate about the exact point where Plautius' force disembarked. Given its proximity to the continent, however, and noting arguments in favour of other potential landing places such as Chichester by Manley (2002, 131) and others, Kent is still widely argued to have been the landing place for this crucial event (Grainge, 117). That being the case, the most likely landing areas would again have been on the eastern coast of the county, the most obvious candidates being the beaches earlier used by Caesar, though given the huge size of the AD 43 fleet (even accepting it arrived in three waves), a much larger area would have been needed. Here it seems likely that the shelter of the then navigable Watsum Channel to the north of Sandwich, together with the safe harbourage of Pegwell Bay with its broad expanses of beach, would also have been used. As Moody (2008, 141) says:

> Given the size of the operation, it is unlikely that a single location can be identified for the Roman landings. More probably, the ships landed where they could, in the network of harbours, beaches and trading ports on the east and western sides of the Watsum and troops secured themselves, by units, over a wide area.

Once ashore, Plautius secured his beachhead by building a huge 57ha marching camp, the remains of which can still be seen today at the site of the later Saxon Shore fort at Richborough. Some 640m of the defensive ditch have been revealed to date. The sophistication of this fortification is indicated by the presence of a gate tower found by archaeologists on the western side.

Plautius now began his breakout, his 40,000 men snaking along the south side of the North Downs, where he could expect the most sunlight during the day. This was also the most fertile and heavily populated part of LIA Kent, with the newly gathered harvest available to plunder.

Finally, he tracked down his elusive foe, defeating Caratacus and Togodumnus separately in two small engagements in eastern Kent, after which the Dobunni (a tribe based in the Welsh Marches who had supplied troops to support the Catuvellauni) became the first of the British kingdoms to sue for peace. Consolidating for a short period after his victories, Plautius then continued westwards, quickly reaching Bluebell Hill overlooking the Medway Gap, where the river Medway cuts through the North Downs. There, instead of continuing along the route of the Pilgrim's Way as it turned north before crossing the winding river at Cuxton, he instead headed directly westwards, aiming to cross at one of two then well-known fording points. These were at modern Snodland and Aylesford, the former marking the tidal reach of the Medway at the time (Kaye, 2015, 232), and both close to each other.

It is here or nearby that I believe the famous river crossing battle described by Dio took place. This is an important engagement to consider in a work about Agricola's later campaigns in the far north given it shows the native Britons to be a seriously tough opponent, something often glossed over in narratives of the Roman conquests in Britain. To that end, I record Dio's commentary on the engagement in full (*Roman History*, 0.20):

(Plautius) advanced farther and came to a river. The barbarians thought that the Romans would not be able to cross it without a bridge, and consequently bivouacked in rather careless fashion on the opposite bank; but he sent across a detachment of Germans, who were accustomed to swim easily in full armour across the most turbulent streams. These fell unexpectedly upon the enemy, but instead of shooting at any of the men they confined themselves to wounding the horses that drew their chariots; and in the confusion that followed not even the enemy's mounted warriors could save themselves. Plautius thereupon sent across Flavius Vespasian also and his brother Sabinus, who was acting as his lieutenant. So they, too, got across the river in some way and killed many of the foe, taking them by surprise. The survivors, however, did not take to flight, but on the next day joined issue with them again. The struggle was indecisive until Gnaeus Hosidius Geta, after narrowly missing being captured, finally managed to defeat the barbarians so soundly that he received the *ornamenta triumphalia*, though he had not been consul.

There is much to unpack in this short description. In the first instance, this was clearly a far closer-run battle than Dio would have us believe. It took the Romans two days to force the crossing, even after Plautius' initial stratagem in sending the 'Germans' to swim the river. My interpretation here is that he actually sent them to cross the Medway further downstream, aiming to outflank the Britons, perhaps at a location nearer to modern Rochester. This shows the native forces were perhaps better prepared than Dio describes. The Germans he details have often been identified as Batavian auxiliaries, given such troops similarly swam across the river Po near to Placentia during the civil wars of AD 69 (Southern, 2013, 68). Among the auxilia in Plautius' army, these would have been elite warriors, further showing he viewed the Britons on the opposite bank as a serious threat. In terms of such troops swimming in armour, the likelihood is they used inflated pigskins to float across the river, a tactic familiar to the Batavians given their origins in the Rhine Delta (Elliott, 2016, 115).

Whether they were Batavians or not, however, the tactic clearly didn't work as it took an extraordinary act of bravery on the part of the officer Geta on the second day of the engagement to turn the tide in favour of the Romans. We know this because of the *ornamenta triumphalia* awarded to him. This was the highest award possible for a military officer, and one that in Republican times would have allowed him a real triumph in Rome. In imperial times, it was usually reserved for army commanders, so clearly his actions were dramatic indeed. As Moorhead and Stuttard say (2012, 48), 'That the Roman's eventual victory hung in the balance, turning on the fierce and determined fighting of Geta's men, suggests a hard-contested bloody struggle.'

With the Romans finally triumphant, the defeated British host withdrew northwards, quickly crossing the Thames, where they deployed on the north bank and prepared to fight a second battle defending a major river crossing. Plautius was unrelenting in his pursuit and soon the Roman army was arrayed in force opposite. The location of the ensuing engagement is again a matter of conjecture, with some arguing it was near to modern Westminster (Moorhead and Studdart, 2012, 48). However, in recently published work I have argued in favour of a location further to the east on the line of the medieval Higham–Tilbury ferry. This was the lowest fordable point on the Thames during the Roman period (Elliott, 2016, 116). It also most closely fits Dio's description of it being 'at a point near where the Thames empties into the ocean and at flood-tide forms a lake' (*Roman History*, 60.20). If this indeed was the location of the Thames-crossing battle, then Plautius would have reached it by marching north down the Medway past modern Cuxton and Strood, then continuing northwards through modern Higham and Church Street.

In short order, Plautius hit the line of the Thames and once more deployed his troops to force a river crossing. He'd learned from the first crossing battle, though, and determined to make good use of all of the forces at his disposal. First, he deployed the legionaries immediately opposite the Britons to pin them in place. Next, he used the war galleys and transports for the first time on campaign (the Medway crossing battle had been above the tidal reach of that river, with his ships unable to help there). In the first instance, he used the ships to ferry auxilia to the north bank of the Thames, downriver of the Britons. He then used his engineers to build a bridge of boats upriver of the Britons. Legionaries from one of the legions then quickly crossed over there. Finally, with legionaries to the west of the Britons and auxilia to the east, Plautius launched the assault with his main force directly across the river. Supported by *ballista* and missile-armed marines on his war galleys, victory was swift and brutal, the broken Britons again fleeing north, this time for their capital. The Romans once more pursued vigorously, though the primary sources say that many of the fleeing Britons used their knowledge of the local marshy terrain to make good their escape. In their eagerness, many of the pursuing Romans got into difficulty, some being ambushed and killed.

Plautius now paused and consolidated his position, having learned that Togodumnus was dead and Caratacus had fled to the west to find sanctuary with the Silures and Ordovices tribes in Wales. He was weary of over-extending his lines of supply and so built another huge marching camp before resupplying his army using the fleet. At the same time, he sent for Claudius to join him to share the final victory. The emperor, waiting near Boulogne-sur-Mer, crossed the Channel quickly and arrived at Plautius' camp with elephants from his imperial menagerie to intimidate the native Britons. The force then broke camp and headed north at speed for Camulodunum, arriving in late October. The lightning strike smashed all before it and the Catuvellauni quickly sued for peace, eleven other British tribes also submitting to Roman rule. Claudius then declared the province of Britain founded, established Camulodunum as its capital and appointed Plautius its first governor. He then left, never to return, having stayed just sixteen days.

Post-Claudian Conquest Campaigns in Britain

At the point Claudius left his new province it only comprised southeastern Britain. However, the emperor made it clear to Aulus Plautius before his departure that his newly conquered territory must be expanded swiftly. The new governor responded immediately, guided by the tribal landscape set out before him. Already the territories of the Cantiaci, Catuvellauni and Trinovantes had been assimilated by Rome to establish the core province. Looking further afield, the Romans now followed a familiar pattern of imperial conquest. First, those confederations and tribes politically closest to Rome became client kingdoms. This was a formal process where the king or queen of the nation in question became a *clientes* of the empire in a procedure called *rex sociusque et amicus* (translating as becoming an official king/queen, ally and friend of Rome). Such kingdoms continued to function 'independently', but under the guidance of Rome, and often with Roman troops deployed in their territory. These arrangements were usually with a specific king or queen rather than the kingdom itself, the latter more often than not being incorporated into the empire after the ruler's demise (Southern, 2013, 75). In Britain, at the point of the initial breakout campaigns from Claudius' original province, known *clientes* there included the Regni on the south coast, the Atrebates in the Thames Valley (both possibly under the same ruler by this time, thought to be Tiberius Claudius Cogidubnus, an heir of Verica), the Iceni in north Norfolk, and perhaps the Brigantes in the north.

Before launching his first campaign Plautius tasked *legio* XX *Valeria Victrix* with building a fortress at Camulodunum, where he also established a *colonia* for retiring veterans. Their rear secure, the legionary spearheads then set out in short order, using corridors of safe passage through the client kingdoms where necessary to target those British confederations and tribes yet to submit to Rome. Each of the three remaining legions headed in a different direction, with Plautius' own *legio* IX *Hispana* advancing north. Skirting the territory of the Iceni, it soon reached the river Nene in modern Cambridgeshire, where it established a vexillation fort at Longthorpe (Roman name unknown). This built, the legion continued northwest through the lands of the Corieltauvi to found another vexillation fort at Leicester (Roman *Ratae Corieltauvorum*) on the river Soar. Continuing through Corieltauvi territory, it then switched to a northeastern route where, above the Wash, it built a legionary fortress at Lincoln (Roman *Lindum Colonia*) on the river Witham. There the IXth legion was based for a generation.

Meanwhile, *legio* XIV *Gemina* headed northwest deep into the Midlands, establishing vexillation forts at Great Chesterford (Roman name unknown), Mancetter (Roman *Manduessedum*) and Alchester (Roman name unknown). Finally, and most famously, *legio* II *Augusta* under the future emperor Vespasian (AD 69 to AD 79) struck out for the still hostile southwest. Once in theatre, Suetonius goes into great detail about the hard-fought campaign, saying that the senior *legate* 'fought 30 battles, subjugated two warlike tribes [the Durotriges and Dumnonii], captured more than 20 *oppida* [fortified native urban centres], and took the Isle of Wight' (*The Twelve Caesars, Vespasian* 4).

Vespasian headed directly for the coast, where his speedy advance was greatly aided by the use of the British fleet to provide close support in the littoral zone along the seaboard and downriver systems. This included exercising military control there, scouting and raiding ahead of the land forces, carrying out all of the logistical heavy lifting, and building fortified harbours to supply the troops as they advanced (Elliott, 2016, 120). An extreme example of this was the capture of the Isle of Wight (Roman *Vectis*) early in Vespasian's campaign.

Archaeological data supporting the rapid progress of Vespasian's offensive from that point comes in the form of large-scale Claudian-period storage buildings and Claudian pottery on the site of the later Roman settlement of *Clausentum* (today a suburb of Southampton) at the tip of the Bitterne Peninsula. From here, supplies arriving via the regional fleet would have been ideally placed for forward deployment up the river Itchen to the advancing legions and auxilia. Vespasian's ongoing progress can be tracked today by each new coastal base he established during his westward progression. The next step from Bitterne can be found at Wimbourne in Dorset, where he built an early vexillation fort with an associated port and storage facility, this time on Poole Harbour. Weymouth Bay would then have been the location of the next fleet base given its proximity to the major military engagement site at Maiden Castle, where Vespasian's legionaries famously stormed the extensive hill fort defended by the Durotriges. Then heading deeper into Dumnonian territory, a key fleet base was established at Topsham, immediately to the south of the later legionary fortress and *civitas* capital of Exeter (Roman *Isca Dumnoniorum*, of which it became the port). After four seasons of intense campaigning, with Vespasian using this combination of land-based shock troops supplied by his new series of fortified harbours, the southwest was conquered and incorporated into Britannia.

Plautius returned to Rome in AD 47, accompanied by Vespasian. The Romans could be forgiven for thinking at this point that the conquest of Britain was following the same pattern as Caesar's conquest of Gaul. Soon they expected the whole main island of Britain to be filling the emperor's *fiscus* treasury with taxes as one large province. However, nothing could be further from the truth, with years of campaigning still to come.

At the point of Plautius' departure, the territory of the new province had been greatly expanded. Britannia now comprised the region below a line from the river Severn to the river Trent, excepting the territories of the Regni, Atrebates and Iceni client kingdoms. This new stop line is often called the 'Fosse Way Frontier' after the major Roman road that later ran along its length from the legionary fortress at Exeter to that at Lincoln. This routeway derived the name by which it was later known from the Latin word *fossa*, meaning ditch. This not only reflects its origins as the late AD 40s stop line of the initial Roman campaigns of conquest in Britain, but also indicates that for at least some of its length the ditched barrier remained visible hundreds of years later. Back to the late AD 40s, along the 'Fosse Way Frontier' a number of vexillation forts were then built, for example at Newton on Trent and Great Casterton (Roman names unknown), joining already established bases including Longthope and Leicester. These forts later became logistics bases for the next phase of conquest into the west and north.

By this time, manifestations of *Romanitas* had begun to emerge across the conquered territory, with the former native British nobility encouraged to learn formal Latin, wear togas on official business and invest in grand stone-built public building enterprises, conveniently for the Romans funded with loans from the leading senatorial families back in Rome. More practically, given the always-urgent need to make a new province pay its own way, Roman patterns of local government were also imposed. As Oosthuizen (2019, 27) details:

> The (new) administration of Roman Britain was based on a set of nested hierarchies: broadly speaking from vicus, a small local centre [as opposed to the vici civilian settlements associated with Roman forts], to pagus, the locality, to civitates, a region often reproducing a prehistoric territory [as for example with the Cantiaci in modern Kent].

The next governor in Britain was called Publius Ostorius Scapula, he arriving just as winter set in, in AD 47. His first task was to pacify those areas already conquered by Rome below the 'Fosse Way Frontier', in the first instance disarming any Britons still under arms. This included the client kingdoms there and prompted the first revolt against the new Roman presence in Britain, this among the Iceni in north Norfolk. The rebels there fortified themselves in a promontory with a narrow entrance, sometimes identified as Stonea Camp in the Cambridgeshire Fens, later the site of a Roman agricultural imperial estate. Ostorius knew there was real danger here as a native victory could begin to unravel the Roman conquests in Britain to that date. He advanced swiftly on the rebels and defeated them in short order, only needing his auxiliaries to do so with his cavalry fighting dismounted.

Ostorius now turned his attention to the expansion of imperial territory north and west of the 'Fosse Way Frontier' stop line. First, he campaigned against the Deceangli tribe in northwestern Wales, with the Roman fleet deploying to the Dee Estuary to protect his littoral flank and supply his troops along the coast and down the local river systems. To support this extensive campaign the governor built a large 18ha supply base at Rhyn Park in modern Shropshire on the English side of the river Ceiriog. However, his campaigning in Wales was cut short when he was called away to deal with a disturbance among the northern Brigantes. This large confederation, whose name translated as 'High Ones' or 'Hill Dwellers', had yet to feel the might of Rome. Their territory covered a huge region in the north, including modern Yorkshire excepting the east coast, Lancashire, Cumbria, Northumberland and southwestern Scotland. Their power is evident in the size of the pre-Roman tribal capital located at Stanwick in North Yorkshire, this an enormous *oppida* enclosing almost 300ha surrounded by 9km of ditches and ramparts (Moorhead and Stuttard, 2012, 93). Given the scale of his opponents here Ostorius took no chances, marching north with a large force of legionaries and auxilia, swiftly wiping out any opposition and then putting to death the ringleaders.

Matters in the north resolved, Ostorius then returned to Wales, where this time he targeted the Silures and Ordovices tribes in the south and centre who between them were still harbouring the fugitive Caratacus. First Ostorius redeployed *legio* XX *Valeria Victrix* from Colchester to Kingsholm near modern Gloucester (Roman *Glevum*), where he built a vexillation-sized fort. This location became a key site for the various campaigns of conquest in Wales given it was the lowest easily bridgeable point on the river Severn, while also being navigable for the seagoing transport vessels of the fleet. Once the campaign was underway, with the XXth legion driving hard into the territory of the Silures, the governor then deployed *legio* XIV *Gemina* to the Welsh Marches. From there they opened a new front against the Ordovices. Progress for both legions and their auxiliaries was slow, but eventually Roman military prowess prevailed, with the tribes submitting after Caratacus was defeated when the Romans assaulted the fortified site he was defending deep in Ordovician territory.

The rebel leader fled once more, this time leaving behind his wife and daughter to be captured by the Romans. Heading north, in AD 51 he eventually arrived at the court of Cartimandua, queen of the Brigantes. Here she was presented with a dilemma. The Roman conquest of Britain was still in its early years, with resistance evident in many areas, even below the 'Fosse Way Frontier'. To that end, handing him over to the Romans would be an embarrassing loss of face to those Britons still fighting Rome. However, after the failed unrest in Brigantian territory at the beginning of Ostorius' governorship (the event that may have placed her on the throne there) she was clearly aware of the military might of the empire. In the end, she made the pragmatic choice to hand the former leader of the Catuvellauni over to the Romans in chains. Caratacus was later presented to Claudius, with the emperor deciding to spare him. He was allowed to live out the rest of his life in Rome, where he made a positive impression on the nobility and people there. Meanwhile, Tacitus says Cartimandua was rewarded with great wealth for her support for Rome (*The Histories*, 3.45).

Back in Wales, if Ostorius thought the region pacified he couldn't have been more wrong as the Silures now rose in revolt. The governor made it known he intended to exterminate the whole confederation as a punishment, this unsurprising given Rome's usual attitude to recalcitrant foes. As Mattingly says (2006, 89):

A key ingredient in the Roman approach to war was their ruthless attitude, which frequently extended to their use of exemplary force. Rebellious peoples were slaughtered or enslaved without qualms, massive resources being poured into the crushing of even small groups of dissenters.

On this occasion this was a mistake as, with nothing to lose, the Silures now fought a vicious guerrilla campaign (Southern, 2013, 88). On one occasion, they inflicted a major defeat on the Romans, ambushing a sizable force of legionaries when they were building a marching camp. In this engagement, Roman losses were heavy, with the *praefectus castrorum* camp prefect, eight centurions and hundreds of soldiers killed. However, the Silures then made a mistake, allowing themselves to be drawn into a set-piece encounter when, having ambushed a Roman foraging party, Ostorius arrived with a sizeable force of legionaries and wiped the Britons out. Despite this setback, the Silures still refused to submit, knowing the fate that awaited them. The conflict fizzled on unresolved, its ultimate outcome the death of Ostorius in AD 52, worn out by years of campaigning in Wales and the north.

Britannia's next governor was Aulus Didius Gallus, who relocated *legio* XX *Valeria Victrix* to a new legionary fortress at Usk (Roman *Burrium*) in southeastern Wales, *legio* XIV *Gemina* to a similar new fortress at Wroxeter (Roman *Viroconium Cornoviorum*) and *legio* II *Augusta* to the existing fortress at Gloucester. Both the new sites were specifically chosen for the access provided to the Bristol Channel by the rivers Usk and Severn respectively, with maritime supply remaining vital to Rome's continued military success in its Welsh campaigning. This observation is reinforced by the next two forts built as the campaign continued – these vexillation-sized structures at Chepstow (Roman name unknown) on the mouth of the river Wye and Cardiff (Roman name unknown) on the river Taff.

The gruelling Welsh campaigns continued throughout the AD 50s. However, the most noteworthy event in Didius' time as governor in Britain was his intervention in Brigantian territory, where Rome had to engage once more. There, in the mid-AD 50s, a schism occurred between Cartimandua and her husband Venutius. We have no insight into what caused this, but we do of the outcome, he being banished from the northern kingdom. Soon he was raising a force to invade the queen's territory. This was a serious threat to the Roman client kingdom, with Tacitus calling him the leading British military leader now Caratacus had been captured (*The Annals*, 12.40). Didius realised the queen was under threat and quickly intervened. At first, the governor sent *exploratores* scouts and auxiliaries, but soon realised he'd misjudged the seriousness of the threat. He therefore deployed a full legion to the north – either *legio* IX *Hispana* or *legio* XIV *Gemina* – and soon the situation was under control after a series of decisive clashes, with Venutius again banished. The queen later divorced him and married his armour-bearer, a man called Vellocatus.

By this time, the never-ending conquest campaign in Britain was proving onerous back in Rome, with Suetonius saying that after Claudius died in AD 54 the new emperor, Nero (AD 54 to AD 68), for a time considered abandoning the province altogether (*The Twelve Caesars, Nero*, 18). However, he eventually decided his forces would stay and the province continue, though only because he feared the negative publicity if he withdrew.

Didius departed back to Rome in AD 57 and was replaced by Quintus Veranius Nepos, a noted military leader with a hardman reputation. Here, clearly Nero had determined that if Rome was to stay in the main island of Britain then all resistance in Wales must be crushed once and for all. However, the new governor only had time to lead a few skirmishes against the still-resisting Silures before he died in office.

His replacement was one of the truly great British governors, Gaius Suetonius Paulinus, appointed by Nero in AD 58. Another seasoned military leader, he set to work in his new province immediately, picking up where Verianus had left off in Wales. First, to consolidate his position in Silurian territory he built a series of forts to secure the key valleys in the interior, which the natives had been using to access the rich farmlands along the coast. Then, in AD 60, he targeted the region he determined to be the real centre of resistance to Roman power in Wales. This was Anglesey, deep in the heart of Ordovician territory, the mysterious island that was home to the druids, leaders of LIA religion in pre-Roman Britain. It was also a place of refuge for the thousands of Britons fleeing the gradual scouring campaigns of the Romans, not only in Wales but elsewhere in the main island of Britain.

As with Vespasian's conquest of the Isle of Wight a decade earlier, here Paulinus staged a Claudian invasion in miniature, with an army of around 20,000 men. This included *legio* XIV *Gemina*, most of *legio* XX *Valeria Victrix* and an equivalent number of auxiliaries. The governor was a meticulous planner and built hundreds of flat-bottomed boats in the estuary of the river Dee to transport his legionaries and auxilia foot troops across the shallow Menai Straight, with the auxiliary cavalry swimming across. However, his amphibious assault was heavily opposed, despite the war galleys from the regional fleet enfilading the landing zone with artillery and other missile weapons. Tacitus here provides a detailed description of the desperate engagement, saying (*The Annals*, 14.29):

> On the beach stood the adverse array, a serried mass of arms and men, with women flitting between the ranks. In the style of Furies, in robes of deathly black and with dishevelled hair, they brandished their torches; while a circle of Druids, lifting their hands to heaven and showering imprecations, struck our troops with such an awe at the extraordinary spectacle that, as though their limbs were paralysed, they exposed their bodies to wounds without an attempt at movement. Then, reassured by their general, and inciting each other never to flinch before a band of females and fanatics, they charged behind the standards, cut down all who met them, and enveloped the enemy in his own flames. The next step was to install a garrison among the conquered population, and to demolish the groves consecrated to their savage cults: for they considered it a duty to consult their deities by means of human entrails.

So far so good for the new governor. However, next he faced an existential threat to the survival of the province from a totally unexpected direction. This was the AD 60/61 revolt of Boudicca, queen of the Iceni in north Norfolk. I pick this up in the next chapter, given Agricola's own direct involvement in this campaign early in his military career. Meanwhile, I cover the subsequent governors in Roman Britain prior to Agricola's arrival in Chapters 4 and 5, as their activities formed the immediate backdrop to his own campaigns in the far north.

Chapter 4

Early Life and Career

Having set the scene for Agricola's story, I now turn to his biographical narrative. In this chapter, I first detail his family background, upbringing (this set against Nero's execution of his father shortly after his birth) and early senatorial career. Next, I look at the role he played in suppressing Boudicca's revolt during his first visit to Britain as a military tribune. I then follow his career development through postings in Rome, Asia and Spain. Finally, I set out the role he played during the AD 69 'Year of the Four Emperors' and its immediate aftermath. Note that in telling the story of this turbulent period of Roman history, the dating of events is complex and convoluted, based on often contradictory primary sources that generations of historians have since tried to thread together, often to support their own agendas. What you read here is my own personal take on events, focused only on those that impacted Agricola directly.

Agricola's Family and Early Career

Tacitus makes the historian and reader's life as easy as it is possible to get when introducing Agricola for the first time. He says (*The Agricola*, 4.1):

> Agricola had his origins in the old and famous colony of *Forum Julii*. Both of his grandfathers were procurators of the Caesars and were the equivalent of nobility in the equestrian order. His father, Lucius Julius Graecinus, was a member of the Senate and won fame by his practice of eloquence and philosophy ... [while] his mother was Julia Procilla, a paragon of feminine virtue.

There is much to unpack here. First, Agricola's family were aristocratic members of the Julii *gentes* clan, as was another more famous namesake,

Gaius Julius Caesar. The Julii were one of Rome's oldest patrician *gentes*, this phrase referring to a group of related families who found common cause on the great issues of the day. They originated in Alba Longa, 19km southeast of Rome, an ancient city in Latium near Lake Albano in the Alban Hills. In the later Republic, when it became fashionable for each clan to associate themselves with a divine origin, the Julii aligned themselves with Iulus, son of Aeneas and founder of the town, claiming him as their clan founder. Additionally, in the origin myths of Rome, Aeneas himself claimed to be the son of Venus and Anchises, the former an association embraced tightly by the Julii. Caesar himself used both mythical connections wholeheartedly whenever it provided a political advantage, as Agricola did later.

The Julii moved to Rome after Alba Longa's destruction by Rome's third king, Tullus Hostilius, in the mid-seventh century BC. They were an unremarkable *gentes* for most of their existence before the time of Caesar. Little is known about the twelve clan members who were elected as magistrates in the first two centuries of the Republic, excepting Gaius Julius Iulus, who became consul in 489 BC. The next member to rise to prominence was a Julius Caesar who became a *praetor* during the Second Punic War. He was the first in the family to have the *cognomen* Caesar; it was later claimed that this derived from the Punic word for elephant (*caesai*) after he killed one in battle. Shortly afterwards the clan split into two distinct lines, each registered to a different tribe in the Roman voting census. The next clan member to rise to prominence was Lucius Julius Caesar, who reached the consulship in 157 BC. He came from the more successful branch. Next, Sextus Julius Caesar became consul in 91 BC, while Lucius Julius Caesar became consul in 90 BC, he playing a key role in bringing the Social War to an end, as detailed in Chapter 1. In the same year, the latter's younger brother Gaius Julius Caesar Strabo (the last a nickname meaning 'squinty') became an *aedile*, a junior public official with responsibilities including public entertainment. However, it was Caesar himself, born in 100 BC, who rose to become the greatest Roman of all, at least as viewed today. This didn't stop his assassination in 44 BC, though his great-nephew Augustus did establish the Julio-Claudian dynasty under which Agricola lived for much of his life.

Next, the family's home town was *Forum Julii* ('marketplace of the *Julii*'). Confusingly, there are three first-century AD candidate sites for this settlement. These are modern Fréjus, in the Provence-Alpes-Côte d'Azur region of southeastern France, modern Cividale del Friuli, in the Friuli-Venezia Giulia region of northeastern Italy (a town established by Caesar), and Voghera, in Lombardy, northwestern Italy (a town established by Augustus). Fortunately, recent archaeological evidence suggests that Tacitus is here referring to the first candidate. That is the interpretation I use ongoing.

Agricola's *Forum Julii* was located on the Mediterranean coast in the Roman province of Gallia Narbonensis, to the east of the regional mercantile powerhouse Marseille (Roman *Massilia*). The site was originally settled by Ligurians around the natural harbour of Aegytna, with the remains of their defensive wall still visible on nearby Cap Capelin and Mont Auriasque. It was then occupied by Phoenician colonists, shortly after they founded Marseille around 600 BC. Later, it became an important Gallic port, finally falling under Roman control after the establishment of their first Gallic province, Gallia Transalpina in 121 BC. Shortly after, Narbonne (Roman *Colonia Narbo Martius*) was founded as a new regional capital in 118 BC.

Fréjus became a key town as the Republic expanded further north into Gaul, and south into Spain. Importantly, it sat on an important crossroads where the *Via Julia Augusta* imperial trunk road from Italy to the Rhone valley met the *Via Domitia* linking Italy to Spain along the Mediterranean coast. Of note in the Roman world, it was the birthplace in 67 BC of the poet Cornelius Gallus. The town's association with the Julii began when Caesar decided to refound it in AD 49 as *Forum Julii*, his new capital of Gallia Transalpina. Later, it was here where Octavian repatriated the war galleys he captured at the Battle of Actium in 31 BC, and where after becoming emperor in 27 BC he settled many veteran legionaries from *legio* XIII *Augusta* (Pollard and Berry, 2012, 72). For a short time, the settlement then acquired the additional suffix *Octavanorum Colonia*, with *Forum Julii* becoming the capital of his new province of Gallia Narbonensis in 22 BC. Importantly, it then became a key port for the *Classis Misenensis*, the second largest of the Augustan regional fleets that was headquartered at Miseno (Roman *Misenum*) in the Bay of Naples.

Much of the Roman-built environment still visible in Fréjus today dates to the reign Tiberius, when the town underwent a further expansion, this including the *Lanterne d'Auguste* lighthouse, amphitheatre, theatre, public baths and main aqueduct. The town's 3.7km wall circuit was built shortly after, this enclosing an area of 35ha, making use of the foundations of earlier Phoenician and Gallic fortifications. By that time, the town's population had grown to 6,000, reflecting its great wealth. This was derived from a number of economic vectors. These included:

- Its importance as a port.
- The local mining of green sandstone and blue porphyry in huge state-run *metalla* quarries.
- A thriving *garum* fish sauce industry.
- Region-wide viticulture and arable farming.

To hold the post of the procurator there, as with Agricola's grandfathers in the early first century AD, was thus very prestigious.

At some stage in the early AD 30s Agricola's father was promoted from equestrian to senatorial rank by the emperor Tiberius. Both Tacitus and Seneca provide interesting detail about his character. Today we would perhaps call him independent minded, even fond of his own voice, traits that later didn't endear him to Caligula. As detailed, Tacitus says he was known for his eloquence and philosophy. Meanwhile, Seneca says he was noted for declining the offer of financial assistance from two powerful local magnates who wanted to help finance games in the arena he was organising in *Forum Julii* (*De Benificiis, Dialogues and Essays*, 2.21.5). This was the senatorial equivariant of showing off his personal wealth. Elsewhere, Seneca also details Graecinus writing a sarcastic commentary about the philosopher Aristo (*Epistulae Morales ad Lucilium, Dialogues and Essays*, 29.6). Of note, he also wrote a two-volume manual on viticulture (Birley, 2005, 72). We have no idea which service he performed to achieve his promotion to the top level of Roman society, but soon he was making his name as a patrician.

The only other family member of this generation we have any detail of is Graecinus' younger brother Marcus Julius Graecinus, who set up his elder brother's funerary monument in Rome. This provides our only detail of the public positions held by Agricola's father. It says (CIL vi.41069):

> To Lucius Julius, son of Lucius, Anienis, Graecinus, tribune of plebs, *praetor*, Marcus Julius, son of Lucius, Anienis, Graecinus, *quaestor*, had this set up.

Agricola was born on 13 June AD 40, most likely in Rome (Birley, 2005, 72). Shortly after this his father was executed by Caligula, with Seneca saying this was 'for the sole reason that he was a better man than a tyrant found it expedient for anyone to be' (*De Benificiis, Dialogues and Essays*, 2.21.5). Agricola never knew his father and was raised by his mother, first in *Forum Julii*, then in *Massilia*, where she also owned property, and finally on her family estates near *Albintimilium* in Liguria, northwestern Italy. This was where she was living at the time of her untimely death in AD 69, as detailed below. Tacitus' comment about her being 'a paragon of feminine virtue' was intended to show to his largely male readership her matronly qualities of morality, frugality and dignity. However, the key fact to note here is that the family maintained its wealth even after Graecinus had suffered his grim fate, with no sign of a *damnatio memoriae* by the emperor, himself to be assassinated seven months later.

Agricola's early life was typical for a young aristocratic child, aside from his father's premature death. When he was due to be born Graecinus would have summoned any nearby male relatives in Rome to the family home to legally 'witness' the birth by waiting with him outside the birthing chamber. However, the only male actually present in the room where the mother was confined was a doctor, and even then only if required, given the expense. The other main attendants at the birth were the midwife, any nearby female relations and the female slaves of the house. Once the baby was born, it was placed on the ground by the delivering midwife and inspected for any abnormalities to assess the child's chances of survival. Agricola's birth seems to have been uncomplicated, with the baby vigorous and healthy. Graecinus then officially accepted his new son into the wider family, with fires lit on the altars in the household *lararium* shrine. The birth date was then recorded, and nine days later, a formal ceremony of purification called *lustratio* was performed. This was designed to rid the child of any evil spirits that had entered him during the birthing process. Agricola was then given his *bulla* special charm by his father, usually made of a precious metal in a leather pouch that was placed around his neck. After that, the child was formally given his or her name. Graecinus gave his son the full *tria nomina* used by the elites in Roman society. This comprised:

- The *praenomen* first name, used to identify the individual in informal conversation.
- The *nomen* main name, indicating his *gentes*.
- The *cognomen*, which identified the particular branch of the *gentes*, though in some cases could also be a family nickname.

In giving the full *tria nomina* to Agricola his father was making a clear statement to his peers, showing overtly what he had achieved in life to that point.

Of Agricola's upbringing after his father's death, Tacitus says (*The Agricola*, 4.12):

> He was brought up under his mother's tender care. He passed his boyhood and youth being trained in all the liberal arts. He was shielded from the temptations of bad companions, partly by his own sound instincts, and partly by living and going to school from his early years in *Massilia*, a place where Greek refinement and provincial puritanism meet in a happy blend.

Multiple contemporary sources provide detail about an elite Roman child's upbringing and education. Each stage of a child's life was important in the Roman world, and Agricola's birthdays would always have been celebrated by his family. These festivities included, once more, the lighting of fires on the household altars in the *lararium*, and also the hanging of flower garlands, drinking sweet wine and eating ritual cakes. Although very young children were viewed by the Romans as non-humans given the scale of infant mortality across all levels of Roman society, when they reached their first birthday freeborn children began to gain certain legal rights. This was a stage called the *anniculus*.

The various steps of a freeborn child's upbringing then broadly tracked those of modern children. At the age of 5, the *infantia* infant stage ended. For the next two years, Agricola was given increasing responsibilities around the home. Tasks included looking after the household animals and general chores. At this age, children were also differentiated based on gender for the first time, with the social and educational pathways of boys and girls separating.

Only 10 per cent of Roman society was literate, and education was of great importance to free Romans, being compulsory for the children of the aristocracy and desirable for other citizens who could afford it. Here, Julia Procilla and her family made sure Agricola received the best education they could afford, for example moving to *Massilia*, where the finest schooling in the region could be found.

Primary schooling for Roman boys began at the age of 7, either in the home with a *pedagogus* private tutor, or sometimes in a school that was usually the home of the tutor. Given that Agricola's mother specifically moved to *Massilia* for his education, we can assume the latter was the case here. At this early stage in a child's education they were taught basic literature in both Latin and Greek using a wax tablet and stylus, and also arithmetic using an abacus. Another focus at this age was on the traditions and rituals of Rome.

After his primary education, Agricola went to a more advanced school in *Massilia*. Here he was educated as a *discipuli* student. The tutor at this stage was called a *gramaticus* in Latin, or *grammarian* in Greek. Pupils of this age were taught more advanced literature, and the 'seven liberal arts' of geometry, advanced mathematics, music, astronomy, grammar, logic and rhetoric. The latter was thought particularly important for a young man who wanted to make his way in life in the Roman world, where an ability to speak well in public was expected of all men born free. Specifically, when being taught rhetoric pupils learned to study literature, read aloud, comment on etymologies and subject matter, explain literary devices and work out analogies. The renowned first-century AD Spanish-born rhetorician Marcus Fabius Quintillianus, better known as Quintilian, distilled these five aims down to two, saying pupils should develop a working knowledge of the poets, and learn how to speak in public (*Institutes of Oratory*, 1.4.2). Here, Agricola also developed a love for philosophy that stayed with him for the rest of his, with Tacitus saying (*The Agricola*, 4.13):

> I always remember how he would often tell us that in early manhood he would have drunk deeper of philosophy than a Roman and a Senator should, if his mother in her prudence had not dampened the fire of his passion.

Here we see his mother as a permanent presence during his upbringing, this being unusual among Roman aristocracy but reflecting the family trauma of his father's execution. Meanwhile, physical training also played a key role in the education of boys at this age, they being taught martial skills, running and swimming. They were also taught how to ride a horse, initially bareback.

Schooling for Roman children was onerous, repetitious and prone to regular corporal punishment for even the smallest error. Because of this, it was common for families with slaves, such as Agricola's, to send one with the child to school to ensure that no abuse took place. This was usually the slave who supervised the children in the home. Boys were also taught seven days a week with no weekend off. No doubt, the young Agricola was delighted when his schooling ended with his graduation at the age of 16. Around the same time, he also underwent an important ritual that transitioned him to manhood. This involved the removal of his *bulla* and his child's tunic.

Agricola embarked on his public service career when he turned 18. This was along the *cursus honorum* set career path for aristocratic Roman men of senatorial and equestrian rank. Though the various posts, and associated ages to hold them, changed over time, in Agricola's day they were as follows (Turney, 2022, 43):

- *Vignitivir*, for equestrians at 18.
- Military or civilian tribune, for senators at 18 and equestrians at 20.
- Quaestorship at 25. As detailed above, this was the rank held by Agricola's uncle when he set up the funerary monument in Rome to his father.

- Tribunate of Plebs or *aedileship*, the latter responsible for public buildings and festivals, at 27. This was non-mandatory for senators.
- Praetorship, either as a military commander or senior elected magistrate, at 30. The latter was the most senior position held by Agricola's father.
- Governor of a lesser province, or *legatus legionis* commanding a legion, at 30. Only for senators at this time.
- Consulship at 32. Only for a senator, who from this point could then become governor in a major province. Such was the case with Agricola in Gallia Aquitania and Britannia.

By law, there were minimum intervals between holding successive offices, and it was forbidden to repeat an office. However, the rules were frequently ignored, particularly in times of crisis. A prime example was Marius when consul seven times.

Tacitus begins his narrative on Agricola's adult life with his appointment as a military tribune, most likely with Exeter-based *legio* II *Augusta* in Britain. He says (*The Agricola*, 5.13): 'He served his military apprenticeship in Britannia, to the satisfaction of Gaius Suetonius Paulinus, that sound and thorough general, and was picked by him to be tried out on his staff.' This gives us a firm date range for Agricola's time as a military tribune in the province given Paulinus was governor in Britain from AD 58 and AD 62. Some have argued here that Agricola may have arrived in Britain slightly earlier to serve under either Didius or Verianus, Paulinus' predecessors, but there is no hard evidence for this. That would have also placed him in post younger than the usual *cursus honorum* minimum of 18 for the role.

Agricola clearly impressed Paulinus on the first of his three visits to Britain. Tacitus provides more detail here, saying (*The Agricola*, 5.13):

Agricola was no loose subaltern, to turn his military career into a debauch, nor did he make his tribuneship and inexperience an excuse for amusing himself and taking leaves. Instead, he got to know his province and be known by the army; he learned from the experts and followed the best models; he never sought a task for self-advertisement, never shirked one through cowardice. He was always energetic; careless never.

Tacitus portrays Agricola here as a model junior officer. However, he was about to be tested in battle in the most extreme of circumstances. This was because, while on Paulinus' staff, he found himself on the front line of the Roman fightback against the Boudiccan revolt.

Boudicca and Paulinus

The blood-soaked rebellion of Boudicca is arguably the most famous event in the story of the Roman occupation of Britain. It almost ended the Roman presence in the islands here, and saw the legionaries and auxilia fighting in the most challenging conditions. Defeat would have meant the destruction of four legions on a scale surpassing even Varus' defeat in Teutoburg Forest in AD 9.

The context behind this dramatic event was the earlier death of the Iceni king Prasutagus, Boudicca's husband. A Roman client king, in his will he left his kingdom to his two daughters, and also to the emperor Nero. As detailed in Chapter 3, ruling *clientes* of the Romans usually left their kingdom entirely to the emperor after their deaths, and Nero reacted predictably when he heard news of Prasutagus' unusual arrangement. The dead king's will was ignored and the territory of the Iceni quickly folded into the expanding province of Britannia. It is now that Boudicca enters history, with Dio describing her appearance as very much the warrior queen, saying (*Roman History*, 62.2):

> She was very tall and stern; her look was penetrating; her voice harsh; a mass of auburn hair fell to her hips and around her neck was a heavy golden torc; she wore a patterned cloak with a thick cape over it fastened with a brooch.

Boudicca protested against the treatment of her kingdom. Tacitus says the Roman response was brutal in the extreme (*The Annals*, 14.31). He details Iceni territory being pillaged by centurions, the dead king's household ransacked by slaves, Boudicca herself lashed and her two daughters raped. It is worth noting here that Dio gives a completely different and far more mundane reason for Boudicca leading her revolt, saying (*Roman History*, 62.2):

An excuse for the revolt was found in the confiscation of the sums of money that Claudius had given to the foremost Britons; for these sums, as Decianus Catus, the procurator of the island, maintained, were to be paid back. This was one reason for the uprising; another was found in the fact that Seneca [one of Nero's key advisors], in the hope of receiving a good rate of interest, had lent to the islanders 40,000,000 *sesterces* that they did not want, and had afterwards called in this loan all at once and had resorted to severe measures in exacting it.

Whatever the cause, the result was incendiary in the extreme. Tacitus says Boudicca first addressed her people, setting them on course for savage rebellion. He has her say (*The Annals*, 14.35):

It is not as a woman descended from noble ancestry, but as one of the people that I am avenging lost freedom, my scourged body, the outraged chastity of my daughters. This is a woman's resolve; as for men, they may live and be slaves.

Dio also has the queen exhort the masses to revolt, grasping a spear and then saying (*Roman History*, 62.3):

Have we not been robbed entirely of most of our possessions, and those the greatest, while for those that remain we pay taxes? Besides pasturing and tilling for them all our other possessions, do we not pay a yearly tribute for our very bodies? How much better it would be to have been sold to masters once for all than, possessing empty titles of freedom, to have to ransom ourselves every year! How much better to have been slain and to have perished than to go about with a tax on our heads! Yet why do I mention death? For even dying is not free of cost with them; nay, you know what fees we deposit even for our dead. Among the rest of mankind death frees even those who are in slavery to others; only in the case of the Romans do the very dead remain alive for their profit. Why is it that, though none of us has any money (how, indeed, could we, or where would we get it?), we are stripped and despoiled like a murderer's victims? And why should the Romans be expected to display moderation as time goes on, when they have behaved toward us in this fashion at the very outset, when all men show consideration even for the beasts they have newly captured?

Soon Boudicca's ferocious insurrection had ignited most of the southeast above the Thames against the Romans, with all of the local aristocracy involved, not just those of the Iceni. Marching south at the head of an army 120,000 strong according to Dio, she first targeted Colchester, then the provincial capital (*Roman History*, 62.2). The nearest Roman legion was *legio* IX *Hispana* in the Midlands, still holding the northeastern line of the 'Fosse Way Frontier'. Its *legate* Quintus Petillius Cerialis, a future governor in Britain (see Chapter 5), moved quickly to lead a large force comprising vexillations of legionaries and auxiliaries to intercept Boudicca. This arrived too late to save Colchester, which by that point had already been torched, with great loss of life, including a large number of Roman veterans and their families burned alive as they sought shelter in the Temple of Claudius there. This had been built to celebrate Plautius' earlier victory, its enormous foundations still visible beneath modern Colchester Castle. Cerialis' force was then decisively defeated by Boudicca's army, the *legate* fleeing for his life alongside his cavalry, he leaving his legionaries to their fate. He then remained incongruously holed up in a nearby fort until the insurrection had been finally defeated.

At this point, Agricola was still with Paulinus in north Wales. There the Romans were hoping to complete the conquest of Anglesey. This was quickly abandoned when the governor heard of Boudicca's revolt in the east. Here was real jeopardy for Paulinus, campaigning further from Rome than any other Roman military leader at the time. He acted immediately, turning back and heading for Wroxeter in the Welsh Marches. There he picked up the western end of Watling Street, by that time almost complete and running through St Albans to London (Roman *Londinium*), and then running onwards to Richborough on the east Kent coast (today, the A5 and A2 broadly track its route). He was accompanied by *legio* XIV *Gemina*, some vexillations from *legio* XX *Valeria Victrix* and a few auxiliary units including two *ala* of cavalry.

Reaching High Cross in modern Leicestershire, where Watling Street crossed the Fosse Way, Paulinus then sent for the Exeter-based *legio* II *Augusta* (likely Agricola's home unit) to join him. However, the legion's *legatus legionis* and second-in-command were away, with its *praefectus castrorum* in charge. This was a man called Poenius Postumus. He ignored the call and brought shame on the legion. He clearly thought the province was about to fall and wanted to stay on the river Ex. From there he knew he could evacuate his troops if necessary. Elsewhere, by this time a few stragglers from *legio* IX *Hispana* had also found their way to Paulinus. This gave him a total force of around 6,000 legionaries from the 3 legions, 4,000 foot auxiliaries and around 1,000 mounted auxiliaries.

Tacitus says Paulinus then marched in person to London, the recently founded major trading port on the river Thames, from where the provincial procurator Catus Decianus had already fled to Gaul as Boudicca and her growing force continued its march south towards the town. It is useful to quote the historian in full at this point given the real sense of menace he presents as the new province fell into chaos (*The Annals*, 14.33):

> Paulinus ... with wonderful resolution, marched amidst a hostile population to *Londinium*, which, though undistinguished by the name of a colony [it was styled by the Romans a municipium mercantile town], was much frequented by a number of merchants and trading vessels. Uncertain whether he should choose it as a seat of war, as he looked round on his scanty force of soldiers ... he resolved to save the province at the cost of a single town. Nor did the tears and weeping of the people, as they implored his aid, deter him from giving the signal of departure and receiving into his army all who would go with him. Those who were chained to the spot by the weakness of their sex, or the infirmity of age, or the attractions of the place, were cut off by the enemy.

The key reference here is the description of the local population as hostile when Paulinus was marching down Watling Street through the Midlands. This confirms that the Catuvellauni certainly, and most likely the Trinovantes to their east, had joined the Iceni in the great revolt. In these circumstances, Paulinus' force would have been constructing defended marching camps at the end of each day's march as they travelled southeast. It is therefore unlikely that, if Paulinus did indeed travel in person to London, he took his whole army. More likely, he either travelled with a staff team and bodyguard, or sent an advance guard to London in his place to assess the situation with the authority to evacuate if needed.

In the event, when Boudicca did arrive in London, any remaining Romans or Romano-British were butchered and the town burned to the ground. Boudicca then targeted the new *municipium* of St Albans (Roman *Verulamium*), razing this also. The primary sources say that 80,000 were killed in the three sacking events to this point, indicating the scale of the insurrection and its rank savagery. However, the stage was now set for Roman retribution, and on a devastating scale.

By now, Boudicca's force had grown to 230,000, according to Dio (*Roman History*, 62.8), though in the unlikely event this is anywhere near accurate, no more than 120,000 were warriors, the rest being camp followers. Even at the lower end of speculation for the size of her army, this was an enormous force to keep in the field, and Boudicca knew a meeting engagement with Paulinus would be needed quickly to keep her warriors together. She also knew that if the governor was defeated, the Romans might abandon the province for good. Boudicca therefore advanced northwest along Watling Street to seek out the Roman army.

As the Iceni queen progressed, she received intelligence about the size of Paulinus' force and, given the disparity is size, no doubt felt the outcome of the forthcoming battle was a foregone conclusion. In that, she was wrong, as the wily Paulinus was ready for her and chose the place to make his stand very carefully. This was in a bowl-shaped steep defile, with woods on either side and rear, and an open end facing Boudicca's line of advance along Watling Street. The woods protected his flanks and limited the frontage of the line of battle, negating the British superiority in numbers and playing to the martial superiority of his own legionaries.

The exact location of the battle site is unknown, though all the leading candidates are along the line of Watling Street, hence the engagement often being referred to as the Battle of Watling Street. These sites are at Mancetter, High Cross, where Paulinus had awaited the arrival of *legio* II *Augusta* in vain, Church Stowe in Northamptonshire (my own preference), and Markyate in Hertfordshire. All four sites also have a significant water source, essential with so many engaged in the battle.

Early Life and Career 75

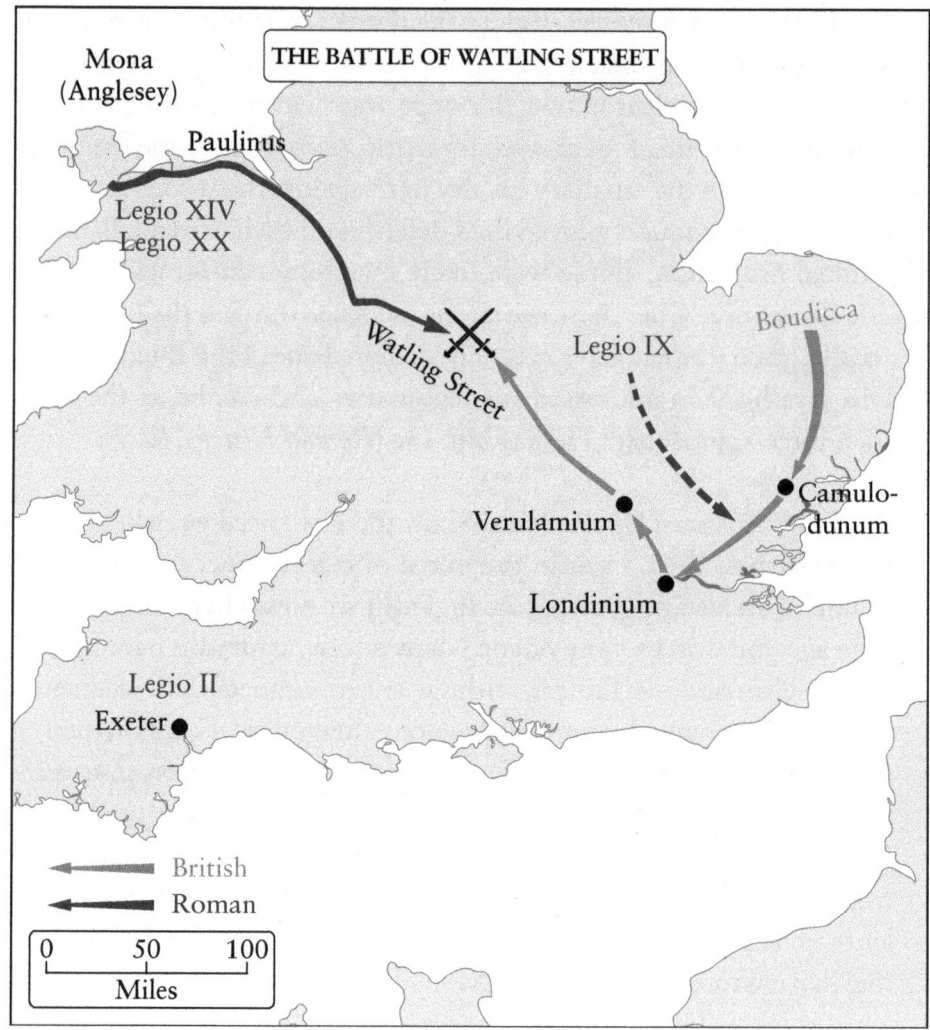

Map 2.

Paulinus arrayed his legionaries and auxilia uphill of the Britons. Both Dio and Tacitus give their own descriptions of his deployment. The former says (*Roman History*, 62.8): 'He separated his army into three divisions, in order to fight at several points at one and the same time, and he made each of the divisions so strong that it could not easily be broken through.'

Meanwhile, Tacitus says (*The Annals*, 34.1): 'The legionaries were posted in serried ranks, the light-armed troops on either side, and the cavalry massed on the extreme wings.'

Neither mention a reserve, though Paulinus would likely have kept at least his guard cavalry back to help deal with any breakthrough of his battleline. What is clear is that the ridge was held by a strong force of legionaries and auxilia foot arrayed for battle, supported by the legionary artillery, and with the auxiliary cavalry hard against the woods on either flank. Finally, Paulinus deployed field defences on each extreme flank for additional protection. These were likely marching camps, with that at Castle Dykes near Church Stowe strong evidence this was the location of the battle, given it would have naturally anchored one of the Roman flanks.

Dio says he then addressed his legionaries and auxilia as the huge British force approached. He has him say (*Roman History*, 62.9):

Up, fellow-soldiers! Up, Romans! Show these accursed wretches how far we surpass them even in the midst of evil fortune. It would be shameful, indeed, for you to lose ingloriously now when but a short time ago you won by your valour. Many a time, assuredly, have both we ourselves and our fathers, with far fewer numbers than we have at present, conquered far more numerous antagonists. Fear not, then, their numbers or their spirit of rebellion; for their boldness rests on nothing more than headlong rashness unaided by arms or training. Neither fear them because they have burned a couple of cities. Exact from them now, therefore, the proper penalty for these deeds, and let them learn by actual experience the difference between us, whom they have wronged, and themselves.

Boudicca deployed her enormous force opposite, though in much denser formation, with the chariots in front manned by her own elite warriors. So confident were the Britons of victory that the families of the warriors joined the baggage train at the rear of her battle line to watch events unfold. She now exhorted her own army to more slaughter, and then opened the battle with a wild uphill charge with both the chariots and foot warriors. The former rode across the front of the Romans, hurling insults and javelins, before turning square on to close for hand-to-hand combat. The foot troops followed close behind. Soon Boudicca had lost control of her army as each noble and warrior strove to get to grips with the Romans.

Agricola as governor in Britannia. Note his high-quality muscled cuirass. (© *Graham Sumner*)

Marcus Favonius Facilis, legio XX *Valeria Victrix* centurion based in Colchester, wearing finely decorated *lo* *hamata* chainmail. Almost certainly a veteran of the AD 43 Claudian invasion of Britain. (© *Graham Sum*

teran legionary of *legio* II *Augusta* wearing *lorica segmentata* and imperial Gallic helmet. Note his fully closed *calcei* boots, more suitable than *caligae* legionary sandals in the British climate. (© *Graham Sumner*)

Auxiliary *eques* on campaign in Britain. His green saddlecloth is notably expensive given it would have required double dyeing. (© *Graham Sumner*)

Agricola and Tacitus on the Great Hall frieze of Roman generals and emperors in National Galleries Scotland. (*Public domain*)

Statue of Agricola in his birthplace in Fréjus (Roman *Forum Julii*) in modern France. (*Rafał Klisowski via Wikimedia Commons/CC BY-SA 3.0*)

Domitian, third, last and least successful of the Flavian emperors. Assassinated in AD 96. (*Castro Pretorio via Wikimedia Commons/CC BY-SA 4.0*)

Vespasian, founder of the Flavian dynasty. (*Carole Raddato via Wikimedia Commons/CC BY-SA 2.0*)

Fragments of a dedicatory inscription found near the *forum* of *Verulamium*, modern St Albans. The references Agricola during the reign of Titus, and is translated below as RIB 3123. (*Carole Raddato via Wikimedia Commons/CC BY-SA 2.0*)

'To the Emperor Titus Caesar Vespasian Augustus, son of the deified Vespasian, Pontifex Maximus, in the 9th year of tribunician power, acclaimed Emperor 15 times, consul for the 7th time, designated for the 8th time, censor, father of his country; and to the Caesar Domitian, son of the deified Vespasian, consul for the 6th time, designated for the 7th time, member of all the priestly colleges; when Gnaeus Julius Agricola was imperial propraetorian legate.'

Mamucium, the Flavian vexillation fort founded by Agricola. Together with its *vicus*, today it has grown into mighty Manchester. (*Author's copyright*)

Fine tombstone of a Roman cavalry *eques* from Corbridge (Roman *Coria*), now in the Tullie House Museum and Art Gallery, Carlisle. Note the shield grip, and overt attempt to diminish the native Briton at bottom by showing his naked buttocks. (*Author's copyright*)

A full legion on the march, with senior officers and standard-bearers to the fore. Recreated in Lincoln Museum. (*Author's copyright*)

The Colosseum. The ultimate monument to the Flavian dynasty in Rome. (*Author's copyright*)

Forum, Pompeii. Looking north towards mighty Vesuvius. The destruction of Pompeii with the volcano's cataclysmic eruption in AD 79 was a major event in the Roman world as Agricola began his first major campaign in the far north of Britain. (*Author's copyright*)

Statue of Mars, legionary fortress, York (Roman *Eboracum*). Founded by the IXth legion under the governor Cerialis in his conquest of Brigantian territory. (*Author's copyright*)

Principate legionary, resplendent in *lorica segmentata*, imperial Gallic helmet and *scutum*, wielding a *gladi hispaniensis*. (*Painted by the author*)

Principate legionary. Note the *singulum* military belt with *baltea* straps covering the groin area. (*Painted by the author*)

Highly decorated Roman centurion. (*Painted by the author*)

...egionary *scorpio* bolt-shooter, used to great effect by Agricola in his campaigns in the far north of Britain. (Painted by the author)

Three veteran Roman legionaries carrying much of their kit in this commemorative slab found at the Roman Antonine Wall fort at Croy Hill. (*Author's copyright*)

The price of imperial failure in the AD 69 'Year of the Four Emperors'. Vandalised silver bust of Galba. (*Author's copyright*)

An incredible survival from the classical world. An intact Roman legionary *scutum*, found at Dura-Europus on the eastern frontier. (*Author's copyright*)

An almost complete Roman legionary's *lorica segmentata* cuirass. Found at the site of the AD 9 Varian Disaster in the Teutoburg Forest, Germany. (*Author's copyright*)

The *forum Romanum*, centre of political life in ancient Rome. (*Author's copyright*)

The Cramond Lioness, found at the Roman fort and military harbour on the Forth. What the Romans really thought of the Britons in the far north. The feeling was mutual. (*Author's copyright*)

Statue of Gnaeus Julius Agricola, on the terrace above the Great Bath in the Roman Baths, Bath, Somerset. (*Author's copyright*)

Fine example of an imperial Gallic legionary helmet. Note the extra protection provided by the brow guard, cheek guards and neck guard. (*Author's copyright*)

By way of contrast, the discipline of the legionaries and auxilia now shone through. The battle proper began with the Roman artillery opening fire as soon as the Britons were in range, first the *ballistae* and then *scorpiones*. Given the nearby proximity of the various logistics bases being used by the Romans to support their campaign in Wales, it seems likely there were a larger number of artillery pieces available to Paulinus than usual. Further, having chosen his battlefield, it is certain he would also have set down range markers to ensure the accuracy of his artillery bombardment. Then, as the range narrowed, auxiliary archers and slingers also joined the barrage. By this point, the Britons, increasingly disordered by the concentrated missile fire, had begun their ascent up the steep hillside towards the main Roman deployment. The legionaries now threw their lighter *pila* – 6,000 iron-barbed javelins arcing high in the air in a steep parabola and then dropping onto the heads of the Britons, many without helmets. The auxiliary infantry joined in with their own *lancea*. Then, at point-blank range as the flagging Britons reached the Roman battleline, the legionaries unleashed their second, heavier *pila*. These flew in a flat arc, hammering into the front ranks of Britons, who came to a shuddering halt in a tangle of dead horses, overturned chariots, bodies and wounded.

Paulinus saw the British advance falter and seized his chance to take the initiative. He now ordered the legionaries to move forward in a series of *cuneus* wedge formations, with centurions and standard-bearers to the fore. The auxiliaries followed. Swords were drawn and shields set hard forward. The wedges then charged downhill into the dense mass of Britons, causing slaughter everywhere and forcing the natives into a huge, desperate crush where the warriors couldn't use their weapons. A massacre ensued as the Britons broke and tried to run away. However, they were trapped on the field by the surrounding families and baggage train. All were hacked down where they stood, the slaughter desperate.

The result was a mighty victory for Paulinus, with Tacitus saying (*The Annals*, 14.35):

> The troops gave no quarter even to the women: the baggage animals themselves had been speared and added to the pile of bodies. The glory won in the course of that day was remarkable, and equal to that

of our older victories: for, by some accounts, little less than eighty thousand Britons fell, at a cost of some four hundred Romans killed and a not much greater number of wounded. Boudicca ended her days by poison. Meanwhile Postumus, camp-prefect of *legio* II, informed of the exploits of the men of *legio* XIV and *legio* XX, and conscious that he had cheated his own legion of a share in the honours and had violated the rules of the service by ignoring the orders of his commander, ran his sword through his body.

Dio's account of Boudicca's fate differs from that of Tacitus. He says that (*Roman History*, 62.12): 'After the battle Boudicca fell sick and died. The Britons mourned her deeply and gave her a costly burial; but, feeling that now at last they were really defeated, the survivors scattered to their homes.'

Thus ended Boudicca's revolt in the desperate Battle of Watling Street, with Roman victory overwhelming and total.

In the aftermath of Boudicca's defeat, Nero hurriedly sent 2,000 more legionaries to Britain from the German frontier, largely to replace the casualties in *legio* IX *Hispana*, together with 1,000 auxiliary cavalry and 8 units of auxiliary foot. Turney convincingly argues here that among the leaders of the emergency reinforcements was Titus, son of Vespasian and future Flavian emperor (2022, 60). Certainly, Suetonius says Titus served in Britain as a military tribune, and he is known to have been based in Germany around this time (*The Twelve Caesars*, *Titus*, 41). If he did travel to Britain, he may have met Agricola, given the latter remained on Paulinus' staff after the defeat of Boudicca.

The new troops helped Paulinus stamp out the last flames of resistance in Britain. This was carried out with such vigour that in the Iceni's north Norfolk homelands the region remained underdeveloped for many years, with some of the urban plots in the later *civitas* capital at Caistor St Edmunds (Roman *Venta Icenorum*) never used.

Sadly for Paulinus, he didn't receive the plaudits he might have expected after his mighty victory. This was because the absent procurator Decianus, still hiding in Gaul, was quickly replaced by Nero with a new man named Gaius Julius Alpinus Classicianus. We know him well from the archaeological record, given the enormous altar-shaped funerary monument erected by his wife, Julia Pacata, in London. This was later reused in one of the bastions added to the Severan land wall of London towards the end of the second century AD, with two surviving sections now on display in the British Museum (RIB 12). Classicianus was critical of Paulinus' post-revolt punitive actions against the Britons, fearing it might spark another revolt. He reported this to the emperor, who sent his own freedman Polyclitus to conduct an investigation. Though we don't have full details of his findings, the investigator did report that Paulinus had lost some ships from the regional fleet. This was excuse enough for Nero to relieve him, his replacement the more conciliatory Publius Petronius Turpilianus. However, Paulinus didn't return to Rome in disgrace, given that high-quality building materials dating to the mid-AD 60s feature both his and Nero's names alongside symbols of victory, and a man with his name was nominated as consul for AD 66.

With a degree of calm restored to Britain, rebuilding and repair began, with consolidation once more the order of the day. In the first instance, the provincial capital was moved from the *colonia* at Colchester to the *municipia* of London on the north bank of the Thames. This triggered a rebuilding programme there, paid for by the imperial *fiscus* treasury, the first manifestation being the construction of the 1.5ha Neronian fort at modern Plantation Place on Fenchurch Street. This was found during rescue excavations by Museum of London Archaeology (MOLA) in the early 2010s. The fortification was a timber and earthwork structure, similar in design to a standard Roman marching camp, though more robust in its construction.

The governors who followed Paulinus in the AD 60s are often criticised for not living up to his martial prowess. However, as Jones and Mattingly argue, the likes of Turpilianus and his own successor, Marcus Trebellius Maximus, were clearly obeying a new set of orders. Rather than continue the expansion of Roman-controlled territory, this was to regarrison the province and complete the pacification of the natives in the newly conquered territories north of the 'Fosse Way Frontier' (1990, 71). The strategy was clearly successful as by the mid-AD 60s, Nero was able to pull the veteran *legio* XIV *Gemina* out of the line in Britain for redeployment east.

By this time, the territory of the new province had greatly expanded beyond the 'Fosse Way Frontier' stop line of the late AD 40s. Below it, the various client kingdoms, including the Regni, Atrebates and Iceni, had now been subsumed into Roman-controlled territory. Above it, to the northeast, the lands of Corieltauvi south of the Humber were now also part of the province, and perhaps even land belonging to the Parisi to their north. The lands of the Dubonni and Cornovii in the Welsh Marches were now also part of Britannia, providing the springboard for more campaigns in Wales, some more successful than others. Evidence this region became a new frontier zone for the campaigns there is evident with the construction around this time of two new branches of Watling Street from Wroxeter, one heading south to Caerleon (Roman *Isca Augustus*) and one north to Chester (Roman *Deva Victrix*). Both sites featured new fortifications, the latter a key location for Agricola in his later campaigns in the far north of Britain. All of the above detail allows us to roughly establish the northern frontier of the province as the AD 60s came to an end. This was now on a line from the river Dee on the west coast to the Humber Estuary on the east, excepting much of Wales (especially in the north), whose total conquest to that point remained elusive.

Rome, Asia and Spain

Agricola likely left Britain at the same time as Paulinus, or shortly afterwards. Arriving back in Rome, he was soon married. This was to Domitia Decidiana, who Tacitus says was the 'child of an illustrious house', adding that the union 'lent him both distinction and material aid to his ambitions' (*The Agricola*, 6.15). The inference here is her family connections and wealth boosted his career chances as he progressed along the *cursus honorum*, with Turney suggesting her father was the hugely wealthy Romano-Gallic aristocrat Domitius Decidius, who had been head of the *fiscus* treasury under Claudius (2022, 61).

We see the positive impact of Agricola's new family ties in his next appointment when elected in AD 62 to serve in the super rich province of Asia as a *quaestor*. This was under its proconsul Otho Titianus, elder brother of the future emperor Marcus Salvius Otho and an imperial favourite of Nero. Domitia moved with Agricola to the provincial capital

Pergamum, their marriage there evidently a happy one, with Tacitus saying, 'they lived in rare accord, maintained by mutual affection and unselfishness' (*The Agricola*, 16.1). Their first child, a son, was born in late AD 62 but died in infancy, while their second child was the daughter later to marry Tacitus. Both were born in the Asian capital.

Agricola remained in Asia until late AD 64, when he and the family returned to Rome. He clearly delayed this as long as possible given Nero's increasing unpopularity – a very shrewd move as he avoided the famous Neronian fire, which began on 13 July, and the subsequent brutal persecutions of the Christians in the city.

Once back in Rome, Agricola continued to keep a low profile and spent the following year quietly before becoming Tribune of Plebs in AD 66, and then *praetor* in AD 67. In each post, he proved a true survivor in an age when many leading nobles fell foul of Nero's increasingly wild mood swings, keeping his head down rather than losing it. Tacitus provides excellent anecdotal detail here, saying (*The Agricola*, 6.17):

> He passed the interval between quaestorship and Tribune of Pleb, and his actual year in office as tribune, in quiet inactivity; he understood the age of Nero, in which an absence of initiative proved a good philosophy. His praetorship ran the same quiet course, for no administration of law had fallen to him. Over the games and other vanities of his office he compromised between economy and abundance, steering clear of extravagance but not missing popular approval.

Agricola came close to crossing Nero only once. This was in the spring of AD 68, the year after his praetorship. Here, he was tasked by Servius Sulpicius Galba, governor of Hispania Tarraconensis and senior governor across the whole Iberian Peninsula, with carrying out an inventory of temple treasures in Rome. This was in response to allegations by the Senate that Nero was misappropriating funds from there (Kean and Frey, 2005, 56). Tacitus says Agricola fulfilled the task well, calling his investigation a 'striking success' (*The Agricola*, 6.18). Agricola no doubt only accepted this risky post because of the man who commissioned him. With the Julio-Claudian dynasty spiralling to its end, Galba was the man of the hour. The 'Year of the Four' emperors was about to begin.

Year of the Four Emperors

By the summer of AD 68 the population of Rome, including the Senate, had had enough of Nero and his violent, unpredictable ways. In particular, they were alarmed at his response to the AD 64 fire, which had destroyed much of the city's centre. This was to use it as an excuse to build a new, hugely expensive palace complex away from the Palatine Hill on the nearby Oppian Hill. He called this his *Domeus Aurea*, 'golden house'. Unsurprisingly, the construct cost spiralled out of control (Kean and Frey, 2005, 54). Soon the *fiscus* imperial treasury was under enormous pressure, causing a sudden surge in inflation. Nero's response was to devalue the gold *aereus* by reducing its weight by 10 per cent. When this failed to compensate for his extravagant spending, he took to extorting money from the wealthy, eventually accusing many of treason. More often than not, these were found guilty and put to death, with their estates confiscated by the emperor. Here, Nero's *praefectus praetorio* Ofonius Tigellinus played the leading role as accuser, prosecutor and often judge. These were the lethally murky waters being cannily navigated by Agricola once back in Rome.

A backlash in public opinion soon followed. Nero's response was to take himself out of the imperial spotlight in Rome and head to the cultural-powerhouse province of Achaea. Kean and Frey describe what happened next (2005, 54):

> While there he involved himself in a frenzied whirl of athletic competitions [including the Olympic Games] and musical diversions in which he always desired to be awarded the first prize. Reality was no longer a concept Nero understood, so he did not care that in Greek competition merit, not social standing, was supposed to be rewarded; he even won first prize in competitions he never attended.

Detached from reality amid his fawning Greek admirers and hangers-on, Nero then proclaimed the freedom of the Greeks at the Isthmian Games, emulating the gesture of Titus Quinctius Flaminius over 200 years earlier. This was an empty deed given the Senate would never agree to it, but it did stir up further unrest in the provinces elsewhere, including Gaul, Spain and North Africa. His plans to travel further east were then curtailed by the First Jewish Revolt, which broke out in Judea, and soon Nero was speeding back to Rome after learning of serious unrest in the capital when Clodius Macer, the governor of Africa Proconsularis, cut off the *cura annonae* grain supply. More worryingly, Macer was using his region's only legion, *legio* III *Augusta*, to carry out his orders. This was a full mutiny. More bad news awaited Nero when he arrived back in Rome. There he learnt that Tigellinus had abandoned him after narrowly avoiding a lynch mob and was hiding on his rural estate outside of Rome, claiming he was suffering from an incurable illness.

Macer's revolt began a cascade of similar insurrections, great and small, around the empire against Nero. However, it was the rebellion of Gaius Julius Vindex, the governor of Gallia Lugdunensis, that proved the end for the Julio-Claudian dynasty. This prompted Galba in Spain to follow suit, though soon after, Vindex found himself fighting the Neronian loyalist Lucius Verginus Rufus, governor of Germania Superior, and his Rhine army. This included three elite northern frontier legions, *legio* IV *Macedonia*, *legio* XXI *Rapax* and *legio* VII *Primigenia* (Pollard and Berry, 2012, 52). Rufus personally led them against Vindex and defeated the rebel in spring AD 68 near modern Besançon (Roman *Vesontio*) in eastern France, close to the Jura Mountains.

This left Galba to march on Rome alone, where at his behest Agricola had earlier carried out his temple-funding investigation. When news reached Nero in the imperial capital of Galba's approach, he realised, in a rare moment of later-life clarity, that his chances of survival were now slim. With part of the army in revolt, and the Roman public set firmly against him, the Senate decided to act, and on 8 June declared Nero a public enemy. At the same time, they announced their support for Galba, though at that point didn't declare him emperor. Nero, fearing his end was near, fled Rome in disguise the following day, though only made it just past the Servian walls when his escape route was cut off. Knowing torture and a grim death would be his fate if Galba captured him, but lacking the courage to take his own life, he asked a loyal freedman called Epaphroditus to kill him. This he promptly did. The dead emperor was then buried anonymously by his long-suffering mistress Acte in the Abenobari mausoleum on a quiet side of the Pincian Hill, this just outside the city walls. Thus ended the Julio-Claudian dynasty, with a sad whimper, not a mighty bang.

Galba and his army arrived in Rome in early October to find it in chaos. This was because, in the months since Nero's death, Tigellinus' co-*praefectus praetorio* Gaius Nymphidius Sabinus had declared himself the legitimate successor to the throne. This was based on a completely made-up claim he was the illegitimate son of Caligula. Nymphidius, never acknowledged by the Senate, didn't last long. As soon as Galba arrived, the Praetorians backed him and killed Nymphidius. Galba then deployed his legionaries across the imperial capital, finally restoring order. Now the Senate officially declared him emperor, with Macer making it known that Galba had his backing too, he restoring the *cura annonae* at the same time.

Galba next adopted the title *caesar*, the first time an emperor had used it to legitimise imperial power, setting a trend many successors would follow. However, it was all to no avail as a series of missteps by a man Tacitus calls a 'mediocre genius' led to his swift downfall (*The Histories*, 1.49). Suetonius is less kind, providing far more detail. He says (*The Twelve Caesars, Galba*, 4.12):

> His double reputation for cruelty and avarice went before him; men said that he had punished the cities of the Spanish and Gallic provinces which had hesitated about taking sides with him by imposing heavier taxes, and some even by the razing of their walls, putting to death the governors and their imperial deputies along with their wives and children. Further, that he had melted down a golden crown of fifteen pounds weight, which the people of Tarraco had taken from their ancient temple of Jupiter and presented to him, with orders that the three ounces which were found lacking be exacted from them. This reputation was confirmed and even augmented immediately on his arrival in Rome once he had secured his position. For having compelled some marines [from the Misenum-based *Classis Misenensis* regional fleet] whom Nero had made regular soldiers to return to their former position as rowers, upon their refusing and obstinately demanding an eagle and standards, he not only dispersed them by a cavalry charge, but even decimated them. He also disbanded

a cohort of Germans, whom the previous emperors had made their bodyguard and had found absolutely faithful in many emergencies, and sent them back to their native country without any rewards.

Galba then turned on his supporter Macer in North Africa, convinced by his close advisors that the governor of Africa Pronsularis was plotting to remove him. Despite there being no hard evidence for this, Macer was swiftly assassinated on imperial orders.

Alarm bells now started ringing in the upper echelons of Roman society, and a new candidate emerged for the purple. This was Otho, governor of Hispania Lusitania and an erstwhile ally of Galba who had marched with him to Rome. Otho had a personal vendetta against Nero given the latter had forced Otho to divorce his wife (and Nero's former mistress) Poppaea Sabina so that she could marry the emperor. Her death in AD 65 when heavily pregnant, after being kicked in the abdomen by Nero, only worsened Otho's animosity.

Otho had been expecting to be named Galba's heir as a reward for his support against Nero. Galba instead chose leading nobleman Lucius Calpurnius Piso Frugi Licinianus, announcing the move on 10 January AD 69. On paper, this was a shrewd choice given a need to bolster his support in the Senate. This was after word reached Rome that two Rhine legions in Germania Inferior under the command of regional governor Aulus Vitellius had refused to recognise the new emperor. Vitellius had only just been appointed by Galba in one of his first acts in power, on paper a clever move given Vitellius had no experience of senior military command and had a reputation for gambling and gluttony (Kean and Frey, 2005, 59). However, encouraged by his two leading *legates* Aulus Caecina Alienus and Fabius Valens, Vitellius decided to make his own move for the throne. Soon he'd rallied support from the other legions along the Rhine, a total of nine finally declaring him emperor.

Annoyed at being passed over as heir, the ambitious Otho now took advantage of the confusion on the Rhine to make his own bid for power. Here he had an advantage over Vitellius as he was already in the imperial capital. That put him in close proximity to the Praetorian Guard, whom he bribed to remove Galba. Given the latter had yet to pay the guard a donative for supporting his earlier bid for power, they quickly switched sides. Otho was declared emperor on 15 January, with the 73-year-old Galba then hunted down and murdered in the *forum Romanum*. His severed head was then paraded around Rome atop a pole, a clear message to the Senate, who quickly ratified Otho's elevation. Licinianus was also assassinated by the guard at the same time to secure Otho's position.

Otho proved an even poorer choice as emperor than Galba, with Suetonius particularly damning. He says (*The Twelve Caesars, Otho*, 11.1):

> He is said to have been of moderate height, splay-footed and bandy-legged, but almost feminine in his care of his person. He had the hair of his body plucked out, and because of the thinness of his locks wore a wig so carefully fashioned and fitted to his head, that no one suspected it. Moreover, they say that he used to shave every day and smear his face with moist bread, beginning the practice with the appearance of the first down, so as never to have a beard.

For a Roman patrician, such an effete description was a brutal put-down. Sadly for Otho, he also began his reign with a series of poor decisions. In particular, he allowed Nero's statues, many of which had been removed, to be reset in place, and returned the dead emperor's freedmen to work in the imperial palace. After this, the Roman public then began to mock him as 'Nero Otho', a title the vain new emperor loathed.

To that point, aside from his temple investigations the previous spring for Galba, Agricola and his family had managed to remain out of the limelight as the first wave of political violence hit the imperial capital. Sadly for them, this was not to last. Here Tacitus provides the detail, saying (*The Agricola*, 7.19):

> That year dealt a grievous blow to Agricola's heart and home. The men of Otho's fleet, while savagely plundering territory in Liguria during their piratical career, murdered Agricola's mother on her estate, and pillaged the estate and a large part of her fortune, which was the motive for the murder.

As detailed earlier, at the time Julia Procilla was residing on her family holdings in *Albintimilium*, presumably thinking it safer than Rome. Birley argues the grim event took place in March or early April AD 69 (2005, 74). Understandably, Agricola immediately turned against Otho.

Agricola's heartbreak over the loss of his mother was set against even more dramatic developments in Rome. In early March, Otho had received word that Vitellius was on the march south to challenge him. Indeed, his advance guard under Caecina and Valens was already in Cisalpine Gaul in northern Italy. Given their route of approach may have been along the Mediterranean shoreline, this might explain why the Othonian fleet had ravaged the Ligurian coast, costing Agricola's mother her life. Otho now called any loyal troops within a reasonable distance to his standard. At first, this was only the Praetorian Guard and *cohortes urbanae* from Rome, and legionaries and auxilia from Pannonia on the upper Danubian frontier. This gave him a force of around 9,000 men. He also recalled legionaries and auxilia from Moesia on the lower Danube, though knew they would take time to arrive. To give them a chance of joining him he then tried negotiating with Vitellius, offering to make him his adoptive son-in-law. However, Caecina and Valens interceded, ensuring there would be no bargain, and waited for Vitellius to arrive to join them with the bulk of his Rhine army. The primary sources say this would have given the Vitellians up to 60,000 men, an improbable figure, though clearly they heavily outnumbered Otho.

The new emperor now had no choice but to fight, heading north on 14 March, where he aimed to hold the line of the Po River while still waiting for the Moesian troops to arrive. He used a small diversionary strike north of the river to delay Vitellius, while he and his general staff arrived at Brescello (Roman *Brixellum*). He then established his main military camp nearby at Calvatone (Roman *Bedriacum*) between modern Verona and Cremona. Learning Vitellius had ordered a bridge to be built over the Po, Otho then ordered his main force forward to prevent its completion. However, while advancing along the *Via Postumia* in column the Othonian forces, including their baggage train, was intercepted on 14 April by a Vitellian army that had crossed the river under Caecina and Valens near modern Cremona. The First Battle of Bedriacum ensued, with the emperor's forces quickly routed and the survivors fleeing back to Brescello. There, upon learning the news of his army's defeat, Otho chose to take his own life rather than prolong the civil war. By default,

Vitellius now became emperor. However, Otho's last selfless act was in vain. This was because Vitellius' own nemesis was already on the way to challenge him for the throne. This was Vespasian, soon to be the first Flavian emperor.

We have no detail of Agricola's specific activities during this chaotic period, only a mention in Tacitus that when he heard news of his mother's death and the devastation of their estates at *Albintimilium*, he 'set out to pay his last respects' (*The Agricola*, 7.19). Turney believes this shows Agricola headed back to Liguria to begin the lengthy process putting the family affairs in order after the trauma of the 'pirate' raid (2022, 74).

Interestingly, despite his desire for revenge on Otho, he didn't immediately side with Vitellius. Tacitus says this was 'because, in his deliberations, he was overtaken by news of Vespasian's bid for empire, and without a moment's hesitation joined his party' (*The Agricola*, 7.19).

Vespasian was stationed in Judaea when Nero committed suicide, leading the Roman response to the First Jewish Revolt. There he initially gave his support to Galba after Nero's death. However, when he learned of Galba's death at the hands of the Praetorians he decided to act himself. On 1 July AD 69 he was proclaimed emperor by his Judaean legions while visiting Alexandria. Gaius Licinius Mucianus, governor of Syria, quickly gave him his support, with all the remaining eastern legions joining the Flavian cause. Vespasian then tasked Mucianus with leading a strong vanguard of eastern legionaries and auxilia in a march on Rome to seize the throne from Vitellius (Otho having already fallen). On the way they were bolstered by three of the legions Otho had called on to join him from Moesia. These were *legio* II *Gallicia*, *legio* VIII *Augusta* and *legio* VII *Claudia*.

Having failed to arrive in time to save Otho, and then being forced to swear allegiance to Vitellius, these now declared for Vespasian. The troops had already reached Aquileia on the northeastern Adriatic coast of Italy, so were able to apply immediate pressure on Vitellius (Kean and Frey, 2005, 63). This persuaded two other legions in the region to declare for Vespasian, *legio* VII *Gemina Galbiana* and *legio* XIII *Gemina*. The latter in particular had cause to detest Vitellius, having been on the losing side at the First Battle of Bedriacum and then as a punishment forced to build amphitheatres for Valens and Caecina. These five legions, led by Marcus Antonius Primus, commander of *legio* VII *Gemina Galbiana*, then marched on Rome without waiting for the eastern legions under Mucianus to arrive. All was now set for the final showdown between the Flavians and Vitellians.

As soon as Vitellius received the news that Antonius was leading five legions to the imperial capital, he dispatched Caecina (now consul) with three legions, *legio* I *Italica*, *legio* XXI *Rapax* and *legio* XXII *Primiginiam*, together with vexillations from seven other legions and over a thousand auxiliaries, to intercept him at Verona, which he knew the Flavians must pass through to begin the march directly south. Caecina had orders to attack immediately when he sighted the enemy, given Vitellius knew Mucianus was on the way behind Antonius, and behind him Vespasian with the remainder of the eastern legions. However, the Vitellian commander declined to do as ordered as, unbeknownst to Vitellius, he had already decided to defect to the Flavians. Along with Sextus Lucilius Bassus, *praefectus classis* of the Ravenna-based *Classis Ravenna* Adriatic regional fleet, he had already reached out to Antonius with a view to switching sides. Sadly for Caecina, when he and the admiral put the idea to their own legionaries and auxilia they refused to follow them and put Caecina in chains. Bassus had much better fortune, narrowly escaping and then handing over the *Classis Ravenna* to the Flavians. The fleet's marines, who from that point fought on land for Vespasian, were later rewarded by the emperor, he forming *legio* II *Adiutrix* from their ranks in AD 70. Meanwhile, Bassus was rewarded for his loyalty by promotion the following year, when he became the governor of Judaea as the First Jewish Revolt ground to its sanguineous end. It was he who, leading Roman forces in the region, destroyed the Jewish strongholds at Machaerus and Herodium, though he died on the way to besiege the final centre of Jewish resistance, Masada.

Back to the chronological narrative, at the point when Caecina had tried to switch sides, Vitellius' other highly experienced leader Valens was ill in Rome. Only now, with Caecina under arrest, did he head north to take over command. Sadly for Vitellius, he was to arrive too late.

Leaderless, and not waiting for Valens to arrive, the Vitellian troops continued their advance on Verona, still following Vitellius' original orders. They passed through Cremona, where their scouts located Antonius and his army at Calvatone, to the immediate west. The Flavian commander was the first to respond, sending a cavalry column to challenge the Vitellian vanguard. A general engagement then began on the morning of 24 October. This lasted two days and is today called the Second Battle of Bedriacum, though it was actually a far more fluid engagement that took place over a wide area.

In the first instance, Antonius' legionaries and auxiliaries had the better of the fighting, with the Vitellian troops retreating to their marching camps around Cremona. Antonius pursued immediately, his forces advancing along the *Via Postumia* towards Cremona. There they were opposed by a powerful Vitellian force, now reinforced by the veteran *legio* IV *Macedonica*, though they still had no army commander given that Valens had yet to arrive. Battle recommenced and continued into the night. This proved a particularly brutal affair, with the Flavian *legio* VII *Gemina Galbiana* suffering heavy casualties and losing its *aquila* eagle standard, though this was later recovered by a centurion at the cost of his life. However, finally Antonius' forces gained the upper hand just before dawn broke. The turning point was the rising of the sun, which prompted the Flavian legionaries of *legio* III *Gallicia* to lift their arms to heaven in praise, as was their custom. The Vitellian forces misread this as a greeting for new Flavian reinforcements, lost heart and were driven back to their camps. These were then stormed by Flavian troops, after which Cremona fell to Antonius. The city, full of Vitellian loot from the earlier raiding along the Ligurian coast, was brutally sacked over a four-day period, with huge loss of civilian life. This was the unintended consequence of Antonius belatedly ordering his troops not to take any Cremonians as slaves on pain of death after the sacking had begun, his troops then panicking and killing their captives to escape punishment.

His victory complete, Antonius continued to Rome, where Vitellius had already agreed to abdicate. However, this was to no avail given his surviving troops chose to fight on. Then, on 20 December, the Flavians arrived and immediately launched an assault on the city. Kean and Frey take up the story of Vitellius' ignominious end (2005, 61):

> The emperor disguised himself in dirty clothing and hid in the imperial doorkeeper's quarters, leaning on a couch and a mattress

against the door for protection. Dragged from his hiding place by the Flavians, he was hauled off to the *forum Romanum*, where he was tortured, killed and his body tossed into the Tiber.

Vespasian, the last man standing as a contender for the throne, was recognised as emperor by the Senate on 22 December. So began the Flavian dynasty, with the 'Year of the Four Emperors' at an end.

Agricola's actions in later AD 69 are unclear, excepting his overt support for Vespasian. His options were to remain in *Albintimilium*, where work continued to set things back in order, go home to *Forum Julii* to protect his family's estates there, or go to Rome. There is no evidence at all of the latter, which was highly dangerous given his support for the Flavians before their final victory. The first two options are therefore the most likely. Birley argues in favour of *Forum Julii*, noting that the provincial governor, Valerius Paulinus, was a long-term friend of Vespasian and prominent Flavian supporter from the beginning of his campaign for the throne (2005, 75). He was also well known to Agricola. It was Paulinus who, in October AD 69, seized *Forum Julii* in the name of the Flavians. This was important given the town's key transport links, as detailed earlier, it sitting on the important crossroad where the *Via Julia Augusta* from Italy to the Rhone valley met the *Via Domitia* linking Italy to Spain. Indeed, it had earlier seen a clash between troops supporting Otho and Vitellius. Once he declared for the Flavian cause, Paulinus then convinced several key surrounding towns to join Vespasian too. He then went on the offensive against Vitellian troops in the region, eventually capturing Valens.

Though we are uncertain of Agricola's actions at this time, we do know what happened to him after the final Flavian victory. This was two sequential big promotions, the second of which took him back to Britain. Here, Tacitus picks up the story, providing excellent detail (*The Agricola*, 7.19):

> The initial policies of Vespasian were in the hands of Mucianus, since Domitian was still a young man and exploited his father's success only to indulge himself. Mucianus sent Agricola to levy new troops and, when he had performed that task with scrupulous zeal, put him in command of *legio* XX *Valeria Victrix* [based in Britain].

Tacitus mentions Domitian here, given Titus was still in Judaea and would shortly begin his siege of Jerusalem. Meanwhile, it is also evident that the former Syrian governor Mucianus had been well rewarded for his loyalty to Vespasian. Tacitus provides a useful pen portrait, saying (*The Histories*, 9.1):

> He was a curious mix of self-indulgence and energy, courtesy and arrogance, good and evil. Excessively self-indulgent in his spare time, yet he showed remarkable qualities when actively employed on a task. In public you would praise him, but his private life was criticised. Yet by a subtle gift for intrigue he exercised great influence on his subordinates, associates and colleagues, and was the sort of man who found it more congenial to make an emperor than to be one.

Here was the ultimate patrician-level fixer needed to bind together the political classes in Rome after the bloody Flavian victory.

We have no further detail regarding Agricola's activities levying new troops after Vespasian's victory. However, it may have been he who formed *legio* II *Adiutrix* from the marine veterans of the *Classis Ravenna* after their service for Vespasian in the civil war. Later, he would lead them together with the three other British legions when governor there during his third stay in the province. For now, though, his next move was his second visit there, to take over command of *legio* XX *Valeria Victrix*.

Chapter 5

Return to Britannia

With a new dynasty in power in Rome, a new set of directives went out to the military around the borders of the empire. This was to go back on the offensive against the enemies of Rome, and conquer new territory. Vespasian, the veteran general and highly experienced administrator, knew the best way to ensure the support of the Senate and people of Rome was through martial success. Gone was the AD 60s consolidation period under Nero. Now new territory needed bringing under Roman control. In particular, Vespasian looked to the one region of the empire where he knew conflict could be found. That was Britain.

There, after the post-Boudiccan rebuilding period under Turpilianus and Trebellius, a new series of Flavian governors unleashed a fresh onslaught on northwestern Wales and, for the first time in strength, the north. These were Marcus Vettius Bolanus (late AD 69 to AD 71), Quintus Petillius Cerialis (AD 71 to AD 74), Sextus Julius Frontinus (AD 74 to AD 78), and finally Agricola himself (AD 77 to AD 85). By the time he was appointed governor, the latter had already served the first two as *legatus legionis* of *legio* XX *Valeria Victrix* during his second visit to Britain, before his later and final visit as governor.

As always when narrating the classical world, the exact dating of the events detailed below is often problematic and what you read here are my own interpretations based on the available historical and archaeological data.

A final point to note here before I go into forensic detail about Agricola's later campaigning activities in Britain is the impact an earlier event had on the psyche of the Roman military. This was the AD 9 Varian Disaster, called the *Clades Variana* by the Romans, when three entire legions plus supporting auxilia were lost while campaigning north of the Rhine in the Teutoburg Forest. This shocking event, when over 30,000 men were lost under Publius Quinctilius Varus around modern Kalkriese, had such a psychological impact on the imperial capital that plans to expand the empire's frontiers in the northwest of continental Europe were shelved for generations. More importantly, it scarred the self-assurance of the legions. From that point, and for centuries to come, all Roman military leaders strove to avoid the example of the disgraced Varus. Roman military campaigns had always paid attention to intelligence gathering and logistics. Now, that was far more the case. Thus, when Agricola led *legio* XX *Valeria Victrix* in Britain, and later the entire Roman military establishment there, his planning and attention to detail were of the finest quality, in part thanks to the long shadow cast by Varus' ignominious defeat.

Legatus Legionis

When Agricola arrived in Britain in March AD 70 to take command of *legio* XX *Valeria Victrix*, the legion was in revolt (Birley, 2005, 76). This is not as surprising as it might sound. First, the entire empire had just endured the turmoil of the 'Year of the Four Emperors'. Second, on occasion Roman military units did rebel when provoked by extreme events. For example, Tacitus details *legio* IX *Hispana* and two others based in a single legionary fortress on the Danube frontier in Pannonia rebelled in AD 14 due to the poor conditions there (*The Annals*, 1.16). Meanwhile, in a British context, the military there also had form, and far more recently. Tacitus paints a picture of the troops in Britain being underused by Turpilianus and Trebellius. Clearly no fan of either, or the late Neronian policy of consolidation in Britain, he says of the former (*The Annals*, 14.39): 'Turpilianus abstained from provoking the enemy, was not challenged himself, and conferred on this spiritless inaction the honourable name of peace.'

The Roman troops holding the northern frontier, at this time along a line from the river Dee in the west to the Humber Estuary in the east, certainly appear to have had too much time on their hands. This was because later, under Trebellius, real trouble broke out. Tacitus is also unflattering about him, saying he was 'somewhat indolent, and a man who never ventured on a campaign' (*The Histories*, 4.48). Given that Roman legions and their supporting auxilia were, in effect, industrial-scale killing machines, this was not the kind of martial leadership they expected. Soon a full rebellion began, with Tacitus adding (*The Histories*, 1.60): 'The trouble reached such a point that Trebellius was insulted by the auxiliary soldiers as well as by the legions, and deserted by the auxiliary foot and horse who joined Coelius.'

The latter was Marcus Roscius Coelius, who was then *legatus legionis* of *legio* XX *Valeria Victrix*, with Tacitus saying in the same passage that the two men had a long-standing feud. By this point, the 'Year of the Four Emperors' was well underway, with Nero and Galba dead and Otho and Vitellius at war with each other. Things then got worse in Britain when Vitellius, at the height of his struggle with Otho, withdrew 8,000 troops from the province to fight for him on the continent. Turney notes here how large a percentage of the British military establishment this was, with the province at the time only having three legions plus auxilia after Nero had withdrawn *legio* IV *Gemina* (2022, 80). Given the conflicted loyalties of the military units in Britain as the various imperial warlords fought for the throne, we can't be sure if those joining Vitellius were supporters of Trebellius or Coelius. Whichever it was, the withdrawal of the troops prompted the former to take action. He now challenged Coelius directly. This proved a poor decision, as Tacitus details (*The Histories*, 1.60):

> Trebellius charged Coelius with stirring up mutiny and destroying discipline; in return Coelius reproached Trebellius with robbing the legions and leaving them poor, while meantime the discipline of the army was broken down by this shameful quarrel between the commanders; and the trouble reached such a point that Trebellius fled to Vitellius.

Turney argues the two other *legatus legionis* in Britain now also declared their support for Coelius, making him provincial governor in all but name (2022, 81).

On arrival in Rome, Trebellius expected Vitellius would support him, but that wasn't the case. Instead, he was quickly removed from post in later AD 69, his replacement being Marcus Vettius Bolanus. The latter, a leading senator with wide military experience, had served with distinction as a *legatus legionis* in Armenia in AD 62 fighting the Parthians. He was then consul in AD 66, proconsul in Macedonia in AD 67, and by the time Vitellius took the throne was described by Statius as 'one of those in close attendance' on the new emperor (*Silvae*, 5.2). It is Statius who details Bolanus' martial prowess in most detail, providing a highly favourable commentary.

Not so Tacitus, who again is no fan of a new governor arriving in Britain, this time Bolanus. Specifically of the latter's time in the province, he provides three pithy comments. First, he says (*The Agricola*, 8.1): 'Bolanus governed more mildly than suited so turbulent a province.' Second, directly referencing the rebellious state of the British military at the time of his appointment, Tacitus says (*The Agricola*, 16.1): 'Nor did Bolanus, during the continuance of the civil wars, trouble Britain with discipline. There was the same inaction with respect to the enemy, and similar unruliness in camp.' Finally, he adds (*The Histories*, 2.9): 'Bolanus never enjoyed entire peace in Britain.'

As we shall see, Statius is far nearer the truth given Bolanus proved to be the first of four highly effective Flavian warrior governors in Britain.

Bolanus arrived in the province before the end of the year, bringing *legio* XIV *Gemina* back with him. Here, Vitellius believed it was surplus to requirements on the continent after his defeat of Otho, whom the legion had supported. No doubt, the 8,000 troops also withdrawn from Britain to fight with Vitellius also returned. However, sadly for the new emperor, his reign proved short-lived, and by the year's end, he was dead and Vespasian emperor. The latter wisely decided to keep the recently appointed Bolanus in position in Britain, knowing his martial experience would prove vital in securing the northwestern flank of his newly won empire while he consolidated his position on the continent. From that point, Bolanus showed true loyalty to the Flavians.

Soon the new governor was at work in Britain. His first task was to bring the military back under control. Here he was helped by the arrival of *legio* XIV *Gemina*, the veteran legion that had played the key role in defeating Boudicca. Also, given Vespasian's strong reputation as a military leader, his accession was well received by most of the troops in Britain, especially *legio* II *Augusta*. This was the legion he had led to glory during the AD 43 Claudian invasion of Britain, and the subsequent breakout campaign in the South West. Tacitus provides the detail here, saying (*The Histories*, 3.4): 'In Britain a favourable sentiment inclined toward Vespasian, because he had previously been put in command of the Second legion there.'

Before long, Bolanus had wrangled most of the British military establishment back under his control, except one legion. This was *legio* XX *Valeria Victrix*, still under the command of the problematic Coelius.

Bolanus wanted rid of Coelius as soon as possible and asked Vespasian to remove him from office. The emperor promptly did so, recalling the *legate* back to Rome. There, although his progress along the *cursus honorum* continued, Coelius was slow to achieve the high offices expected of a man who had led a legion. Clearly, his time in Britain had marked him out as trouble.

Vespasian chose Agricola as Coelius' replacement to lead *legio* XX *Valeria Victrix*, showing that by this time he was viewed as a true Flavian troubleshooter. When Agricola arrived in March AD 70, he found the legion still hesitant in declaring its support for Vespasian (Tacitus, *The Agricola*, 7.21). However, Agricola now showed great wisdom. Instead of confronting the legionaries, he chose to win over their trust. Turney neatly summarises this approach, saying (2022, 91):

> Perhaps Agricola tells them flatly that he will not have a repeat of their behaviour and that they have dishonoured the eagle under which they fight. That he needs the XXth in campaigning shape, loyal and true, as the Brigantes need to be dealt with. That he is willing to overlook their mutiny and forego the punishment ordered by the emperor on the condition that they damn well pull their socks up and start acting like soldiers.

The approach worked, with Tacitus saying that 'with a rare restraint he soon found in his legion the loyalty he had created' (*The Agricola*, 7.21). The legion was now back under orders, and ready to play a full role in the conquest of the north.

Agricola's new charge was a veteran legion, founded around 31 BC by Augustus when still known as Octavian. It then played a leading role in the Cantabrian Wars in northern Spain from 25 BC to 19 BC, before moving to the legionary fortress of *Burnum* in modern Croatia in AD 6 (Pollard and Berry, 2012, 99). There it adopted a new *cognomen*, *Valeria*, after the name of its commander, Illyrian governor Marcus Valerius Messalla Messallinus. The legion gained fame in the region by defeating a rebellion led by Bato of the local Daesitiates tribe (Cassius Dio, *Roman History*, 55.30). A second *cognomen*, *Victrix*, was added after a redeployment to *Carnuntum* on the Danube in Pannonia. From here, it led Tiberius' AD 8 campaign against the Marcomanni north of the river. The legion was then deployed to the Rhine as an emergency replacement after the Varian Disaster in AD 9, moving first to Cologne (at the time Roman *Oppidum Ubiorum*, later *Colonia Claudia Ara Agrippinensium*) and then to Neuss (Roman *Novaesium*). From there it campaigned deep into German territory north of the Rhine as part of Tiberius and Germanicus' campaigns of retribution in AD 9 and AD 10, after which it withdrew to hold the frontier again, joining four other legions there. Next, in AD 15 it was one of the three legions under Caecina Severus that struck deep into Germany once more, this time against the Marsi. This was the same campaign where Germanicus led four legions against the Chatti. After this, *legio* XX *Valeria Victrix* again withdrew to the Rhine frontier. There it remained, sometimes on the offensive, sometimes the defensive, until the reign of Caligula.

For some reason the new emperor held a grudge against the legion. As he advanced through northern Gaul during his planned, though aborted, invasion of Britain in AD 40 he let it be known he planned to discipline them. Suetonius hints this may have been because of an earlier slight by the troops against his father Germanicus, though provides no further detail (*The Twelve Caesars, Caligula*, 48.1). However, the legion got wind of the emperor's plans and armed itself, forcing Caligula to back down. Soon the emperor had other things to worry about and matters were quickly resolved. The legion was then one of the four that invaded Britain under Plautius as part of the AD 43 Claudian campaign. Here it played a leading role, with the new province declared in Colchester in October.

In the aftermath of this great Roman success Plautius ordered *legio* XX *Valeria Victrix* to build his new legionary fortress at Colchester. This then acted as the fulcrum for the initial series of Roman breakout campaigns in Britain. The legion then stayed there to act as theatre reserve while *legio* II *Augusta*, *legio* IX *Hispana* and *legio* XIV *Gemina* expanded the new province to the southwest, northwest and north. However, soon it was on the front line again, playing a key role in the various Roman campaigns in Wales. It was based there when the Boudiccan revolt broke out in AD 60/61, with Paulinus leading vexillations from the legion alongside *legio* XIV *Gemina* in his final encounter with Boudicca.

Little is known of the legion's activities after this until the trouble during Trebellius' governorship, with Agricola's arrival as *legatus legionis* finally setting it back on a firm footing within the Roman army in Britain. It is uncertain where the legion was based when Agricola arrived, with Birley saying that (2005, 76):

> It has been generally supposed that it had moved from Usk (Roman *Burrium*) to Wroxeter (Roman *Viroconium*) when the latter fortress was evacuated by *legio* XIV *Gemina*. But it may have been based first at Gloucester from AD 67 to AD 75.

Bolanus was quickly in action on arrival in Britain. The context was trouble in the north, again caused by Cartimandua's former husband Venutius. Taking advantage of the turmoil on the continent in AD 69, he staged another revolt among the Brigantes, this time with the help of allied and unconquered tribes from the far north. Again, the queen's position was in peril, and again she appealed to Rome for help. However, given Bolanus had only just arrived and was still bringing order to the British legions, he sent north a flying column of auxiliary cavalry who managed to extract Cartimandua back to safety within the borders of the province to the south. This is a classic example of what today we would call a special operation, especially given the distances travelled through hostile territory, with the Brigantian capital located at Aldborough in North Yorkshire (Roman *Isurium Brigantum*), some 120km north of the then frontier.

Later, larger formations of Roman troops under Bolanus fought even further north in Brigantian territory, with Statius (*Silvae*, 53.1) having the governor campaigning in the 'Caledonian Plains'. This is often interpreted as a reference to the Scottish Borders. While the Romans failed at this point to remove the Brigantian usurper Venutius from power, his insurgency focused Roman attention on the far north of Britain for the first time proper, and within a decade much of Brigantian territory up to the Solway Firth–Tyne line had been incorporated into the Roman province. It is highly likely that *legio* XX *Valeria Victrix* under Agricola played a full role in these later campaigns of Bolanus. Meanwhile, Venutius' ultimate fate is unrecorded.

Bolanus remained in Britain until the spring of AD 71, before his recall to Rome, where Vespasian rewarded him with patrician rank (Statius, *Silvae*, 5.2). Later, he became proconsul in Asia, one of the most important governorships in the empire. Both are strong evidence that, far from being inactive in Britain, as Tacitus suggests, Bolanus had made a good impression as governor of a province Vespasian knew well (Birley, 2005, 62).

Bolanus' replacement was the same Cerialis who earlier faced disgrace after his woeful performance with *legio* IX *Hispana* fighting Boudicca in the aftermath of the sack of Colchester. However, he then rebuilt his reputation in the 'Year of the Four Emperors', being an early convert to Vespasian's cause given he was a relative through marriage. Famously, he presented himself to the Flavian leader in Umbria in late autumn AD 69 after disguising himself as a peasant to evade capture by Vitellian troops.

However, at first things didn't go well for Cerialis. He was given command of a large troop of auxiliary cavalry and ordered by Vespasian to advance on Rome. Sadly for the Flavians, he was intercepted by a Vitellian force and heavily defeated on the outskirts of the imperial capital (Tacitus, *The Histories*, 3.79). Nevertheless, Vespasian stayed loyal to his kinsman and the following year he was appointed consul, tasked with leading the Roman forces fighting the Batavian revolt on the Rhine. This rebellion had broken out in AD 69, again against the backdrop of the 'Year of the Four Emperors'. Here, an auxiliary officer and Batavian prince called Gaius Julius Civilis led the Batavi and their German allies in a large-scale rebellion against Roman rule. Initially it was highly successful, with two Roman legions destroyed. However, when Cerialis arrived in theatre in AD 70 at the head of an enormous army, numbers told and he won a famous victory, and the revolt was crushed. It was also here that Cerialis was reintroduced to the British military, given the *Classis Britannica* regional fleet transported *legio* XIV *Gemina* from the province to join his army (the legion was not to return to Britain).

Cerialis was rewarded with the governorship of Britain, arriving with another new legion for the province, *legio* II *Adiutrix*. His orders were simple: provide the new Flavian dynasty with martial success by conquering the north of Britain, with Venutius' earlier rebellion providing the opportunity. He began immediately on arrival, heading north to set about the Brigantes (Tacitus, *The Agricola*, 17.1). In the first instance, he ordered *legio* IX *Hispana* from its legionary fortress at Lincoln into Yorkshire, where the troops constructed a new fortress at York, deep in Brigantian territory on the river Ouse. This was classically playing card shaped and very large, enclosing an area of over 20ha and able to host the 5,500 men of the legion. Its original defences were a ditch and 3m high turf/clay rampart topped by a palisade, with wood-built towers and gates. Then *legio* II *Adiutrix* moved into the vacated fortress at Lincoln to act as a strategic reserve. Next, Cerialis split the *Classis Britannica* into two divisions, one on the west coast, which gathered in its old hunting ground off the north Welsh coast, the other on the east coast off the Humber Estuary. The former was tasked with supporting a drive up the northwest coast by Agricola and *legio* XX *Valeria Victrix*. Meanwhile, the latter had orders to support a similar drive up the northeast coast by the units of the *legio* IX *Hispana* led by Cerialis himself. Here, Agricola was clearly acting as Cerialis' second-in-command. Finally, before the campaign began, the governor redeployed part of the *legio* II *Adiutrix* from Lincoln to the river Dee, where a new naval facility and fort was constructed at Chester. This had a dual purpose: to provide a base for the west coast division of the fleet, and to secure Agricola's left flank from any threat from northern Wales.

In this campaign the *Classis Britannica* played a key role, controlling the littoral zone along both coasts to secure the exposed maritime flanks of the legionary spearheads, providing the transport and supply function to keep the land forces moving, and scouting out ahead to provide timely intelligence of any gathering opposition. We have strong archaeological data to support this, which shows new Roman harbours being built at Wilderspool (Roman name unknown), Kirkham (Roman name unknown), Lancaster (Roman name unknown), Ravenglass (Roman *Itunocelum*) and Kirkbride (Roman name unknown) on the west coast in addition to Chester, and Brough-on-Humber (Roman *Petuaria*) and South Shields (Roman *Arbeia*) on the east coast.

Cerialis' campaign followed a familiar pattern, with each legionary spearhead marching inland to subdue Brigantian tribes as they arrived at each estuary on the coast. Thus, rivers including the Dee, Esk, Ellen and Wampool in west, and Humber, Tees and Tyne in the east, provided highways for the invader to take the fight to the enemy. In this way, Agricola and Cerialis wrestled regional control, slice by slice, of territory from the Brigantes. The progression of the campaign over two to three years is well evidenced by the multitude of vexillation fortresses built as the operation unfolded, the end never in doubt. The final stand was at the Brigantian capital of Stanwick, with the Romans victorious. Some argue it was here that Venutius met his end. Our sources are silent at this point regarding Cartimandua, so it is unclear whether she regained her crown or not, but we do know that by the time Cerialis returned to Rome in early AD 74, the whole of the north of England (and potentially southern Scotland) was occupied by Roman forces, with the province extending its frontier further north than ever before.

Based on dendrochronological evidence, one of the final acts of the campaign was the founding of a vexillation fort at modern Carlisle (Roman *Luguvalium*) by Agricola. Afterwards, with his success leading his legion and playing a key part in the great Roman victory evident to all, Agricola was cannily modest, if one believes his son-in-law. In a classic example of Roman hagiography, Tacitus says (*The Agricola*, 8.1): 'Agricola conducted himself modestly, attributing his success to his general [Cerialis], who had made the plans.' Thus, Agricola ensured Cerialis took the credit for Rome's victories in the north, avoiding the jealousy of a governor close to Vespasian. This was shrewd indeed, especially in the wake of a brutal civil war.

Cerialis' replacement was Frontinus, another soldier governor and Flavian favourite who had fought for Vespasian in AD 69. He was famed in his lifetime as a military man of letters, composing a well-regarded book on strategy called *Strategems*, which was later heavily used as source material for Aelian's more famous *Tactics*. Arriving in Britain at the beginning of AD 74, with the north for now pacified by Cerialis,

Frontinus turned his attention to the unfinished business in Wales. Here, despite the campaigns of earlier governors including Paulinus, the native tribes were still proving troublesome, especially the Silures in the south. Using *legio* II *Augusta*, Frontinus mounted another lightning Roman campaign, using the river Severn and Bristol Channel to protect his left flank, where, once again, the regional fleet played a major role in the now familiar roles of littoral control, transport and scouting. Within three years, all opposition in the south of Wales had been crushed, with a string of forts built across the central and southern peninsula to help enforce the rule of Rome. A number of these were on riverine estuaries, again showing the importance of the *Classis Britannica*, including locations such as Carmarthen (Roman *Moridunum*) and Cefn Gaer (Roman name unknown). Finally, to secure the region even more firmly he permanently redeployed the *legio* II *Augusta* from Gloucester to Caerleon on the river Usk, where they built a large legionary fortress and harbour to oversee southern Wales and the Bristol Channel. Frontinus similarly had *legio* II *Adiutrix* develop the vexillation fort and harbour at Chester into a full legionary fortress to keep an eye on northern Wales and the Irish Sea. It is likely that from this point, units of the *Classis Britannica* were permanently based at these two sites in southern and northern Wales. North Wales continued to be a problem, though, and was the first target of the next warrior governor in Britain, Agricola.

Governor

Agricola returned to Rome in late AD 73, before Cerialis' departure early the following year. His service in Britain clearly impressed the Flavians, with Vespasian promoting him to patrician rank on his arrival home. Agricola was then given another major promotion, this time as governor of Gallia Aquitania. Tacitus emphasises the scale of this promotion, saying it carried the prospect of a consulship, 'for which the emperor had marked him out' (*The Agricola*, 9.1).

Gallia Aquitania was an important province, today the region of southwestern France, with its Atlantic coast facing the Bay of Biscay. Named after the regional Aquitani tribe at the time of the Caesarian conquest of Gaul, it was bordered by Gallia Lugdunensis to the north,

Gallia Narbonensis to the west and Hispania Tarraconensis across the Pyrenees to the south. Within Roman Gaul, it was part of the wider region nicknamed *Gallia Comata* ('long-haired Gaul'), along with Gallia Lugdunensis and Gallia Belgica, as opposed to *Gallia Bracata* ('trousered Gaul'), which comprised Gallia Narbonensis on the Mediterranean coast.

When governor in Gallia Aquitania, Agricola was based in Bordeaux (Roman *Burdigala*), this after Vespasian declared the city the new provincial capital early in his reign. The province was wealthy, with extensive *metalla* industries run by the military, including gold and silver mining and iron manufacturing, an extensive linen industry, and large agricultural estates growing millet and wheat. Viticulture was also extensively practised, with fine wines exported upriver on the Loire and its tributaries to northern Gaul and Britain, and overland to central Gaul for onward transport down the river Rhone to the Mediterranean.

Given the importance of provincial governorships to Agricola's career, both in Gallia Aquitania and later in Britain, understanding this role is important. The emperor in Rome could not rule such a vast empire directly given the huge distances involved and speed of transport. Therefore, power was devolved from the emperor to each province through their governors (or proconsuls in a senatorial province) and procurators in two separate chains of command. This system was designed to prevent one or the other accruing too much power and challenging imperial authority. Appointment as a governor was one of the most senior posts on the *cursus honorum*, and a precursor to serving a term as a consul in Rome.

The governor was the emperor's military and legal representative, and usually of senatorial class. He headed an executive body called the *officium consularis*. In most provinces this included an *iuridicus* legal expert, *legates* from any legions based there, senatorial-level military tribunes from any auxiliary units, and equestrian-rank officers. Meanwhile, the procurator, usually an equestrian, was the emperor's financial representative tasked with making the province pay. He had a personal staff of equestrian and freedmen administrators called *procutatores*, known collectively as his *caesariani* (Birley, 2005, 300). These personnel were registrars, finance officers and superintendents. The procurator's specific responsibilities included the collection of all taxes within the province, for example the land tax (*tributum soli*), duty on the carriage of goods on public highways (*portorium*) and the poll tax (*tributum capitis*). They were also responsible for the collection of rent from any imperial estates in the province owned by the emperor, the management of all major *metalla* mines and quarries (to run these the procurator appointed one of his staff, known as a *procurator metallorum*) and distributing pay to public officials and the military.

One might note here how small the executive teams of the governor and procurator were, in total no more than sixty staff in a normal province. To give context, in Roman Britain this amounted to only 0.0017 per cent of the estimated population of 3.5 million, compared to around 25 per cent in public employ today. Clearly, this was an insufficient number of officials to run the province, and therefore both teams were bolstered by the appointment of military personnel assigned from the provincial military presence to assist with official duties. Those appointed to the *officium consularis* were known as *beneficiarii consularis*, and those to the procurator's staff *beneficiarii procuratoris*.

Tacitus provides a detailed account of Agricola's time in Gallia Aquitania, saying that while at first many peers thought he might struggle in this civilian role given his largely military experience to that date, he won over the province by 'performing his duties both readily and equitably' (*The Agricola*, 9.2). Once more, just as in Britain with *legio* XX *Valeria Victrix*, we see the pragmatic Agricola in action. Tacitus provides enigmatic insight, saying (*The Agricola*, 9.4): 'He succeeded where few succeeded. He was strict but often merciful, with his familiar manner not lessening his authority nor his strictness reducing his popularity. He avoided rivalry with colleagues, and disputes with procurators.'

After a successful three years as governor in Gallia Aquitania, Agricola was recalled to Rome in late AD 76. There it was already being rumoured he was set to be appointed governor of Britannia (*The Agricola*, 9.1). However, first he was appointed consul by Vespasian, likely in early AD 77, when he was 36. In that year he also had happy family news, with Tacitus here speaking in the first person (*The Agricola*, 9.1): 'In his consulship he betrothed to me, in my early manhood, his daughter Julia, a girl of rare promise, and after its close gave her to me in marriage.'

The year AD 77 was clearly a busy one for Agricola given that, in the early summer, he was also appointed to the College of Pontiffs. This was the religious council whose members were the highest-ranking priests in

Rome, led by the emperor himself as Pontifex Maximus. Agricola was now at the very apex of patrician society, and in early autumn was finally awarded the governorship of Britannia (Birley, 2005, 78).

Agricola arrived in his new province in late summer AD 77 with his wife Domitia. Birley says it is not impossible that Tacitus accompanied him as a *tribunus angusticlavia* to serve in one of Britain's legions, along with his new wife (2005, 77). However, we have no direct evidence for this. If he did, he was likely soon seconded to serve in Agricola's *officium consularis* as a senior *beneficiarii consularis*, making him an eyewitness to many of the events he narrates during Agricola's time as governor in Britain.

Agricola travelled to Britain from Boulogne-sur-Mer, headquarters of the *Classis Britannica*, where the fine legionary-sized fortress atop high ground north of the Liane estuary provided excellent accommodation for his fleeting stay before passage. After a short crossing of the English Channel, the party arrived in Britain at Richborough, then a thriving port and set to become the imperial gateway into the province after Agricola's later northern triumphs. From there they travelled overland to London along Watling Street. This mercantile town had been made the provincial capital in the AD 60s in the aftermath of the Boudiccan revolt, and was still being rebuilt after its destruction in the rebellion. It seems likely the post-revolt 1.5ha Neronian fort built near modern Fenchurch Street was still there. The building of this fortification had required a resetting of the pre-Boudiccan street grid in London, which soon filled out with new public and private buildings. Agricola may have stayed in an early iteration of the governor's palace on the Thames river front below today's Cannon Street railway station, and would have attended administrative gatherings in the new *basilica* and *forum*, an early version of which was being built beneath modern Leadenhall Market.

However, Agricola didn't stay in London long. His orders were very specific. These were to conquer more territory for Rome in the north of Britain, this time the main island's farthest extremities there. First, though, he had unfinished business in Wales. There, the Romans had been engaged in a holding operation in the north after Paulinus had been forced to abandon his campaign to conquer Anglesey by Boudicca's insurrection. Therefore, before he deployed north, Agricola needed to secure his rear by finishing the campaign Paulinus had started.

Soon he was marching at speed along Watling Street with his mounted guard, heading for northwest Wales. No doubt, they were impressed when they passed the battlefield monument halfway on the journey at modern Church Stowe in Northamptonshire, built recently to celebrate Paulinus' earlier victory over Boudicca. Carvings and ashlars from this can be seen today inside St Michael's church there.

The Ordovices were the final tribe holding out against Roman rule in north Wales. Agricola lost no time targeting them. Once he reached Wroxeter, the key Roman town in the Welsh Marches, he sent orders to all military units in the vicinity to join him, both legionaries and auxiliaries. He then launched a lightning strike into his target battlespace. This was territory Agricola knew well, having earlier fought there with Paulinus in the pre-Boudiccan revolt campaign, and later with *legio* XX *Valeria Victrix* when leading the western flank of Cerialis' campaign against the Brigantes. Tacitus provides excellent detail, particularly highlighting how tough his opponents were, and how late in the year the campaign season this was, which surprised not only his opponents but also his own troops. He says (*The Agricola*, 18.1):

> Shortly before his arrival the Ordovices had almost wiped out a squadron of cavalry stationed in their territory, and this initial stroke had excited the province. Those who wished for war welcomed the lead, and waited only to test the new governor. The summer was far spent, the auxiliaries were scattered over the province, the legionaries took it for granted there would be no more fighting that year. Everything, in fact, combined to hamper or thwart a new campaign, and many were in favour of simply keeping an eye on the danger. Even so, Agricola decided to go and meet the threat. He drew together detachments of the legions and a force of auxiliaries. As the Ordovices did not venture to meet him in the plain, he marched his men into the hills, with himself in the front of the line to lend his own courage to the rest by sharing their peril, and slaughtered almost the entire nation.

Within a month, Agricola had driven any Ordovices survivors back to Anglesey, the last bastion of native resistance. Tacitus once more takes up the narrative, emphasising Agricola's skill at overcoming adversity, in this case a lack of maritime transport to get his troops over the Menai Straight. He says (*The Agricola*, 18.61):

> He decided to reduce the island of Anglesey, from which Paulinus had been recalled by the revolt of Boudicca. But as often happens when plans are hastily conceived, he had no ships; it was the resource and resolution of the general that took the troops across. Agricola carefully picked out the auxiliaries who were familiar with the fords and had a tradition of swimming with arms and horses under control, and made them discard all their equipment. He then sent them in so suddenly that the enemy, who had been thinking in terms of fleet, ships and naval warfare, completely lost their heads. They sued for peace and surrendered the island, and Agricola won great reputation and respect.

Thus fell the Ordovices, last of the British tribes to resist the might of Rome below the northern frontier, which by this time was set along a line between the Solway Firth and Tyne following Cerialis' earlier campaigns. Wales was now pacified and fully incorporated into the empire, with Agricola building a series of forts in the north there to replicate those built further south by Frontinus. The new forts included Caerhun (Roman *Canovium*), Caernarfon (Roman *Segontium*) and Caer Gai (Roman name unknown). A Roman fortified site has also been recently found at Cemlyn Bay on Anglesey that may also be Agricolan (Turney, 2022, 136).

Cannily, Agricola played down his success in Wales, hoping to win over the local nobility through largess. Tacitus says, 'he did not even use laurel-wreathed dispatches to announce his achievement', adding that his modesty only increased his fame (*The Agricola*, 18.62). Finally, with the onset of winter, Agricola returned to London where he spent the next few months clamping down on alleged abuses of Roman power across the province. Here Tacitus provides excellent detail, saying (*The Agricola*, 19.63):

He eased the levy of grain and tribute by distributing the burden fairly, and put an end to the tricks of profiteers that were more bitterly resented than the tax itself. Before his arrival ... the provincials had actually been compelled to wait at the doors of closed granaries, in order, moreover, to buy grain and so discharge their duty by payment.

Soon Agricola's charm offensive began to bear fruit, with Romanitas firmly embedding itself in Britain, especially in the south and east of the province where the military presence was less visible. Tacitus again takes up the story, saying (*The Agricola*, 21.65):

To induce a people uncivilised and therefore prone to fight, to grow pleasurably inured to peace and ease, Agricola encouraged individuals and assisted communities to build temples, forums and proper town houses. He praised the keen and scolded the slack, and competition for honour worked as well as compulsion. Furthermore, he trained the sons of the leading men in the liberal arts and preferred the natural ability of the Britons over the trained skill of the Gauls. The result was that in place of distaste for the Latin language came a passion to command it. In the same way, our national dress came into favour and the toga was everywhere to be seen.

In a typical Roman conceit, Tacitus then concludes that the Britons' adoption of 'porticoes, baths and sumptuous banquets' were actually manifestations of vice and were 'in fact part of their enslavement' (*The Agricola*, 21, 68). Here we can read the opposite, with Agricola's son-in-law actually claiming it was his father-in-law who had finally tamed the Britons.

In spring AD 78, Agricola headed north again, this time along newly built Ermine Street, aiming for Lincoln and recently established York. With orders from Vespasian to conquer the far north of Britain, his attention now turned to the heart of darkness there (as the Romans perceived it). First, though, he needed to secure the Brigantian territory previously conquered by Cerialis. This was an instructive decision, indicating that while the territory in the north of modern England was now officially part of the province of Britannia, in reality the natives there were less keen on being part of the Roman world. This feeling was clearly mutual, as notably the only reference to native Britons in the Vindolanda tablets calls them *Brittunculi*, meaning 'wretched little Britons'.

Agricola's AD 78 activities in Brigantian territory were, in effect, the pre-campaign phase for his later assaults on the far north. He took the task seriously, deploying the whole of *legio* IX *Hispana* from York, and vexillations from his other three legions in the province, *legio* II *Augusta*, *legio* II *Adiutrix* and *legio* XX *Valeria Victrix*. Later, these formed the core of his strike force in the far north. In addition, large numbers of auxiliary troops also joined him, both in Brigantian territory in AD 78 and later in modern Scotland.

Such a huge military force quickly subdued any remaining resistance to Roman rule on the provincial side of the northern border. This included building a large number of vexillation forts throughout the region to secure the key transport routes, *metalla* resources and most fertile agricultural land there (Tacitus, *The Agricola*, 20.1). Many of these fortifications were along a new Roman road built from York that eventually reached the Firth of Forth, today called Dere Street.

Contemporary Roman sites built on Dere Street broadly track Agricola's AD 78 campaign. The first place of interest is Aldborough (Roman *Isurium Brigantum*) in North Yorkshire, later the *civitas* capital of the post-conquest Brigantes. Here Agricola built a fort guarding the point where Dere Street crossed the river Ure (Ottaway, 2013, 249). Heading further north along the road, another fort was built at Catterick (Roman *Cataractonium*), again in North Yorkshire, where the road crossed the river Swale. Mattingly says this base became the long-term transit camp for those heading to the northern frontier and beyond, from Agricola's time onwards (2006, 147).

Continuing north, the next site reached is at Piercebridge, where a fort was built at the crossing of the river Tees, with another constructed slightly further north at Binchester (Roman *Vinovia*) in County Durham guarding the Dere Street river crossing of the river Wear. Moving on, an auxiliary fort was built at Ebchester (Roman *Vindomora*) in County Durham protecting the crossing of the river Derwent. Finally, just short of the northern frontier, a fort was established at Corbridge (Roman *Coria*). This later became the most northerly town in the Roman world, and was another key logistics hub for the Roman military in the north throughout the occupation. Dere Street forts even further north are considered in later chapters.

Intriguingly, the Antonine itinerary also shows a branch of Dere Street heading south from York, 19km on to a place called *Delgovicia* (today unknown), and then a further 36km to a location called '*Praetorium*' (again unknown). This last is the name given to the house of the commander in a Roman fortress, so might indicate the presence of a military base of some kind. However, given both sites have yet to be found, we have no idea if they are Agricolan.

It also seems likely it was Agricola in this campaign who built the Stanegate Road. This physically set out the line of the first official Roman frontier in the north of Britain. The route was a strategic military trunk road running east–west along the line of the Solway Firth–Tyne isthmus from the fort Agricola built at Carlisle under Cerialis to his new fort at Corbridge. Along its length, to control access to and from the far north, a series of vexillation-sized forts were then built, again as part of the same campaign, each one day's march from the next. Well-known examples include Chesterholm (Roman *Vindolanda*) in Northumberland and Nether Denton (Roman name unknown) in Cumbria. Noted here should be the dramatic and dislocating impact the building of this frontier highway had on the local population. The process took no account at all of local Brigantian land ownership, the road simply following the most ergonomic geological and geographic route, its line later fortified by Hadrian with his wall. From the point Agricola built this road, those to the south were part of the Roman world, while those to the north were not, and were 'other'. A modern analogy would be the building of the Berlin Wall in 1961.

Many of the other forts built in the north during Agricola's AD 78 consolidation campaign are also well known. These include the auxiliary cavalry fort at Malton (Roman *Derventio Brigantum*), a key road crossing of the river Derwent in North Yorkshire, the vexillation fort at Bainbridge (Roman *Virosidum*) in Upper Wensleydale, and the vexillation forts at Castleshaw (Roman name unknown) and Manchester (Roman *Manucium*) in Greater Manchester.

Agricola in Scotland

At the end of the campaigning season, with his rear in both Wales and northern England now secure, Agricola withdrew to York to overwinter. Then, at the beginning of AD 79, his legionary *agrimensor* surveyors were back on the northern frontier. There they began planning the northern extension of Dere Street that would run through the Scottish Borders to the Forth. Agricola's first major assault on the far north was about to begin.

Chapter 6

Campaigns in the Far North: AD 79/80

Agricola fought seven campaigns in Britain while governor. His initial two, in Wales and against the Brigantes, have already been considered. Here I now detail the first and second of his five in the far north, those in AD 79 and AD 80. His chief aim in these, and in his later campaigns in this far northern battlespace, was to provide the Flavian dynasty with the martial success it so desired. Indeed, he was to prove the dynasty's greatest military leader, serving all three Flavian emperors, Vespasian, Titus and Domitian, such was the length of his tenure in Britain.

In this chapter, I first detail the battlespace and its peoples in the far north of Britain in the late first century AD. This includes their military capability. Next, by way of counterpoint I consider the army and fleet Agricola used in the far north. I then discuss marching camps, so important in all Roman campaigning in enemy territory, and particularly so here. Finally, I provide full insight into both the AD 79 and AD 80 campaigns.

The Far North, and its Peoples

In terms of native settlement north of the frontier in the Flavian period, little had changed since the LIA. As Mattingly details (2006, 422): 'In most areas, social organisation was characterised by dispersed small settlements, suggesting a high degree of social fragmentation into family groups or clans.'

To some extent, settlement patterns there did have distinct similarities to the northern region of the Roman province to the south, particularly in today's Scottish Borders, Fife and the upper Midland Valley. This is not surprising given commonality with the Brigantes further south, whose lands had only just been conquered by the Romans and then brutalised with the building of the Stanegate frontier. For example, the round houses of southeastern Scotland, the most common type of dwelling there as with the Brigantes in the south, used dry stone walls in their construction, with an internal ring of posts utilised to support an 'attic' to give extra living space (Kamm, 2011, 15). Hill forts were also common both north and south of the frontier, highlighting the ephemeral nature of security in the region before Cerialis pacified the Brigantes in the south, and Agricola later conquered regions further north, though only for a time. Mattingly highlights well-known examples north of the frontier including those at Traprain Law, Dryburn Bridge and Broxmouth. That these fortified sites were, among other things, places of communal refuge is evidenced by the many roundhouses within their perimeters. Meanwhile, their defensive function is clear, with huge defensive circuits featuring ramparts over 6m in height built using dry stone walling techniques. Atop these circumvallations ran a palisade, making the circuits even more imposing. A number of these forts feature their stone walling being vitrified through the use of fire. It was previously thought this was a deliberate measure to strengthen them. However, recent research shows the process actually weakened the defensive structure. Instead, modern interpretations see the vitrification process as a deliberate attempt at slighting the defences, perhaps in the context of Roman offensive operations.

As one travelled further north and west, way beyond the Roman frontier, other types of dwelling begin to appear in the archaeological record. Some of these were unique to Scotland. One example was the wheelhouse, found in the exposed coastal areas of the Western Isles. These featured spokes of stone walling radiating out from the centre of the structure to support a solid outer wall, with the lower section of the dwelling sunk down into a pit. The entrance was a tunnel into the main chamber covered in stone and peat slabs.

The broch was another example of a bespoke Scottish dwelling type in the far north. These were constructed using dry stone walling, with some examples up to four storeys high, making them by far the most imposing structures north of the frontier aside from hill forts. The remains of over 500 of have been found, each built around a central courtyard with a very narrow and easily defendable entrance, and with the inhabitants living in galleries built within. All were constructed between 200 BC and

AD 150, with their standard design indicating they were built by travelling specialist broch builders. Brochs are found all around the Atlantic coast of Scotland, though the largest concentrations are in Caithness, Sutherland and the northern isles.

A final type of dwelling found in the far north of Scotland was the crannog. This was a fortified timber (or stone in the Outer Hebrides) roundhouse with a thatched roof built on piles or an artificial island in a lake, again emphasising the need for security. Crannogs were common in both Ireland and Scotland. In the latter, their remains are found mainly on the west coast, with the highest concentrations in Argyll and Dumfries and Galloway.

The economy of the far north was also different to that in the south, though again note there was more commonality as one neared the frontier. In his wider appreciation of Roman Scotland, Kamm says that many of the advances in economic and manufacturing sophistication in the Roman world, which were visible by the Flavian period in the provincial south, were lacking in Scotland. Specifically, he details that (2011, 15):

> As crafts became more sophisticated and mass production was introduced, particularly of iron objects and pottery, so trade increased and urban development occurred around centres of industry and commerce. This happened from Spain right across central Europe, and in Britain on the East and South East coasts. Scotland remained largely untouched by such advances until the 13th century AD.

One area where the lowlands of Scotland could match the north of Britannia in terms of productivity was agriculture. When travelling through the modern Scottish lowlands researching Agricola's campaigns, it is clear the region features some of the most fertile land in the north of Britain, for example in Fife. Given a lack of economic opportunity is often cited as a key reason why Rome ultimately chose not to invest in the permanent occupation of Scotland, this is important. If the region was productive enough agriculturally, then other reasons need to be considered.

Certainly, geology and climate were important. Here, the defining physical feature in the Agricolan battlespace in the far north was the Highland line running from the Isle of Arran in the southwest to

Stonehaven in the northeast. This separates the Scottish Highlands from the more fertile Midland Valley, including Fife and the Scottish Borders. Beyond were the Northern Highlands to the far northwest above the Great Glen Fault, then below that the Grampian Mountains. This latter extensive range, which geographically comprises two thirds of the Highlands, features (west to east) the Western Highlands, Southern Highlands, Central Highlands and Cairngorms. Even below the Highland line, the lowland region also features significant upland territory. From north to south, this includes the Ochil Hills separating the valley of the Forth from the upper Midland Valley (both to play a key role in Agricola's campaigns), the Campsie Fells, then in the Scottish Borders the Pentland Hills, Lammermuir Hills, Moorfoot Hills, Tweedsmuir Hills, Lowther Hills, Carsphairn Hills and Galloway Hills.

Such challenging terrain made campaigning in the region of modern Scotland particularly problematic for the Romans. Later, Dio described the Maeatae and Caledonians of his day who fought Septimius Severus living in 'wild and waterless mountains and desolate and marshy plains' (*Roman History*, 77.12). In the same passage, he adds: 'as the emperor advanced through the country in the far north he experienced countless hardships in cutting down the forests, levelling the heights, filling up the swamps, and bridging the rivers.'

Thus, even accepting much of the lowland region was fertile then and now, the battlespace was always physically taxing. Additionally, the climate in the far north was more problematic than in the provincial south, particularly rainfall. This is a theme Herodian comments on, saying that because of the continuous wet weather, 'the land of the Briton's there becomes marshy, in addition being flooded by the continuous ocean tide' (*History of the Roman Empire*, 3.14.6). He adds that the incessant rain and mists from the marshes made the air in the far north gloomy and depressing for the Roman soldiery.

Yet even then, this combination of exhausting terrain and harsh weather hadn't stopped the Romans conquering other territories with similar issues. Much of North Africa, the economic powerhouse of the empire by the Flavian period, was inhospitable, mountainous or desertified, yet that hadn't stopped its full incorporation into the empire. Similarly, Trajan later fought two brutal campaigns to conquer Dacia, again overcoming serious geological (for example the Carpathian Mountains) and climate issues to form his new province there. Therefore, a further reason needs to be considered as to why the Romans found the far north of Britain so difficult to conquer.

In my recent research on Agricola's campaigns in the far north another answer has become evident. Naturally, when one considers the campaigns of Agricola, Quintus Lollius Urbicus or Severus when trying to conquer territory in the far north, the focus is often on the Romans themselves. Yet I believe a large part of the answer as to why the Romans struggled in the region lies with their opponents. It is increasingly apparent to me the natives in the far north proved the most belligerent opponents the Romans fought in Britain, or indeed many other places in the empire. This was perhaps on a scale to match the Jewish rebels in Judaea in their three ferocious revolts against Rome. The similarities here of brutal opposition to Roman rule are numerous, as are the Roman responses. For example, Vespasian and his son Titus played crucial roles in crushing the First Jewish Revolt, while seventy years later, Antoninus Pius chose Urbicus as his new governor in Britain, tasking him with (briefly, as it turned out) driving the northern frontier up to the line of the Antonine Wall. Notably, the emperor's choice had earlier won the *dona militaria* decoration for playing a key role in brutally defeating the Third 'Bar Kokhba' Jewish Revolt.

Focusing on the region of modern Scotland, it seems the native leadership throughout the period of Roman occupation to the south had no interest at all in being official participants in the Roman world. As can be seen with the creation of the enormous Maeatae and Caledonian confederations, proximity to the frontier did encourage a coalescence of power as Rome sought to bend the elites in the region to their ways. However, when it came to conquest and incorporation into the empire, the native Britons there simply weren't having it. As I detail later, Agricola did succeed in conquering the far north very briefly, needing a force of 30,000 men to do so, but was then recalled. Urbicus and his immediate successors as governor were content with the incorporation of the Scottish Borders only after building the Antonine Wall, but this too was abandoned after only twenty years. Meanwhile, Severus ultimately failed, given his untimely death in York in February AD 211, despite his overall force numbering

57,000 men. In short, the warriors in the far north of Britain proved to be fearsome opponents of the Romans.

As earlier discussed, Ptolemy sets out the various tribes in the far north of Britain when writing in the mid-second century AD. I recap them here given their importance in understanding Agricola's campaigns in the region. Above the Brigantes north of the Roman frontier, the Votadini were based in the eastern Scottish Borders, the Selgovae in the central Borders and the Novantae in the western Borders. Above the latter, the Dumnonii were based around the Clyde, the Epidii on the Mull of Kintyre, then above both on the west coast were the Creones, the Carnonacae and the Caereni. Above the Votadini on the east coast were the Venicones around the Tay, then above them in Aberdeenshire the Vacomagi and the Taexali. Broadly, throughout the Grampians, were located the Caledonii. At the time Ptolemy was writing, the latter were a specific tribe rather than the huge regional confederation that are first referenced during the reign of Commodus (Dio, *Roman History*, 77.12.1). Next, around the Moray Firth were the Decantae, Lugi, Smertae and finally the Cornacii. Note that in the Flavian period, and indeed later, when Ptolemy was writing, the Maeatae (as with the Caledonian confederation) had yet to appear.

We have little contemporary detail of the appearance of the peoples living in the far north of Britain except one general comment by Tacitus, who may have been an eyewitness to Agricola's campaigns there (see discussion in Chapter 5). He says, 'their reddish hair and large limbs proclaim a German origin' (*The Agricola*, 9.1). This became the standard Roman trope when describing the far northern Britons, with Jordanes writing in the mid-sixth century AD that 'the Caledonians have reddish hair and large loose-jointed bodies' (*Getica*, 2.13). Here he is referring to the later Caledonian confederation, rather than Tacitus' Caledonii.

We also have little contemporary insight into societal structure in the region except a few passing phrases. For example, when later talking of the Maeatae and Caledonian confederations, Dio says (*Roman History*, 77.12.1-4):

> Both inhabit wild and waterless mountains and desolate and swampy plains, and possess neither walls, cities, nor tilled fields, but live on their flocks, wild game, and certain fruits … their form of rule is

democratic for the most part, and they choose their boldest men as rulers.

Dio adds a final cultural anecdote here about the Britons of the far north, again in the context of the Severan campaigns there (*Roman History*, 76.15). This is a reference to his wife Julia Domna talking to the wife of a Caledonian confederation leader named Argentocoxus in which they compare the sexual customs of their cultures. We have no further detail, though clearly he infers they differed.

The armies of the Britons in the far north fought in a manner very similar to those defeated by the Romans in the south. This included a chariot-riding nobility, skirmishing cavalry on small ponies, a levy of largely unarmoured foot troops armed with short spears and shield, and various types of skirmisher. Here Dio provides great insight through analogy when describing the Maeatae and Caledonian warriors who fought by Septimius Severus in his attempts to emulate Agricola 130 years later. Specifically, Dio says (77.12.1-4):

> They go into battle in chariots, and have small, swift ponies; there are also foot soldiers, very swift in running and very firm in standing ground. For arms they have a short spear and shield, with bronze apple attached to the end of the spear shaft, so that when the enemy is shaken it may clash and terrify the enemy; and they also have a dagger.

Dio is describing here an enemy ready to fight a meeting engagement, deployed in battle array. However, more often than not the natives in the far north avoided direct engagement with the legions and auxiliaries of Rome, preferring guerrilla warfare and massed raids, often at night. This is not surprising given the power the Romans could bring to bear in a set-piece battle, where the asymmetry between their troops and the natives would be all too apparent.

Dio also provides a vivid description of the difficulties the Romans faced when engaging the native Britons in their home territory, this again in the context of the Severan campaigns. He says (*Roman History*, 76.13):

> The enemy purposely put sheep and cattle in front of the soldiers for them to seize, in order that they might be lured on still further until they were worn out; for in fact the water caused great suffering to the Romans, and when they became scattered, they would be attacked. Then, unable to walk, they would be slain by their own men, in order to avoid capture, so that a full 50,000 died [clearly a massive exaggeration, but indicative of the difficulties the Romans faced].

Herodian also provides insight here, saying of the same campaigns (*History of the Roman Empire*, 3.14):

> Frequent skirmishes occurred, and in these the Romans were victorious. But it was easy for the Britons to slip away; putting their knowledge of the surrounding area to good use, they disappeared in the woods and marshes. The Romans' unfamiliarity with the terrain prolonged the war.

Additionally, Dio highlights how the Britons in the far north combined ferocity with a deep understanding of how best to utilise the harsh environment in which they lived, saying (*Roman History*, 77.12.1-4):

> They can endure hunger and cold and any kind of hardship; for they plunge into swamps and exist there for many days with only their heads above water, and in forests they support themselves upon bark and roots, and for all emergencies they prepare a certain kind of food, the eating of a small portion of which, the size of a bean, prevents them from feeling either hunger or thirst.

The hunger-preventing food described here has been identified as the heath pea (*lathyrus linofolius*) by Dr Brian Moffat of the Soutra Aisle research centre (2000, 13).

Agricola's Army

In earlier work, I estimated Agricola's overall force in his AD 79 and AD 80 campaigns in the far north comprised some 30,000 men (Elliott,

2016, 133). Both campaigns replicated his AD 88 Brigantian campaign in scope, though on a larger scale. Again, *legio* IX *Hispana* formed the core of his army, together with numerous vexillations from *legio* II *Augusta*, *legio* II *Adiutrix* and *legio* XX *Valeria Victrix*. Some argue the latter three may have participated at near full legion strength. However, a significant holding force would have been needed to secure northern Wales after Agricola's AD 87 campaign there, and the northern frontier too.

Additionally, Tacitus specifically mentions 8,000 auxiliary foot and 3,000 auxiliary cavalry (*The Agricola*, 9.1). To this, we can add the 7,000 *milites*, both marines and sailors, of the *Classis Britannica*. Overall, I estimate that at the outset of his AD 79 campaign Agricola was able to deploy a force comprising 12,000 legionaries, 11,000 auxiliaries of all kinds and 7,000 naval *milites*.

Marching camps

Marching camps were a key feature of all Roman military campaigning from the early 270s BC when the mid-Republican armies appropriated their use from the Hellenistic king Pyrrhus of Epirus. They were built by every Roman military unit at the end of every day's march in enemy territory, and always by the troops themselves, whether legionaries, auxiliaries or naval *milites*. Some then became permanent fortifications, often over a lengthy period and through multiple phases of occupation.

Marching camps play a very important part in tracking Roman military campaigns across the empire given that their archaeological typology can, in best-case scenarios, provide a dot-to-dot track of the route taken by each campaigning force, particularly if their size and dating evidence can be matched to a known campaign and force size. Some marching camp footprints in the landscape are of more use to archaeologists than others based on the state of their preservation. The key factors here are soil quality, and landscape modification by settlement, farming and industry from the post-Roman period onwards. Thus, while we are fortunate in Britain that in Wales, the north of England and Scotland we have many known Roman marching camp sites, fewer have been found elsewhere, even using modern technology and the fact we know they did exist. Key examples of still-to-be-found marching camp sequences include

Caesar's two incursions to southeastern Britain in 55 BC and 54 BC, and the Claudian invasion of AD 43.

In construction marching camps were short-term replicas of a permanent Roman fortification. While temporary by their very nature, often being abandoned after a few days' use at most (though some did become permanent), they nevertheless required substantial amounts of trained military labour in their construction. They were always playing card in shape, featuring at least one and sometimes more surrounding deep ditches, with the spoil then being used to create an internal rampart. Atop this ran a palisade built from the wooden *sudes* (stakes) carried by the troops as part of their engineering equipment, usually two per man (Oleson, 2009, 702). The palisade atop the rampart was either a continuous wooden barrier, or created by the stakes being lashed together to form large caltrops. Meanwhile, the camps also featured various kinds of protected gateway to ensure their resilience against any aggressor. Three broad types of gateway are known, these called *clavicula*, *titulus* and 'Stracathro' (Jones, 2013, 5). The first was a curved extension of the rampart, extending internally, externally or both from the rampart. The second was a stepped-out traverse section of rampart wall, parallel but proud of the circumvallation. The third was a complex hybrid of the two, named after the marching camp at Stracathro near Brechin in Angus, where they were first identified. Of the latter type, Jones says (2013, 51): 'It consisted of an external clavicula ditch with an oblique traverse guarding the entrance gap, possibly accompanied by an internal curving rampart.'

The *titulus* was the most common choice given its comparative simplicity, with the *clavicula* less popular as it was more difficult to lay out accurately. A poorly constructed example of the latter at the northern marching camp at Burnswark illustrates this. Meanwhile, the most complicated type, the 'Stracathro' design, is often associated with Agricola's campaigns in Scotland, though Jones has recently questioned this (2013, 52). Marching camps also often featured wooden towers around the perimeter, always internal and most often at the fort corners and either side of the gateways.

Within this circumvallation would then be set out the key elements of a Roman fortification, all initially temporary, including a *principia* headquarters building, a *praetorium* commander's residence, an *intervallum* inner perimeter road, the *Via Praetoria* road leading from the *praetoria* to the main gate, the *Via Decumana* road leading from the *praetoria* to the rear gate, and the *Via Principalis* main transverse road leading to the *Porta principalis sinistra* left gate and *Porta principalis dextra* right gate (Tibbs, 2019, 15).

Despite the huge amounts of labour required to build such a temporary camp, they were then destroyed if the military force chose to move on, this to prevent their use by the enemy. Here Cowan is instructive. He says that after a night's rest (noting that up to 20 per cent of the soldiery would have been on guard duty at any given time), or longer if the formation was staying in place for an extended period of time, the camp was then rapidly struck, detailing that (2003a, 45):

> In the early morning, camp was struck as quickly and in as orderly a way as it had been constructed. The first trumpet call signalled the striking of the tents; the second to ready the pack animals and destroy the camp; the third to fall into marching ranks.

As detailed, well-defined marching camp sequences are very important tools to help archaeologists and historians track the progress of Roman campaigns, in our case in Scotland. However, one should note that categorising them is not an exact science, despite the desire of generations of antiquarian and modern scholars to do so. Even with the surveying and construction skills evident when the Roman military were building their camps, they still lacked the exacting measurement and alignment technology available in the modern era. Therefore, no two are exactly the same size. Further, as Jones says, 'dating camps is fraught with problems', with complications arising from the differing archaeological techniques used over centuries, and the frequent Roman reuse of the same sites (2013, 109). That being said, it is broadly possible to place many Roman marching camps in Scotland in a specific sequence based on their size. Jones details these as a 12ha sequence, a 25ha sequence, a 45ha sequence, a 54ha sequence and a 67ha sequence (2013, 99). There are other suggested groupings, but these five broadly cover things except for a few outliers. I detail those of likely Flavian provenance here, whichever of his campaigns they date to, for use as a point of reference going forward.

For background, while marching camps were used every time a Roman force travelled through the unconquered far north, the vast majority fitted into a few key campaigns. These may have included the one in the Scottish Borders dating to Bolanus' northern campaign around AD 70 when we have the 'Caledonian Plain' reference (Statius, *Silvae*, 53.1). We then have the Flavian campaigns of Agricola (the furthest penetration north by a distance), the Antonine campaigns of Urbicus and his successors in the AD 150s when driving the northern frontier from Hadrian's Wall to the Antonine Wall line, and the AD 209 and AD 210 campaigns of Septimius Severus. The skill for the archaeologist and historian is to then match the various marching camp size sequences to these campaigns. That is more difficult than it sounds, for while we can make assumptions based on camp and force size, archaeological data to confirm what might seem obvious is actually sparse in many areas.

We are on comparatively firm ground with three of the sequences. Here, in his survey of the Severan campaigns in Scotland, Hodgson argues the 54ha sequence and the 67ha sequence are both Severan from the early third century AD (2014, 38). I agree with this interpretation. Meanwhile, given the only Roman force to campaign above the Highland line in Aberdeen, Aberdeenshire and the Highlands was that of Agricola in his later campaigns there, the sequence of 44ha sites running from the North Sea coast above Stonehaven to the Moray Firth must have been Flavian. I list these latter here, southeast to northwest, with all associated with Agricola's final AD 83 campaign except Raedykes, which may date to the previous year. Note that at many marching camp sites throughout Scotland, where there is more than one phase of occupation, they are often labelled I, II and so on. Given our focus here is purely Flavian, I only follow this convention if relevant:

- Raedykes
- Normandykes
- Kintore
- Logie Dumo
- Ythan Wells
- Burnfield
- Muiryfold

- Auchinhove, with 'Stracathro' style gates and the only one actually in the Highlands.

Some argue that two possible fortified sites even further north at Bellie on the Moray Firth itself are also Roman, and so Flavian given the location. If either were confirmed it would make them most northerly Roman fortified site in the world. However, archaeologists continue to question the Roman provenance of the location, for example Tibbs, who believes the evidence is inconclusive (2019, 182).

Moving south to the upper Midland Valley below the Highland line, dating the marching camps and confirming which sequence they belong to becomes more problematic. Those that were certainly first built during the Flavian period, and so link with the 44ha sequence further north, are as follows (this time southwest to northeast):

- Bochastle, with 'Stracathro' style gates and the site of a later Glenblocker fort, see Chapter 7.
- Dalginross, again with 'Stracathro' style gates.
- Ardoch, part of the Gask Ridge system detailed below, and site of multiple phases of Roman fortified occupation.
- Inchtuthil, later the site of the Flavian legionary fortress built by *legio* XX *Valeria Victrix*.
- Inverquharity, also with 'Stracathro' style gates.
- Stracathro, the 'Stracathro' gate type site.

Another site in this sequence has been identified at Dun on Montrose Bay, which some argue was a naval base for the *Classis Britannica*, though more research is required to confirm this. Meanwhile, to the east in Fife, the marching camp site at Abernethy has also been identified as Flavian.

In terms of size sequencing these marching camps, the first marching camp at Inchtuthil is a tiny outlier at 0.9ha, as is that at Inverquharity at 2.35ha. Dalginross is part of the 12ha series, Bochastle fits best in the 25ha sequence, while the second marching camp phase at Inchtuthil (which some argue was a 'labour' marching camp used by troops building the legionary fortress), and those at Stracathro and Abernethy, are southern additions to the 44ha sequence. The first camp built at Ardoch, the largest of any at this site, is at 52ha similar in size to the later Severan 54ha camps and here a Flavian outlier. This may indicate it was a logistics base for the wider Flavian operations in the far north rather than a traditional marching camp.

All of the above indicates that much of the 12ha, 25ha and 44ha sequences between the Forth and the Moray Firth are Flavian. This does fit with the strategy Agricola adopted in his campaigns in the far north, with his entire force only operating as a homogenous whole once above Stonehaven, as I detail below, hence the string of 44ha forts there. It may also indicate that things in this region of the northern battlespace were, from a military perspective, a mess. This was a huge overall Roman force, operating in a distant, largely unknown territory against the most hostile of enemies. It was a harsh learning experience for all concerned.

Moving south again, the Scottish Borders also features a large number of Flavian marching camps. These are too numerous to detail or sequence here, though of note they include the first two phases of Roman fortification at Newstead near Melrose. Most of these sites once more fit into the 12ha, 25ha and 44ha sequences that are evident further north.

Finally, in terms of Flavian fortifications in the far north, we have the Gask Ridge system of eighteen known signal stations/watchtowers that many believe were built by Agricola. This runs along a spine of land around 70m above sea level between the Highland line and Fife, heading roughly northeast. It begins at Ardoch and ends on the Tay near Bertha. There a fort site may be either Flavian or Antonine, so is not included above. From these Gask Ridge sites there are clear view lines north to the Highlands and south to the hollow of Strathearn and the Forth (Keppie, 2004, 166). As such, it would have performed an early warning function as Agricola's marching camps progressed up to the Highland line and further, able to keep an eye on native British incursions into the Midland Valley battlespace, and also summon reserves from further south. As Coby says in his recent study of the strategy behind the use of Roman fortifications, these locations are ideally placed to allow swift signalling along their line, and to other in-sight fortifications too (2022, 111). Of interest, Turney has argued that these sites, with their commanding views, were actually built to provide a fortified access route into the north, and

Campaigns in the Far North: AD 79/80

may actually date to an earlier 'lost' campaign of Frontinus (2022, 120). In this work, I will stick with Agricola as their originator.

The Campaigns of AD 79 and AD 80

Agricola finally launched his first assault on the far north of Britain in late March AD 79. This was a year set to feature two momentous events in Roman history, namely the death of the 69-year-old Vespasian after a long illness on 24 June, and the eruption of Vesuvius in the Bay of Naples towards the year's end. Of the former, Dio provides the detail, saying (*Roman History*, 17.1): 'Vespasian fell sick, though not if the truth be known of his accustomed gout, but of a fever, and passed away at Aquae Cutiliae in the Sabine country.' The emperor's death would see the accession of his eldest son Titus. Meanwhile, the Plinyan eruption of Vesuvius caused the destruction of many of the key Roman cities in Campania, including Pompeii and Herculaneum.

As detailed earlier, Titus was an experienced warrior famed for his victories in the First Jewish Revolt. His becoming emperor placed an even sharper emphasis on the need for Agricola to secure victories against the Britons for the Flavians. Here he was highly successful. On this first campaign, Dio paints a broad picture, saying (*Roman History*, 66.20): 'Meanwhile war had broken out again in Britain, and Gnaeus Julius Agricola overran the whole of the enemy's territory there.' Tacitus is far more specific, saying (*The Agricola*, 22.1):

> In the third year of his campaigns in Britain [the first in the far north, after his Welsh and Brigantian campaigns] he attacked new tribes, with our ravages on the native population carried out as far as the Taus, an estuary so called.

The reference to the Taus estuary is commonly interpreted as meaning the Tay, which does fit the archaeological evidence for this earliest Flavian campaign in the far north.

Agricola's strategy here paralleled that of Cerialis' when the latter first conquered Brigantian territory. This featured two legionary spearheads forging northwards, one on the west coast and one on the east. Unlike the later advances of Severus' 50,000 men through the Scottish Borders in AD 209 and AD 210, when the army was kept together as a homogenous whole to punch through to the Forth, here Agricola chose to pacify as much territory as possible in one go, operating on a broad front. His initial targets were the northern Brigantes above the Stanegate frontier, the Votadini in the eastern Borders, the Selgovae in the central Borders, the Novantae in the western Borders, the Dumnonii around the Clyde and the Venicones around the Tay. As always, the *Classis Britannica* was on hand just off the coast of each thrust to fulfil littoral control, transport and scouting roles, with Moorhead and Stuttard saying that (2012, 103):

> The fleet was to play a vital role throughout the course of the campaign, sailing ahead to reconnoiter harbours, shadowing the troops as they pressed forward on land, and shipping supplies up from the south. Just as importantly, it was a useful tool in Agricola's arsenal for psychological warfare, as the sight of Roman galleys plying up and down the coast of Scotland, using its sea lanes and its anchorages and beaches as if they were their own, struck fear into the Caledonian's hearts.

Many of the 12ha, 25ha and 44ha marching camp sites in the Scottish Borders, Fife and the upper Midland Valley date to this first campaign, with Tacitus extolling Agricola's skill in choosing their locations. He says (*The Agricola*, 22.1): 'It is widely observed by experts that no general has ever shown a better eye for suitable sites than Agricola.'

The Romans made good use of the camps, with Tacitus saying they were employed as bases to make 'frequent sallies' against the native Britons. Here, careful logistics planning ensured the troops had enough supplies to survive a siege if they chose to stay in place longer than a few days (*The Agricola*, 22.1).

This first season north of the border seems to have been relatively problem free for the Romans, with the natives 'too terrified to molest the army' (*The Agricola*, 22.1). The only negative that Tacitus details was the weather, which he says 'severely buffeted our army' (*The Agricola*, 22.1). No doubt this also proved a challenge to the fleet operating on the west and east coasts. However, Agricola was clearly successful given

Dio says that towards the end of the year Titus was given his fifteenth salutation by the Senate to celebrate Roman success in Britain (*Roman History*, 66.20). Agricola then left garrisons in the north, with some of the camps becoming permanent, one likely candidate being Newstead. Tacitus reports a winter free from trouble in the region, saying that (*The Agricola*, 22.1): 'Winter in these forts was free from fear, and each could take care of itself. The enemy was baffled and near despair.'

This is interesting, given the natural ferocity of native resistance to the Romans in the far north. Clearly, the speed, mass, broad front and sheer energy of Agricola's AD 79 campaign overwhelmed initial native resistance, dislocating community after community. These were then forced to flee northwards or submit to Rome and risk slavery or death. Tacitus adds a key issue for the Britons here was something new from the Romans in the far north of Britain. This was their retaining a strong military presence north of the frontier over the winter, which by its very mention by Tacitus shows this was something novel. In the past, if Roman columns had penetrated that far, they had always returned south at the end of the campaigning season, with the natives then returning to their own territories. That wasn't the case now. Tacitus concludes his commentary on the AD 79 campaign by saying Agricola also ensured his prefects and centurions were given as much credit for his success as he himself received (*The Agricola*, 22.1).

One key point often neglected in commentaries of Roman conquest, with Agricola's AD 79 campaign in the far north a prime example, is the effect this had on the native population, both at the time and after. Fernández-Götz and Roymans are insightful here, saying (2024, 79):

> The Roman conquest would have generated phenomena of ontological [sense of self and place in the world] insecurity, starting with the profound mark left by military defeat on the self-esteem and self-perception of the vanquished. When a way of life is subject to doubt or threatened by another, the doxa (the set of beliefs and social practices that are considered normal in a certain social context) is fractured and undergoes transformation.

Even so, the natives of the far north of Britain proved remarkably resilient after each phase of attempted Roman conquest. Once the political imperative driving the Roman Flavian, Antonine and Severan campaigns in the region diminished, the surviving local peoples there gradually returned from their refuges, often in the Highlands, to reclaim their lands and reestablish local culture.

Back to the narrative, one of the reasons why the Romans left troops to overwinter north of the frontier becomes clear when Tacitus narrates Agricola's second year campaigning in the far north in AD 80. Here he discusses where Agricola might have halted that year 'if the valour of our armies and the glory of Rome had not forbidden a halt' (*The Agricola*, 23.1). This clearly shows his standing orders were to conquer territory and then stay there, not withdraw each winter, his aim to incorporate the newly gained lands into the province in the south. Titus evidently wanted the Flavian conquest in the far north of Britain to be permanent, not temporary.

Interestingly, Tacitus details the specific place he says would have been ideal for any halt. He says (*The Agricola*, 23.1):

> A place within Britannia itself would have been found for halting [if the standing orders had allowed it]. For the Clota and the Bodotria, carried far back inland by the tides of opposite seas, are separated by only a narrow neck of land. This neck was now secured by garrisons, and whole sweep of land to the south was safe in our hands. The enemy had been pushed into what was virtually another island.

Again there is much to unpack here, not least where the isthmus of land between the Clota and the Bodotria actually is. The mention of the province of Britannia might indicate it was within the province itself, which would mean he is describing the Stanegate frontier between the Solway Firth and Tyne. However, that doesn't fit with the narrative of conquest the previous year, especially as Tacitus later also talks of campaigning above the Bodotria. Therefore, in all likelihood, he is speaking of the line between the Clyde and Forth later fortified as the Antonine Wall in the mid-second century AD. The fact he didn't halt there confirms his legionary spearheads did indeed penetrate into Fife and the upper Midland Valley in AD 79. Meanwhile, the final line of the quote seems to confirm his victories that year were total, with Turney calling it the result of a few months of savage conquest during that year's campaigning season (2022, 158). In this region, almost certainly, two of the early sites converted from marching camps to permanent fortifications, in addition to Newstead in the Borders, were at Inchtuthil and Ardoch in Perth and Kinross. Given their later use as key locations by Agricola, both were ideally sited to act as logistics bases to support the campaigning in Fife and towards the Highland line.

It seems clear from Tacitus' commentary that Agricola spent the AD 80 campaigning season consolidating his position in the Scottish Borders, Fife and upper Midland Valley. The one area in this wider region where he seems to have been less successful was in the western Borders, given his focus on the Novantae the following year. Some argue he may even have bypassed the native Britons there, though this seems unlikely given the legionary spearhead we know he specifically deployed on the west coast.

Meanwhile, a key part of this consolidation process was the construction of new military harbours in the battlespace to facilitate the effective use of the *Classis Britannica*. These were located at Kirkbride, Newton Stuart, Glenluce, Stranraer, Gurvan, Ayr and Dumbarton on the west coast, and Cramond on the east, site of the later Roman fort on the southern shores of the Forth. Further north along the east coast a naval base may also have been established at Carpow on the Tay, again later to become the site of a fort. With that, Agricola concluded his second year in the far north, set his troops to overwinter there again, and got ready for another year of campaigning in AD 81, when he turned his attention to the Novantae.

Chapter 7

Campaigns in the Far North: AD 81/82

By this point, after Agricola's far northern assault in AD 79 and consolidation campaign in AD 80, the Romans had control of much of the Scottish Borders, Fife and the upper Midland Valley. The natives, wrong-footed by the Romans remaining in the region over winter after the first invasion, continued to flee north if they could. Agricola next tackled the unfinished business with the Novantae in the southwest Borders. At this point, after a short and brutal campaign there, Tacitus considered invading modern Ireland with a single legion. Here, after the death of Titus, he was denied permission by the new emperor Domitian, last of the Flavians. Domitian had little interest in new Roman adventures over the Irish Sea, instead ordering Agricola to return to the far north. Here, with his AD 82 campaign, he set up his *coup de grâce* at Mons Graupius in AD 83, which I detail in the next chapter. Additionally, in this chapter I also discuss the abortive Roman plans to turn Chester into the provincial capital of an expanded province of Britannia if Ireland had been conquered.

The Novantae Campaign of AD 81

In his third northern campaign in AD 81, Agricola turned his attention to the troublesome southwest of modern Scotland, where he had unfinished business with the Novantae. For this, he gathered the west coast squadrons of the *Classis Britannica*, likely at least a third of its overall strength of 700 ships. He then launched an ambitious amphibious invasion (Tacitus, *The Agricola*, 24.1). In earlier work, I have argued this maritime assault was either northwards across the Solway Firth to the southern coast of Dumfries and Galloway, or westwards across the river Annan in Dumfries and Galloway (Elliott, 2016, 167). Kamm reasons convincingly it was the former, with Maryport (Roman *Alauna*) on the coast of the Lake District a key point of departure (2011, 67). If so, this major Roman fort and harbour was likely Flavian in its origins rather than Hadrianic as usually argued.

This was the fifth major amphibious operation in Britain following the Claudian conquest in AD 43, Vespasian's assault on the Isle of Wight, and the two invasions of Anglesey by Paulinus and Agricola. With this new invasion, Tacitus says the governor was 'on the lead ship', painting a picture of Agricola standing in the prow waiting to leap ashore with the first men, Alexander the Great fashion (*The Agricola*, 24.1).

Kamm believes the most likely landing site, if the fleet crossed the Solway Firth as he argues, was the mouth of the river Nith to the south of Dumfries. He says (2011, 67):

> Here, at Ward Law, on a ridge with fine views of the whole of the Solway Firth, are traces of a Roman fort which could be Flavian. Just to the south of the fort, the naturalist and traveller Thomas Pennant (1726–1798) found in 1772 evidence of a native hill fort, surrounded by a double ditch and guarded on its south side by a steep slope down to the shore.

It is here the Novantae likely tried but failed to resist Agricola's assault. Through analogy with a nearby site we can get a sense of what it was like being on the receiving end of a Roman assault on a native fortification. This is at Burnswark Hill, a 7ha LIA fortification 6km east of Lockerbie. Here, a debate has taken place as to whether data previously considered (from antiquarian and 1960s archaeological excavations) showed an actual Roman siege at the site (likely Antonine in date), or that the site was instead an example of a Roman siege training exercise. The key items of interest were the north and south Roman siege camps there, and also a plethora of *ballista* bolts/balls and lead slingshots found at the site. To reach a conclusion either way the Trimontium Trust recently carried out a new review of the existing research, and secured fresh data. The latter was based on a systematic metal-detecting survey to identify more lead slingshots (with a view to plotting their scatter) and experimental archaeology regarding the use of slings in siege warfare (Reid, 2016, 22).

The results of this research suggest the two camps are a real-world tactical response to the topography in the context of a full siege, and the widespread scatter of slingshots and other missiles (and their quality) suggesting deadly intent. As Reid (2016, 26) says, the evidence shows that:

> there was a massive missile barrage at Burnswark. This was not just restricted to the gateways, but extended along a full half kilometer of native rampart. The simplest explanation for this distribution is that the defenders on the hilltop were suppressed by a hail of sling bullets with an accurate range of 120m and the stopping power of a modern handgun, as well as *ballista* bolts, and arrows. This presumably covered an attacking force sweeping out the three huge gateways and storming the hilltop. Such a combination of missile troops and conventional infantry is likely to have been brutally effective.

Here we see the brutal nature of Roman military activity in the far north of Britain. Further, another factor adds even more insight into the awful experience of the native Britons on the receiving end of this devastation. This is because some of slingshots were hollowed out with a 4mm hole through their centre; this designed to make a screeching noise when slung. As such, it is an early example of psychological warfare on the battlefield, bringing to mind the screaming sirens of diving Junkers Ju-87 Stukas during the Blitzkrieg in the early Second World War, adding to the misery of those on the receiving end.

Returning to Agricola and the Novantae, whatever the exact details of his invasion of their territory, once again the combination of Roman land and naval forces proved highly successful, rapidly concluding matters with the total defeat of the natives in Dumfries and Galloway. Now the Romans had control of the whole region. Here Turney comments on Agricola's heavy reliance on the *Classis Britannica* to support his land campaigns, in particular that against the Novantae. He says (2022, 193):

> It is conceivable that Agricola had more sense of the value of the navy than most governors. He had been raised in *Forum Julii* and Marseille, both busy ports, and at the time of his birth at least, *Forum Julii* had been a main naval base.

Agricola, Ireland and Chester

By this time Agricola knew the various Hibernian tribes across the Irish Sea had been supporting the Novantae prior to his victory over them (Reid, 2023, 60). Tacitus tells us that, on reaching the western coast of Dumfries and Galloway, he personally viewed the Irish coast (*The Agricola*, 24.1), with Kamm saying his likely location was the beach along the Rhinns of Galloway (the Roman *Novantarum Peninsula*, 2011, 66). From there, the Irish coast can be clearly seen across the North Channel of the Irish Sea. Here, Agricola now considered another adventure across the ocean, this time a full-scale invasion of Ireland. Tacitus describes the scene, saying (*The Agricola*, 24.1): 'The whole side of Britannia that faces Hibernia was lined with his forces, with hope rather than fear as his motive.'

He later provides more detail, saying (*The Agricola*, 24.10):

> Often I heard Agricola say that Ireland could be reduced and garrisoned by a single legion and some auxiliary units; also that it would be better for future relations with Britain, if the territory were to be ringed by Roman arms with no prospect of freedom.

Ireland was well known to the Romans by this time through two main vectors. First, as detailed above, the support of the tribes there for the Novantae and their neighbours. Second, through mercantile interaction. Here Haywood provides a useful description of the Irish world at the time, saying (2009, 84):

> Ireland preserved a vigorous La Tène culture. Literary sources record trade between Roman Britain and Ireland, but few Roman objects have been found there. Reports from merchants gave Roman geographers [like Ptolemy] the first reasonably accurate depictions of the islands and its peoples.

Interestingly, the lack of Roman artefacts found in Ireland is in sharp contrast to the unconquered far north on the main island of Britain. This reflects the level of military campaigning there, especially at the time of Agricola. Given there is no evidence the Roman military were ever active in Ireland, except perhaps with the fleet around the coast, the lack of Roman archaeological finds there is understandable.

Agricola's motive in considering the conquest of Ireland was clearly to neutralise it as a base for anti-Roman sentiment in Britain. Tacitus also says a specific opportunity presented itself around this time, detailing that (*The Agricola*, 24.1): 'Agricola welcomed a Hibernian prince, who had been driven from home by rebellion; nominally a friend, he might be used as a pawn in the game.' This might seem very convenient for Agricola. However, Turney argues support for the story can be found in another, very different literary source. He says (2022, 182):

> In Irish legend, recorded by monks in the Middle Ages, one Túathal Techtmar, the son a deposed Irish high king, went into exile and later returned with an army and retook the throne in a great battle. Some versions of the legend place Túathal's exile in Britain. The Annals of the Four Masters gives us the dates for these events (spurious as they may be, even for a vague legend), telling us that he was exiled in AD 56 and returned in AD 76. The facts these dates come within five years of Agricola theoretically having an exiled king at his side is a coincidence hard to ignore.

In terms of practically, a Roman invasion of Ireland was easily within the means Agricola had at his disposal. As detailed above, the Romans had already carried out five major amphibious assaults while campaigning in Britain, two involving Agricola. Now they had a large fleet available on the southwest coast of Scotland after the Novantae campaign. Mason, in his analysis of Roman naval power, says such a fleet, when gathered in Loch Ryan or Luce Bay in Galloway, would only have had to travel 32km to reach Belfast Lough in today's Northern Ireland (2003, 100).

As he made his plans, what did Agricola know of Ireland at the time? The earliest reference in classical literature is that of the Greek geographer, explorer and astronomer Pytheas of *Massilia* who, when exploring northwestern Europe in the 320s BC, called the island *Iérnē* (written as Ἰέρνη in ancient Greek). By Tacitus' day this had been Latinised as Hibernia, with the Romans calling the natives Scoti or Scotti. Ptolemy's mid-second-century AD *Geography* includes the earliest surviving detailed account of Hibernia. In it, he lists sixteen specific tribes, all with territories along the coast. Running clockwise, and starting in the extreme northeast opposite Galloway, these were the Robogdii, Darini, Voluntii, Epdani, Cauci, Manapii, Coriondi, Brigantes, Usdiae, Iverni, Vellabori, Galengani, Auteini, Nagnatae, Erpeditani, and Vennicnii. The later Latin historian Paulus Orosius adds one more, the Luceni, resident between the Vellabori and Galengani. Those closest to Galloway, and so the most likely to have supported the Novantae across the Irish Sea (and later engaged with the Romans), were the Robogdii, Darini or Voluntii. It is unclear which tribe Agricola's prince, or indeed Túathal Techtmar if he was a real historical figure, came from.

Irish systems of government were based on kingship and very similar to those in the far north of Britain, with the position of high king of Ireland frequently recorded in later literature. Settlement patterns were also similar. For example, hill forts were very common, while I have already noted the crannog as a common dwelling in both western Scotland and Ireland. One item of technology at first unique to the west coast of Ireland was a boat called the currach, or curragh. This was a utility vessel built with a wooden frame over which animal skins or hides were stretched. This simple but effective boat building technology was highly scalable, with examples first appearing in the archaeological record in the Irish Neolithic period, which lasted from around 4000 BC to 2500 BC. By Agricola's day, curracha were in use on both sides of the Irish Sea, and were the most common native British vessel to be found there.

Irish armies were similar to those of the northern Britons, featuring a chariot-riding nobility supported by loose formations of foot troops armed with short spears, javelins and daggers. The latter were highly mobile, with later Roman writers saying imperial troops often struggled to intercept them when they raided provincial Britain. Irish armies also made good use of plashed wood edges and bogs when defending their own territory.

The key question to answer here is, why did Agricola not invade Ireland? Clearly, a military operation on this scale would have required imperial approval. No doubt, he sent word to Rome, requesting the emperor's consent. However, here events wrong-footed him. On 13 September, around the time Agricola's high-speed dispatch would have arrived in the imperial capital, at the age of 41, Titus suddenly died of a fever after a short illness.

His successor Domitian, younger son of Vespasian, was completely different to his elder brother. Titus, the renowned soldier, was steady and reliable, just as his father had been. Domitian was far more the self-interested political operator, and notably not a warrior. Dio provides a damning pen portrait when describing the start his reign, saying (*Roman History*, 67.1):

> Domitian was not only rash and quick to anger but also treacherous and secretive; and so, deriving from these two characteristics, impulsiveness on the one hand and craftiness on the other, he would often attack people with the sudden violence of a thunderbolt, but also often injure them as the result of careful deliberation.

Suetonius is even more unfavourable, saying (*The Twelve Caesars, Domitian*, 3.1): 'At the beginning of his reign Domitian would spend hours alone every day doing nothing but catch flies and stabbing them with a needle-sharp pen.' Here was a man not to be trusted and who made enemies, as his later assassination in AD 96 proved.

Domitian clearly had issues with his brother, with Tacitus saying they were never on good terms (*The Agricola*, 24.1). We know this wasn't political spinning by Tacitus on behalf of his father-in-law given that all other contemporary sources confirm it. Turney provides useful context here, saying of the sibling rivalry (2022, 185): 'Titus had enjoyed prestige, responsibility and favour throughout his father's reign, while Domitian had been somewhat side-lined and kept in the shadows, given sinecures and empty titles.'

Here, and in the primary sources, one can detect a growing resentfulness, which eventually bent Domitian's character. Thus, when Agricola's request to invade Ireland arrived in the new emperor's court, the timing couldn't have been worse. After years in his father and elder brother's shadow, Domitian was focused on one thing only: securing his position. Further, even if he had been inclined to consider Agricola's request, the British governor's close association with Vespasian and Titus now counted against him. This was especially the case if plans for a Roman conquest of Hibernia had begun before Agricola took office in Britain, perhaps under Frontinus.

A final factor also working against Agricola came from beyond the grave. This was the recently deceased Flavian fixer Mucianus, the former governor of Syria and leading general for Vespasian in AD 69. While alive, he proved the perfect counterbalance in Rome to Domitian's Machiavellian schemes, given his overt loyalty to Vespasian and Titus. Crucially for Agricola, as we have seen, Mucianus had also been one of his major sponsors at court. For example, it was he who had appointed Agricola to command *legio* XX *Valeria Victrix* in Britain. Later, he then played a leading role in Agricola's appointment as governor in Britian. However, and sadly for Agricola, even though Mucianus died around the same time as Vespasian, he still cast a long shadow at court. Thus, Agricola found himself unwittingly tainted through patronage by Domitian's great rival for Flavian political power. What better way for the new, insecure emperor to flex his imperial muscles than sleight the man his political adversary had championed. Therefore, Domitian gave a firm no to Agricola's request. Instead, the British governor was ordered to refocus back on the far north in his next campaigning season, and wrap things up quickly there (Mason, 2003, 100).

We can now turn to a key location in Roman Britain that provides strong anecdotal evidence to support earlier Flavian interest in Ireland, namely Chester. To recap, this key site had been founded under Cerialis towards the end of his Brigantian conquest campaign. There, *legio* II *Adiutrix* had built a vexillation fort on the river Dee, providing a west coast base for the *Classis Britannica* and securing the west coast advances of Agricola when commanding *legio* XX *Valeria Victrix*. Shortly after, it was then developed into a full legionary fortress by Frontinus, again by *legio* II *Adiutrix*. Notably, this legionary fortress is particularly imposing in its design and, covering 25ha in area, larger and with grander walls than any other Roman fortification in Britain of the period. In his detailed account of Roman Chester, Mason says (2001, 96): 'It is clear that the extra space [within the walls] was required to accommodate a group of "special" buildings belonging to some grandiose scheme for the centre of the fortress, which was halted soon after work started.'

These 'special' structures included a huge, novel 59m² elliptical building with alcoves for imperial statued portraiture, sited to the dextral rear of the fortress *principia*. The fact these buildings were not completed at the time (work on the elliptical building was abandoned for 150 years, later being completed when the fortress was reconstructed in the mid-third century AD), while the essential structures for running the legionary fortress including the *principia*, *praetorium* and barracks were, indicates a change of plan for the site.

Some have argued the large size of the fortress, its fine walls and the 'special' buildings indicate that either Frontinus or Agricola planned to use Chester as a new provincial capital. Given its location, at the centre of a combined mainland Britain and Ireland, it was ideally placed for this role within a larger combined province. However, with Domitian's lack of interest, it was not to be. This then explains why the bespoke buildings were not completed, with the fortress returning to its primary role, housing a legion.

Moorhead and Stuttard believe the new emperor's decision regarding a Roman invasion of Ireland was Agricola's biggest regret as governor in Britain (2012, 103). Now, with new imperial orders, he had to look to the far north again. Soon, planning for a new campaign there was underway.

The Campaign of AD 82: Back to the Far North

In his penultimate year campaigning in the far north of Britain, Agricola changed his strategy. With orders to complete the conquest of the far north as soon as possible, he sought a full meeting engagement with an enemy who, to that date, had pointedly avoided one. Consequently, he abandoned land-based activities on the west coast to concentrate on the east. Here, a key tell is the complete lack of Flavian marching camps in the archaeological record in the west from that point (Fernández-Götz and Nico Roymans, 2024, 74).

This new strategy made sense, given any remaining native population centres were in the far northeast. This was also where any survivors displaced in the AD 79 conquest campaign and AD 80 consolidation year had fled. There, below the Highland line, the fertile lands of the upper Midland Valley were certainly worth renewed conquest. This was partially completed in AD 79 and AD 80, when Agricola had reduced the Scottish Borders, Fife and much of the Midland Valley to Roman vassalage. Such was the success of his 'shock and awe' campaign, his enemy were left 'baffled and near despair' (Tacitus, *The Agricola*, 22.1). Those survivors who had managed flee the Roman onslaught from the Votadini, Selgovae and Novantae in the Scottish Borders, the Dumnonii around the Clyde and the Venicones in Fife now found themselves streaming north through northern Perth, Kinross and Angus, heading for the Highlands and hoping for safety from the Roman killing machine. Above the Highland line, the Caledonii in the Grampians and the Vacomagi and Taexali in Aberdeenshire began to receive these desperate refugees from the south, full of tales of horror at the hands of the Romans.

With his troops still deployed in the north, Agricola was aware of this and sensed total victory. In his view, two legionary spearheads driving up the Highland line southwest to northeast, and along the east coast supported by the fleet, was the logical strategy. At some stage, as the Britons were squeezed into a smaller and smaller region, they would have to turn and fight in open battle. The only question for Agricola was how far north the Romans would have to penetrate before forcing the engagement.

A key tactic in this year was his decision to physically close off access to the mountainous north by building a series of fortifications closing off the glens along the Highland line that gave the easiest access to the lowlands. These are often referred to as Glenblocker forts, with well-known sites including Drumquhassle, Menteith/Malling, Bochastle, Doune, Dalginross and Fendoch. As detailed earlier, Bochastle began life as a 25ha marching camp in Agricola's AD 79 campaign in the far north. Now it became a permanent fort. Others detailed here may also have similarly begun life as marching camps.

For completeness, some argue the Glenblocker forts were built later, for example under Agricola's successor Lucius Sallustius Lucullus in the late AD 80s, after the former's return to Rome. I discount this, given it makes no sense to make such an investment in complex military infrastructure at a time when the Romans were beginning to withdraw from the far north on the orders of Domitian.

The fleeing Britons now found themselves in a race against time as the Romans drove up the Highland line, closing off glen after glen as they ground inexorably northeastwards. It was here Agricola's strategy almost unravelled as some Britons now turned and fought, not *en masse* but in smaller tribal groupings, their very survival at stake. Overcoming the shock of the Roman onslaught in AD 79, and their territories being eviscerated as the Romans consolidated in AD 80, the fighting spirit of the far northern Britons returned. Tacitus has them now attacking military installations, saying (*The Agricola*, 25.1): 'The natives of Caledonia turned to armed resistance. They went so far as to attack our forts, and inspired alarm by taking the offensive.'

These were likely the Glenblocker forts as they were being built, and any marching camps across the wider battlespace. The Britons had some success here as, emboldened, they now began to attack more overtly and challenge the Romans directly in the open, and in ever greater numbers. For the first time since invading the far north in AD 79, Agricola now had a real war on his hands. The governor reacted with his usual vigour, with Tacitus saying that (*The Agricola*, 26.1): 'Agricola now learned the enemy were about to attack in several columns. To avoid encirclement by superior forces familiar with the territory, he likewise divided his own army into three parts and so advanced.' However, he then gives a specific example of a near Roman disaster at the hands of the natives involving the veteran *legio* IX *Hispana*.

This event almost brought shame on the Romans and is important given it is the last time the legion is ever mentioned in a written historical reference, in this instance by Tacitus (the last ever reference to the legion is an inscription above a gateway in York, dated AD 108). Given the importance the AD 82 reference, I record Tacitus' narrative in full (*The Agricola*, 27.1):

> As soon as the enemy got to know of Agricola's division of his army they changed their plans and massed for a night attack on the IXth legion, which seemed to them the weakest [likely through casualties given its key role fighting in the far north since AD 79]. Striking panic into the sleeping marching camp, they struck down the sentries and broke in. The fight was already raging inside the camp when

Campaigns in the Far North: AD 81/82

Agricola was warned by his scouts of the enemies' march. Following closely on their tracks, he ordered the speediest of his cavalry and infantry to harass the assailant's rear and then had his whole army join in the battle cry; the standards gleamed in the light of dawn. The Britons were dismayed at being caught between two fires, while the men of the IXth took heart again: with their lives now safe they could fight for honour. They even effected a sally, and a grim struggle ensued in the narrow passage of the gates. At last the enemy broke under the rival efforts of the two armies, the one striving to make it plain that they had brought relief, the other that they could have done without it.

Reading between the lines in this tale of Roman military bravado, and Tacitus' usual pro-Agricolan narrative, here we see the IXth legion almost overwhelmed and wiped out. However, Agricola's intervention helped the Romans prevail, and soon his campaign was back on track. Eventually, the final Glenblocker forts were completed to seal off the Highlands, with the fleet closing access to the coast. There was now only one way north for the fleeing natives, through a narrow coastal corridor where the Highlands met the sea around Stonehaven. Even passing through there made them vulnerable to predation by the fleet. It also gave Agricola a single target to pursue as he sought his final, decisive battle with the Britons.

In his AD 82 campaign the role of the *Classis Britannica* is perhaps more evident than at any time since Agricola's arrival in Britain. Tacitus provides excellent insight about the vital role played the fleet, detailing it being used to transport troops from the south to replace casualties, harassing the enemy-occupied coast to disrupt economic activity, and maintaining a tight control on the littoral zone as the legionary spearheads advanced (*The Agricola*, 26.1). Tacitus also comments on the risks experienced operating in the treacherous littoral and oceanic waters so far north, highlighting hazards such as the frequent storms and unforgiving tides (*The Agricola*, 26.1). A specific example showing such dangers can today be found in the Grosvenor Museum in Chester. Here, the lower half of a funerary dedication records the loss of a naval *optio* in a storm off the coast of Scotland in the Flavian period. His body was never recovered (RIB 544).

Tacitus continues that at this time, with the Highland line now cut off and the fleeing Britons crowding northwards through the coastal corridor near Stonehaven, the Roman fleet, legionaries and auxiliaries began to share the same marching camps, an unusual development (*The Agricola*, 26.1). This reflected the increasingly hostile territory they were travelling through, both in terms of the elements and opposition, and also the practicalities of keeping the army and fleet supplied so far from the frontier.

In the far north, with refugees flooding into their *oppida* and hill forts, and with the Romans in hot pursuit on land and sea, the native British leaders realised they would have to face the Romans in set-piece battle to settle matters once and for all. Soon planning was taking place to gather a mighty army to challenge Agricola. This set the scene for Agricola's final campaign in the far north the following year.

As the AD 82 campaigning season came to an end, Agricola could reflect on another highly successful year reducing British resistance in his targeted battlespace. All that remained was to pursue the Britons to their last redoubt in the far northeast above Stonehaven. Again, he consolidated over the winter period, maintaining troops in position in the Glenblocker forts, and other fortifications across the region too. This forced any refugees who had fled to the western Highlands, rather than northeast, to overwinter there, a harsh experience for lowland farmers. Meanwhile, the refugees now resident among the Caledonii, Vacomagi and Taexali in Aberdeenshire and along the southern shores of the Moray Firth found what little comfort they could from a brief respite as winter closed down military activity in the south. No doubt the added burden on the local economy of the newly arrived evacuees, already under stress due to the predations of the *Classis Britannica* along the coast, focused the attention of local elites even more on needing to engage the Romans in open battle sooner rather than later. This is exactly what Agricola wanted.

As the Romans settled in to overwinter in the region, their most northerly marching camp was likely that at Raedykes on the high ground above Stonehaven, this set to anchor the 44ha sequence of camps heading northwest the following year. The Romans also built a new series of fortified harbours over the winter along the coast of Angus and in southern Aberdeenshire to support the fleet. This included a key site at Monifieth to the immediate east of Dundee. Many have argued this is the location of the major Roman port detailed by Ptolemy, where he describes multiple *horrea* warehouses being used to support the Roman military (*Geography*, 2.3). It is also likely the fortified harbour at Dun on Montrose Bay was built at this time.

Tacitus and Dio add one final salacious story when concluding their narratives on Agricola's AD 82 campaign. This involved the revolt of some German Usipi auxiliaries who commandeered three *liburnian* galleys of the *Classis Britannica* as the campaign had progressed. Tacitus says (*The Agricola*, 28.1):

> That summer a cohort of Usipi that had been recruited in Germany and transferred to Britain committed a crime so remarkable as to deserve record. They murdered the centurion and soldiers who had been mingled in their ranks to teach them discipline and serve as models and directors, then boarded three *liburnians*, constraining the pilots to do their will. Two of these incurred suspicion and were put to death, the third was set to rowing. As their story was still unknown, they sailed along the coasts like an apparition. When they put into land to get water and other necessities, they came to blows with the local Britons, who defended their property; often successful, they were sometimes repulsed. They were finally reduced to such straits of famine that they first ate the weakest of their number and then victims drawn by lot. And thus they sailed right around Britain. Having lost their ships through bad seamanship, they were taken by pirates and cut off first by the Suebi and then by the Frisii. Some were sold as slaves and passed from hand to hand till they reached our bank of the Rhine, where they gained notoriety from the tale of their great adventure.

Meanwhile, Dio, using Tacitus as his source, says (*Roman History*, 66.1):

> It seems that some soldiers rebelled, and after slaying the centurions and a military tribune took refuge in boats, in which they put out to sea and sailed round the western portion of the country just as the wind and the waves chanced to carry them; and without realising

it, since they approached from the opposite direction, they put in at the camps on the first side again. Thereupon Agricola sent others to attempt the voyage around Britain, and learned from them, too, that it was an island.

Both accounts seem contradictory, including that of Tacitus, who, if not in the region personally, certainly spoke to witnesses. The rebellion of the Usipi due to heavy-handed treatment by Roman officers is clear, as is their seizure of the three *biremes*. However, the implication by Tacitus and Dio that they then circumnavigated the whole main island of Britain before heading up the English Channel and crossing the North Sea to arrive in the far north of Germany (either having been captured by pirates beforehand, of after) is too fantastical. The likely truth here is they headed along the northeastern coast of Scotland, perhaps as far as Caithness. On the way, they endured the hardships described, before either sailing deliberately or being carried by winds and tides back to the far north of Germany. One can therefore discount Dio's suggestion that it was the Usipi who inspired Agricola's order for the *Classis Britannica* to circumnavigate the main island of Britain the following year, unless contemporary Roman opinion believed the German rebels to have done something they had not.

Chapter 8

Campaigns in the Far North: AD 83 and Mons Graupius

Agricola's time as governor in Britain culminated in a mighty battle in the far north at a place Tacitus calls Mons Graupius. This clash, if it did actually take place, is one of the great meeting engagements in British history. It resulted in total Roman victory, after which Agricola ordered his fleet to sail completely around Britain. The governor could now tell Domitian back in Rome that the whole main island had been conquered.

In this chapter, I cover Agricola's final AD 83 campaign in Britain, including a detailed analysis of the Battle of Mons Graupius. I then consider the fleet's post-engagement circumnavigation, Domitian's response to the governor's glad tidings from Britannia, and the immediate aftermath of Agricola's far northern conquests, both in Britain and Rome.

The Build-up to Mons Graupius

The AD 83 campaigning season began with some terrible family news for Agricola. Tacitus tells us that (29.1):

> Agricola suffered a grievous personal loss in the death of the son who had been born the year before. This cruel blow drew from him neither the ostentatious stoicism of the strong man nor the loud expressions of grief that belongs to women. The conduct of war was one of the means he had to relieve the sorrow.

This is the first and last we hear of this son, the second infant boy lost to Agricola and Domitia. The grieving father now threw himself into his military responsibilities, seeking solace in the daily routine of campaigning. Here, partly driven by his grief, he achieved something no Roman leader had done before, or did afterwards: conquer the whole main island of Britain.

Agricola began his AD 83 campaigning season in the far north by deploying the *Classis Britannica* above Stonehaven to predate enemy territory along the coast from Angus to Caithness. By this time, any Britons south of the narrow gap between the coast there and the Highland line were dead, captive, or had returned home to their much diminished settlements now under Roman control in the south. Above the gap, in Aberdeenshire, resided the Vacomagi and Taexali, then throughout the Grampians the Caledonii, around the Moray Firth the Decantae, then heading north up to Caithness the Lugi, Smertae, and finally the Cornacii. Huge numbers of refugees were also seeking shelter in the region. They all now felt the wrath of the Roman fleet, with Tacitus saying (*The Agricola*, 29.2): 'He sent his fleet ahead to plunder at various points and thus spread uncertainty and terror.'

To the south, Agricola next gathered his legionaries and auxiliaries for a final push in the far north. His objective was simple: force a meeting engagement, and totally destroy his enemy. His original force when he first headed north in AD 79 comprised 30,000 troops and naval *milites*. This was built around a core of 12,000 legionaries from *legio* IX *Hispana*, *legio* II *Augusta*, *legio* II *Adiutrix* and *legio* XX *Valeria Victrix*. To these he had added 8,000 foot and 3,000 mounted auxiliaries (these later specifically detailed at Mons Graupius by Tacitus, see below), and the 7,000 *milites* of the *Classis Britannica*. By AD 83, this number had clearly diminished through battle casualties, especially among the legionaries. In particular, it seems the IXth legion was specifically badly affected.

However, through the well-tested Roman system of battle casualty replacement, reserves had arrived in theatre to partially refill the ranks, particularly of the auxilia and fleet whose recruiting ground were closer than those of the legionaries.

To that end, based on analogies with other well-understood Roman military campaigns, I believe Agricola was able to deploy around 28,000 men in his final campaign in the far north, with the auxilia and fleet more or less still at their AD 79 numbers through casualty replacement, but his legionaries diminished and still awaiting many of their replacements. This explains the key role the auxilia were to play at Mons Graupius.

By this time, Agricola's strategy in the far north was forensically focused on defeating the Britons once and for all. Now, for the first time, he drove his legionary spearheads through the narrow gap between Stonehaven and the Highland line into Aberdeenshire and the Grampians. There they hammered their way through native territories in the region, building the 44ha sequence of marching camps running from the North Sea coast above Stonehaven to the Moray Firth. To recap, these were at Normandykes, Kintore, Logie Dumo, Ythan Wells, Burnfield, Muiryfold and Auchinhove (the latter in the Highlands itself). Raedykes, the most southwesterly of these 44ha camps, was, as detailed, likely built the previous year and acted as the launch point for the offensive.

In this final campaign, Agricola's troops penetrated the far north to a greater extent than at any time the Romans had before, or did afterwards. Later, Severus was only to reach Stonehaven before declaring his victory. The most northerly Flavian site that has been securely dated is that at Auchinhove in the Highlands proper, just south of the Moray Firth, featuring the usual 'Stracathro' gateways associated with Agricola's campaigns. In his excellent guide to Roman archaeological sites in Scotland, Andrew Tibbs highlights an interesting feature here, saying (2019, 181): 'It is unusually close to two other [more southerly] camps, which are believed to date to the same period: Muiryfold, less than 3.2km away, and Burnfield, which is 8km away.' Given Roman marching camps are usually one day's march apart, this indicates that these sites were closely connected, perhaps to allow Agricola to mass his force for a specific reason.

Tracing the line of these camps north from the Raedykes to Auchinhove defines the battlespace Agricola's meeting engagement with the Britons at Mons Graupius likely took place, which was notably late in the campaigning season. Turney, for example, argues it was in September – very late for regular campaigning so far north (2022, 235).

Accepting that, we are then faced with a dilemma given we have no idea where the exact battle site of Mons Graupius was. This has led to an intense and ongoing debate. For example, in the nineteenth century it was variously located at nearly every Roman site a few days' march from the east coast above the Tay. However, with the advent of aerial photography from the mid-twentieth century, and more recently data-based historical analysis, the search has become much more specific. Now, the leading candidate site is Mither Tap in the Bennachie range of distinctive hills in Aberdeenshire, these a red granite massif in the eastern Grampians. This interpretation is largely based on etymology, the name of the engagement appearing in Tacitus' *Agricola*. One interpretation suggests the Latin *mons* (mountain or hill) has been paired by Tacitus with a native word some believe to be *Cripius*, the Brythonic name for a comb with distinctive narrow teeth. This suggests a series of peaks, which specifically matches the Bennachie location given the 6.5km long ridge comprises a series of such crests (Campbell, 2010, 66). Anecdotally, this location also matches Tacitus' description of the battle site.

Another alternative might be further north around the grouping of marching camps near Auchinhove referenced by Tibbs, explaining their unusually close proximity. Meanwhile, Birley also suggests an ideal candidate site may have been on the slopes of the 764m tall Ben Loyal in Sutherland, at the most northwesterly tip of the Scottish Highlands. However, given the 'Queen of the Highlands' is over 130km north of Inverness, and there is no archaeological evidence to support a candidacy at such a high latitude, I discount it.

In reality, we have no real idea where Mons Graupius was due to the lack of any archaeological evidence, excepting logic suggesting it was along the far northern Agricolan line of 44ha marching camps, and given it took place at the end of the campaign, likely at its northeasterly tip.

The Battle of Mons Graupius

Wherever the Battle of Mons Graupius took place, it proved decisive. Given that Tacitus provides such a detailed account in *The Agricola*, I choose here to broadly follow his narrative, providing my own interpretation and that of others where more detail is required.

In the first instance, Tacitus describes the response of the native Britons in Aberdeenshire and the Grampians as the legionary spearheads marched inexorably northwards, eviscerating all before them, while the fleet rampaged along the coast. It soon became evident to the surviving

Campaigns in the Far North: AD 83 and Mons Graupius

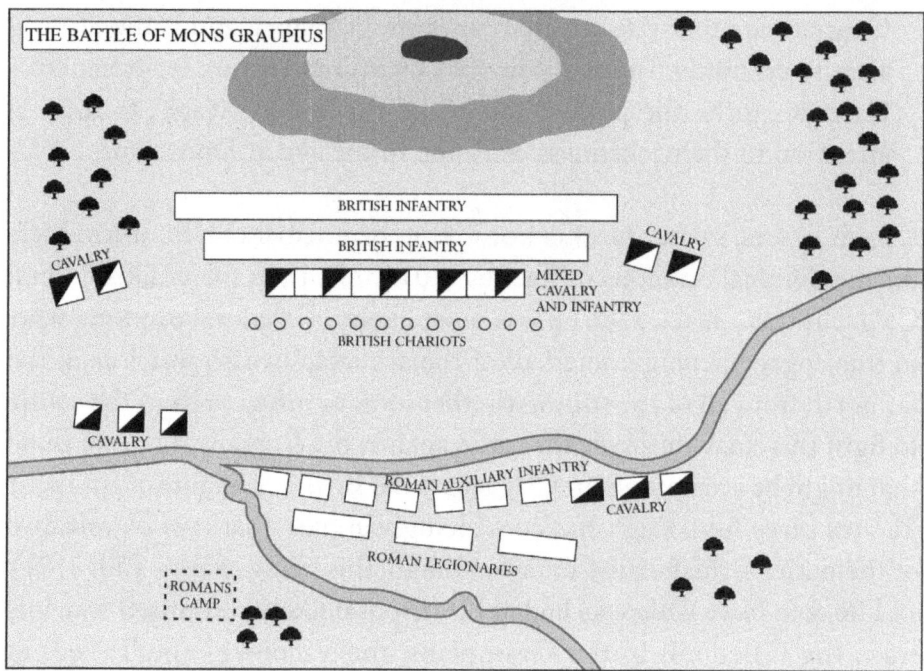

Map 3.

Britons that a final stand now had to be made, which was exactly what Agricola wanted. Tacitus says (*The Agricola*, 29):

> Undismayed by their former defeats, the barbarians expected no other issue than a total overthrow, or a brave revenge. By treaties of alliance, and by deputations to the several tribal regions, they had drawn together the strength of their nation. Upwards of 30,000 men appeared in arms, and their force was increasing every day. Among the chieftains distinguished by their birth and valour, the most renowned was Calgacus. The multitude gathered around him, eager for action, and burning with uncommon ardour.

This is our first mention of the far northern British leader Calgacus. We have no idea if he was a real person or a creation of Tacitus to help his pro-Roman and pro-Agricolan narrative. Turney certainly thinks so, saying (2022, 221):

Calgacus is otherwise attested nowhere in history, and is therefore almost certainly Tacitus' personal creation. Tacitus has created Calgacus to be the perfect foil, to be the 'noble savage', to draw attention to the wickedness of Rome in the age of Domitian.

Kamm agrees, saying he was not a king or a tribal chief but a vehicle for the political opinions of Tacitus (2011, 75). If, in the unlikely event, Calgacus was a real leader, he was most likely a Caledonii overking who, in this engagement, gathered all of the available British warriors in the far north from all of the tribes, whether local or refugees from the south, to fight this final life-or-death battle against the Romans. The one thing that might be accurate about Calgacus is the Brithonic nature of the name Tacitus gives him. Pugh has convincingly argued that it is a derivative of the native British name for swordsman, this being *calgacos* (2013, 81).

The core force Calgacus had at his disposal likely comprised warriors from the Caledonii in the Grampians, the Vacomagi and Taexali in Aberdeenshire and the Decantae around the Moray Firth. They were also joined by the refugees in the region who had fled Agricola's earlier assaults further south. Additionally, warriors may also have joined the British force from further north, including troops from the Lugi, Smertae and the Cornacii.

Notably, the size of the native British army described by Tacitus was larger than that being led by Agricola, given that 7,000 of his overall force of 28,000 in the AD 83 campaign were the naval *milites* of the fleet. Here we may question the real size of Calgacus' army as, once more, Tacitus is narrating a story that emphasises the difficulties overcome by the Romans. Notably, this was the first time a set-piece battle had been fought by the natives of the far north against the Romans, and it seems unlikely the Britons there were able to support such a large force in the field, certainly for long. However, I will use Tacitus' figure for now, given it is the only reference we have to work with.

What is certain is that Roman military tactics and technology far outstripped that of their opponents, though some balance was given by the fact the Britons were fighting in their own terrain and climate, providing a degree of symmetry in the coming encounter not obvious when one simply compares troop quality. To that end, it was imperative

Campaigns in the Far North: AD 83 and Mons Graupius

the Romans were led well on the battlefield. Agricola was keenly aware of the fate of Varus' three legions in AD 9 in the Teutoburg Forest when their commanders had failed them in similarly hostile conditions, and was determined not to make the same mistakes.

Tacitus now has Calcagus address his gathered multitude with a rousing speech, delivered in the finest tradition of Latin oratory. The latter is no surprise given this native British 'sermon on the mount' was likely never delivered. Instead, it is a literary device used by Tacitus to portray the British leader and his warriors as worthy opponents, specifically with an eye on the domestic audience back in Rome. Tacitus has Calgacus say the following, which I record in full, given the level of detail he provides (*The Agricola*, 30–32):

> Whenever I consider the origin of this war and the necessities of our position, I have a sure confidence that this day, and this union of ours, will be the beginning of freedom to the whole of Britain. To all of us slavery is a thing unknown; there are no lands beyond us, and even the sea is not safe, menaced as we are by a Roman fleet. And thus in war and battle, in which the brave find glory, even the coward will not find safety. Former contests, in which, with varying fortune, the Romans were resisted, still left in us a last hope of succour, in as much as being the most renowned nation of Britain, dwelling in the very heart of the country, and out of sight of the shores of the conquered, we could keep even our eyes unpolluted by the contagion of slavery. To us who dwell on the uttermost confines of the earth and of freedom, this remote sanctuary of Britain's glory has up to this time been a defence. Now, however, the furthest limits of Britain are thrown open, and the unknown always passes for the marvellous. But there are no tribes beyond us, nothing indeed but waves and rocks, and the yet more terrible Romans, from whose oppression escape is vainly sought by obedience and submission. Robbers of the world, having by their universal plunder exhausted the land, they rifle the deep. If the enemy be rich, they are rapacious; if he be poor, they lust for dominion; neither the east nor the west has been able to satisfy them. Alone among men they covet with equal eagerness poverty and riches. To robbery, slaughter, plunder, they give the lying name

of empire; they make a solitude and call it peace. Nature has willed that every man's children and kindred should be his dearest objects. Yet these are torn from us by conscriptions to be slaves elsewhere. Our wives and our sisters, even though they may escape violation from the enemy, are dishonoured under the names of friendship and hospitality. Our goods and fortunes they collect for their tribute, our harvests for their granaries. Our very hands and bodies, under the lash and in the midst of insult, are worn down by the toil of clearing forests and morasses. Creatures born to slavery are sold once and for all, and are, moreover, fed by their masters; but Britain is daily purchasing, is daily feeding, her own enslaved people. And as in a household the last comer among the slaves is always the butt of his companions, so we in a world long used to slavery, as the newest and most contemptible, are marked out for destruction. We have neither fruitful plains, nor mines, nor harbours, for the working of which we may be spared. Valour, too, and high spirit in subjects, are offensive to rulers; besides, remoteness and seclusion, while they give safety, provoke suspicion. Since then you cannot hope for quarter, take courage, I beseech you, whether it be safety or renown that you hold most precious. Under a woman's leadership the Brigantes were able to burn a colony, to storm a camp, and had not success ended in supineness, might have thrown off the yoke [I actually have this as a reference to Boudicca and the Iceni, the colony Colchester]. Let us, then, a fresh and unconquered people, never likely to abuse our freedom, show forthwith at the very first onset what heroes Caledonia has in reserve. Do you suppose that the Romans will be as brave in war as they are licentious in peace? To our strifes and discords they owe their fame, and they turn the errors of an enemy to the renown of their own army, an army which, composed as it is of every variety of nations, is held together by success and will be broken up by disaster. These Gauls and Germans, and, I blush to say, these Britons, who, though they lend their lives to support a stranger's rule, have been its enemies longer than its subjects, you cannot imagine to be bound by fidelity and affection. Fear and terror there certainly are, feeble bonds of attachment; remove them, and those who have ceased to fear will begin to hate. All the incentives to victory are on our side.

The Romans have no wives to kindle their courage; no parents to taunt them with flight, and either no country or one far away. Few in number, dismayed by their ignorance, looking around upon a sky, a sea, and forests which are all unfamiliar to them; hemmed in, as it were, and enmeshed, the Gods have delivered them into our hands. Be not frightened by the idle display, by the glitter of gold and of silver, which can neither protect nor wound. In the very ranks of the enemy we shall find our own forces. Britons will acknowledge their own cause; Gauls will remember past freedom; the other Germans will abandon them, as but lately did the Batavii. Behind them there is nothing to dread. The forts are ungarrisoned; the *colonia* in the hands of aged men; what with disloyal subjects and oppressive rulers, the towns are ill-affected and rife with discord. On the one side you have a general and an army; on the other, tribute, the mines, and all the other penalties of an enslaved people. Whether you endure these forever, or instantly avenge them, this field is yours to decide. Think, therefore, as you advance to battle, at once of your ancestors and of your posterity.

Tacitus has the Britons responding to this anti-imperial call-to-arms with wild 'war songs and savage howlings' (*The Agricola*, 33.1). In the Roman writer's narrative, Calgacus then forms up his 30,000 warriors ready for battle, with the hardy and brave pushing to the front (*The Agricola*, 33.2). Agricola then addresses his own army as it looks on at the deploying Britons, with the Roman leader saying (*The Agricola*, 33-34):

If our present struggle were with nations wholly unknown; if we had to do with an enemy new to our swords, I should call to mind the example of other armies. At present what can I propose so bright and animating as your own exploits? I appeal to your own eyes: behold the men drawn up against you: are they not the same, who last year, under the covert of the night, assaulted the IXth legion, and, upon the first shout of our army, fled before you? A band of rogues who have subsisted hitherto because, of all the Britons, they are the most expeditious runaways. Benumbed with fear they stand motionless on yonder spot, which you will render forever memorable by a glorious victory. Here you may end your labours, and close a scene of 50 years by one great, one glorious day. Let your country see, and let the commonwealth bear witness, if the conquest of Britain has been a lingering work, if the seeds of rebellion have not been crushed, that we at least have done our duty.

Tacitus next has the Roman legionaries and auxiliaries shouting their own acclamation at their general's call to arms, with a vigour to match the Britons. Now the business of battle began, with Tacitus providing one of the most detailed accounts we have of Roman deployment on the battlefield. He says (*The Agricola*, 35):

Agricola restrained the ardour of his troops until he formed his order of battle. The auxiliary infantry, in number about 8,000, occupied the centre. The wings consisted of 3,000 [auxiliary] horse. The legions were stationed in the rear, at the head of the entrenchments as a body of reserve to support the ranks, if necessary, but otherwise to remain inactive, that a victory, obtained without the effusion of Roman blood might be of higher value.

There is much detail in this short paragraph, overt or inferred. Notably, this was an unusual deployment for a Roman army in the field. Though it was common for the auxiliaries to engage an enemy before the legionaries were committed, it was not for the legionaries to be deployed *en masse* at the rear. Tacitus' explanation is that Agricola was preserving his legionaries because they were Roman citizens, while the auxiliaries were not. However, given the legionaries were his best troops, and this was the engagement that he believed would finally defeat British resistance, this does not ring true. Clearly, things don't add up in Tacitus' narrative, with the only explanation the fact that the legions were still understrength after a hard campaign, while numbers among the auxilia had been more easily made up through battle casualty replacement. I therefore believe Agricola was hoping his auxiliaries would do the job on their own, as in fact actually happened, given he didn't want to lose one or more of his understrength legions. Here one can again see the long shadow cast by Varus' failure in

Campaigns in the Far North: AD 83 and Mons Graupius   157

AD 9. Agricola would only commit his legions if they were really needed. Fortunately for him, as it turned out, they weren't.

Tacitus now turns his attention to the British deployment. Crucially, he indicates Calgacus ensured his warriors were on high ground above the Roman camps below, and held their position there. One should note the degree of control here, this very different to Boudicca's failure to restrain her troops in the Battle of Watling Street. Specifically, Tacitus says (*The Agricola*, 36):

> The Caledonians kept possession of the rising ground, extending their ranks as wide as possible, to present a formidable show of battle. Their first line was ranged just above the plain, the rest in a gradual ascent on the acclivity of the hill.

Tacitus' description here shows Calgacus' army deployed on a range of steep, mountainous slopes. Agricola's force was deployed below. The Britons numbered around 30,000 men, the Romans around 22,000, with a higher than usual percentage of auxiliaries given the casualties the legionaries had suffered and comparative difficulty replacing their fallen.

Tacitus then provides real insight into the tactics of the Britons as the battle began, this matching exactly those described in earlier encounters further south when Caesar, Plautius and Paulinus fought the Britons. Again, we may be dealing with tropes, with Tacitus perhaps duplicating earlier battle reports. However, even if he wasn't there personally, he certainly had access to his father-in-law's first-hand commentary, together with reports from other Roman eyewitnesses, so I choose to take him at face value. In particular, he says (*The Agricola*, 36.1): 'The intermediate space between both armies was filled with the charioteers and the cavalry of the Britons, rushing to and fro in wild career, and traversing the plain with noise and tumult.'

A missile exchange then began, with the Romans having the advantage here given their legionary artillery, body shields and much higher quality body protection. The British charioteers and foot warriors, with their small shields which Tacitus calls targets, were particularly vulnerable (*The Agricola*, 36.1). In normal circumstances, this should have prompted the Britons to charge down the slope at the Romans to avoid casualties from the artillery bombardment. However, they kept their ground. To force the issue, Agricola now ordered six cohorts of elite auxiliaries forward. Four were of Batavians and two Tungrians, all recruited in the Rhine Delta. These warriors had a fearsome reputation and were soon doing their bloody work, despite the Britons being uphill. Tacitus is notably graphic here, saying (*The Agricola*, 36.1):

> The Batavians rushed to the attack with impetuous fury. Incited by their example, the two other [Tungrian] cohorts advanced with a spirit of emulation, and cut their way with terrible slaughter. Eager in pursuit of victory, they pressed forward with determined fury, leaving behind them numbers wounded, but not slain, and others not so much as hurt.

Tacitus adds here that Calgacus' troops were handicapped by their inferior weapons, which were no match for the *lanceae* spears and *gladii* stabbing swords of the auxiliaries (*The Agricola*, 36). Indeed, some translations have the auxiliaries here actually thrusting their swords into the exposed faces of the Britons.

Tacitus now brings us back to the British chariots, detailing a mounted engagement. This was on one or both flanks of the auxiliary advance against the Roman *equites*, and happened at the same time. Here the result was a different story, with the Britons initially successful against their mounted opponents. Tacitus says (*The Agricola*, 37.1):

> The Roman cavalry, in the meantime, was forced to give ground. The Caledonians, in their armed chariots, then rushed at full speed into the thick of the battle, where the infantry were engaged. Their first impression struck a general terror, but their career was soon checked by the inequalities of the ground and the close ranks of the Romans. Pent up in narrow places, the barbarians crowded upon each other, and were driven or dragged along by their own horses. A scene of confusion followed. Chariots without a guide, and loose ponies, broke from the ranks in wild disorder, and flying every way, as fear and consternation urged, they overwhelmed their own files and trampled down all who came in their way.

Thus, we have the British chariots pushing the *equites* backwards to expose the flanks of the foot auxiliaries. Moorhead and Stuttard call this the moment of greatest danger for the Romans (2012, 114). However, the steadfast Agricola showed no sign of panic. He had faith in his auxiliaries, which soon proved well founded given the British chariots were quickly repelled with heavy losses by the Batavians and Tungrians, with the rocky terrain also counting against the chariots.

Calgacus now faced disaster. The Roman auxiliaries were butchering his foot in the centre, while his chariots had failed to take advantage of their earlier success against the Roman cavalry. In desperation, he now made a last desperate attempt to turn the day his way, ordering his reserve foot warriors high up on the slopes to charge downhill. Specifically, they were ordered to wheel into the flank of the Roman auxiliary foot, indicating they were slightly offset from the line of battle below. However, Agricola easily countered by ordering his now rallied *equites*, and his own personal reserve of guard cavalry, to intercept the British foot while they were on the move. The result was another slaughter.

At that point the Britons broke, with thousands butchered by the Romans as they scrambled to find safety. Over 10,000 perished, with Tacitus describing a dreadful spectacle of carnage and destruction (*The Agricola*, 37.1). A vigorous Roman pursuit followed, and though some Roman troopers were killed by desperate Britons in the mountains, native resistance was finally broken. Agricola allowed the pursuit to continue until nightfall and then recalled his troops to their marching camps for the night. Tacitus says the Romans lost only 360 men overall, including Aulus Atticus, who had commanded a cohort of auxiliary foot and whose 'youthful enthusiasm and mettlesome horse took him deep into the ranks of the enemy' (*The Agricola*, 38.1). Another officer present may have been Julius Karus, whose funerary inscription in Cyrene details he served as an auxiliary prefect in a battle in Britain in AD 83. Tacitus then says Agricola's army, 'elated with success, enriched with plunder, passed the night in exultation', while their shattered opponents, brutalised in defeat, dispersed in all directions, 'men and women wailing together, carrying off the wounded and calling out to the survivors' (*The Agricola*, 38.1).

There is no doubt this was a mighty victory for Agricola, and one carried out without his legionaries engaging too, preserving his elite troops for future operations. As described by Tacitus, the battle was close-run at times, with huge jeopardy for the Romans if they had lost so far north. Defeat would have been total, with few if any survivors. Turney neatly sums up the bone-tired governor's feelings as he reflected on a day's hard fighting, saying (2022, 235):

> Agricola can only have heaved a deep sigh of relief as he looked across the battlefield on a cold September evening, knowing that the dispatch he had to write in his tent would race off to the emperor [most likely by sea down the coast on a fast *liburnian* of the fleet] on the morrow with the best of all possible tidings.

Tacitus then goes into more detail, this time forensic, about the shocking dislocation caused in the region after the defeat of the Britons, beginning with the immediate aftermath of the battle. He says (*The Agricola*, 38.1):

> They abandoned their homes and in fury set fire to them; they chose hiding places, only to abandon them at once [the Roman pursuit clearly aggressive and lengthy]. At times they met to form some sort of common plan, but then split up. Sometimes the sight of their dear ones broke their hearts, more often it enraged them; some, it was well known, laid violent hands on their wives and children as if in pity. The next day revealed more clearly the effects of the victory. An awful silence reigned on every hand, the hills were deserted, houses were smoking in the distance, and our scouts encountered no one. These, sent in all directions, observed the random tracks of the fugitives and determined that the enemy were not massing at any point.

The reference here to domestic violence is notable, though we are likely seeing another of Tacitus' tropisms regarding anyone considered to be non-Roman.

Tacitus next says that, given the lateness of the year, Agricola chose not to chase his shattered opponents on a broad front deeper into the Highlands. Instead, he closed his AD 83 land campaign by leading his army 'into the territory of the Boresti' (*The Agricola*, 38.1). Given this is not one of the tribes detailed by Ptolemy in the far north, these mysterious people have long defied attempts by historians to locate their territory. Turney discusses whether they were the Cornacii in Caithness, the most northerly of Ptolemy's tribes, though this seems unlikely unless Birley was indeed correct in identifying Ben Loyal in Sutherland as a candidate site for Mons Graupius (2022, 242). Others argue Boresti is simply a generic term for the peoples in the campaigning region. Whoever they were, they quickly agreed to submit to Agricola, with the governor taking hostages to ensure their peaceful intent.

Circumnavigation and Consolidation

His victory secure, Agricola now tasked squadrons of the *Classis Britannica* with completing a circumnavigation of the whole of the main island of Britain, perhaps inspired by the adventures of the Usipi rebels the previous year if Dio is correct, though I think it unlikely. Once more, Tacitus provides the detail, saying (*The Agricola*, 38):

> The Roman fleet now sailed round the furthest shores for the first time, and so established that Britain is an island. At the same time it discovered and overthrew some islands, called the Orkneys, which until then had been unknown. Thule too [first referenced by Pytheas, possibly the Shetlands, the Faroes or even Iceland], was sighted.

Tacitus then adds even more tantalising background about the naval taskforce's progress around Britain, saying (*The Agricola*, 38.3): 'the fleet, sped by favouring winds and fame, reached the port of *Trucculensian* from which it had set out to coast the neighbouring stretch of Britannia.'

As with the Boresti, the reference to *Trucculensian* has long been a fixation for historians. In truth, we have no idea where it was, though a harbour somewhere on the southern shores of the Moray Firth may be a candidate given the setting-out reference. Another is the then recently founded fortified harbour at Dun on Montrose Bay, as are Carpow on the Tay and Cramond on the Forth. Some also argue that *Trucculensian* is a mistranslation of *Rutupiensum*, one of the names by which Roman Richborough is known, though this interpretation seems unlikely to me.

The above statements by Tacitus make it clear the British regional fleet did indeed circumnavigate Britain. If further confirmation were needed, we can turn to another contemporary source. Tacitus' contemporary, Plutarch, reports that when attending the Pythean games in Athens in AD 84 he met an individual called Demetrius who was travelling back to Tarsus in southeastern Turkey from Britain (*Obsolescence of Oracles*, 2.1). Demetrius tells Plutarch that:

> among the islands lying near Britain were many which were isolated, having few or no inhabitants, some of which bore the name of divinities or heroes. He himself, by the emperor's order, had made a voyage for inquiry and observation to the nearest of these islands which had only a few inhabitants, holy men who were held inviolate by the Britons.

Once again, there is much to unpack here in a detailed classical reference. First, Plutarch appears to be describing the Outer Hebrides in Scotland given the numerous islands he details, and their remoteness. One could argue the holy men reference points to Anglesey, earlier the final home of the Druids, but any native British resistance there had been wiped out by Agricola's first year campaigning in Britain in AD 77. Next, the reference to the order from the emperor clearly refers to Domitian's senior representative in Britain, his governor Agricola. We may also get a hint here of Demetrius' actual role given the nature of Agricola's orders, namely that he was a high-ranking naval officer, at least a *navarchus* squadron commander and perhaps even the *Classis Britannica's praefectus classis* admiral. We may even be able to provide Demetrius with a *prenomen*, this based on a contemporary bronze plaque on display in the Yorkshire Museum, which was found in the *canaba* civilian settlement at York. This says, 'To the Gods of the legate's residence Scribonius Demetrius set this up', linking this Demetrius either with Agricola (*legate* being a term often used to describe a governor given his role as the emperor's military representative) or the actual *legate* in charge of *legio* IX *Hispana*, then resident in the legionary fortress in York. Meanwhile, a second contemporary bronze plaque, found with the first, says 'To Ocean and Tethys, Demetrius set this up'. Given the proximity of their discovery, it seems likely this is the same Scribonius Demetrius mentioned in the first plaque. Of specific interest, this latter plaque links this Demetrius with the sea.

The feat here of the *Classis Britannica*'s achieving this amazing nautical enterprise cannot be understated. As Turney says (2022, 242): 'The survival of the entire fleet in the conditions they would have faced would be nothing short of remarkable, and might explain something of why Tacitus and other Roman writers place such weight on this event.'

Travelling through the Pentland Firth, separating the Orkney Islands and Caithness, is not to be taken lightly, even today. Nor is traversing the North Channel between northeastern Ireland and southwestern Scotland, especially at the end of the campaigning season, or even perhaps over the winter.

The defeat of the natives across the far north now complete, Agricola could claim that the entire main island of Britain had been conquered. He now set about consolidating his success, once more setting in place garrisons to ensure his conquests in the far north remained under Roman control over the winter. This likely included maintaining troops in the 44ha sequence of marching camps in Aberdeenshire, the Grampians and Moray, and in the Glenblocker forts and Gask Ridge sites further south.

Work fortifying the site at Inchtuthil on the north bank of the Tay also accelerated at this time with *legio* XX *Valeria Victrix* expanding construction there to the scale of a full legionary fortress. Given if completed this would have been the most northerly legionary fortress in the empire, Agricola clearly had designs for it to underpin wider Roman control across the far north, in the same way that York did south of the Stanegate frontier. As detailed below, Inchtuthil was only briefly occupied by *legio* XX *Valeria Victrix* and then evacuated shortly afterwards, no later than early AD 87. Unlike other legionary fortresses in Britain, for example Caerleon, Chester and York, Inchtuthil was not built over in subsequent centuries, and therefore remains to this day one of the most enigmatic Roman sites in Britain. When excavated by Sir Ian Richmond in the 1950s and early 1960s, its internal layout was still largely preserved. It therefore provides the only complete plan of a Roman legionary fortress anywhere in the empire. In design it followed the standard Roman plan, with an external deep ditch with ankle breaker and other field defences sitting proud of an interior turf rampart revetted with stone, atop which would have run a wooden palisade. Timber towers were then constructed at each of the four corners and either side of the four gateways set in each of the four walls. From first-hand experience, when standing inside one can still see the outlines of the *principia* headquarters building, a huge *valetudinarium* hospital covering 5,000m^2, a 3,500^2 *fabrica* legionary workshop, and at least sixty-four barrack buildings. Some estimate the defensive perimeter of the fortress was 10km in length, giving a sense of the scale involved. The fortress location is particularly enigmatic, sitting as it does on a natural plateau above a broad bend on the Tay upriver of Perth. However, of note, the interior section in the eastern part of the fort where the *praetorium* commander's house should be located is empty, showing the structure was never built. Further, the *aedes* chapel of the standards in the *principia* is notably small and has been interpreted as temporary. Taken together, these show that the fortress was never fully completed, its abandonment detailed shortly.

Turney calls the months that followed in far northern Britain a 'winter of content' for the Romans (2022, 245), with Tacitus saying that 'sufficient forces had been allotted for the occupation, and the terror of Rome had gone before Agricola' (*The Agricola*, 38.8). Clearly, the governor's forces had total control of the region, with the natives shattered after recent defeats, especially Mons Graupius. Economic dislocation was total, with Agricola happy to let his troops maintain Roman power in his newly conquered territory. Tacitus then says Agricola himself marched south 'in order to inspire fear in new nations by his very lack of hurry' (*The Agricola*, 38.9). The implication here is that the governor took his time while travelling south though the upper Midland Valley, Fife and the Scottish Borders, with those Roman forces with him in full battle array and with standards aloft, reinforcing Roman authority as they went. Agricola then overwintered in York.

From there, Agricola had more time to curate a fuller report of his tremendous success in the far north for Domitian, the Senate and the people of Rome. As with his earlier note to the emperor in the immediate aftermath of Mons Graupius, this was sent by imperial courier using fast horse relays, which changed mount at *mansio* way stations along major trunkroads, and fast galley when travelling down waterways and along the coast. Late in the year, Agricola's dispatch would have taken around fourteen days to reach Rome, likely arriving in early December (Birley, 2005, 242).

Imperial Response

Sadly for Agricola, when the news did arrive Tacitus says it was not welcomed by an emperor preoccupied with plans and issues of his own. These included multiple major building projects, marital troubles and an abortive campaign in Germany.

In the first instance, Domitian had ordered the construction of numerous monumental buildings in Rome. To an extent, much of this was necessary after the Neronian fire, civil wars in AD 69 and a later fire in AD 80. However, here Domitian saw an opportunity for personal aggrandisement, and was soon reshaping much of central Rome in what was far from a simple rebuilding programme. Indeed, his ambition here was for his vast new structures to be the crowning achievement of a Flavian cultural renaissance. More than fifty new, huge buildings were constructed during Domitian's reign, particularly early on, rivalling the great urban renewal in Rome under Augustus. The most dazzling included an enormous Odeon, his new circus (now the Piazza Navona), and a vast new palace atop the Palatine Hill. Known as the Flavian Palace, this was designed by the emperor's master architect Rabirius. Domitian also restored the Temple of Jupiter Optimus Maximus on the Capitoline Hill, installing a gilded roof at great cost to his *fiscus* treasury. He also completed the Temple of Vespasian and Titus, located at the western end of the *forum Romanum* between the Temple of Concordia and the Temple of Saturn, the Arch of Titus celebrating his elder brother's sack of Jerusalem at the end of the First Jewish Revolt, and most famously, the Flavian Amphitheatre, or as we know it today, the Colosseum. Outside the imperial capital, Domitian also spent lavishly on a variety of other building projects, these even more overtly for his benefit. They include the fabulous Villa of Domitian, an enormous luxury country retreat in the Alban Hills 20km outside Rome. Other personal villas built outside the imperial capital included grandiose examples at *Baiae* on the Gulf of Naples, *Tusculum* and *Antium* in Latium, and *Vicarello* in Etruria.

Meanwhile, an imperial marriage that had started well was now faltering. Domitian had married Domitia Longina in AD 70. She was the daughter of Gnaeus Domitius Corbulo, the legendary Roman general whom Nero had forced to commit suicide in AD 66. Thus, his father-in-law's name was synonymous with military success, something the younger son of Vespasian craved throughout his adult life. His new wife was also very well connected across Roman society, especially at the patrician level, and so the match had seemed perfect at the time. However, their only child died young and by AD 83, they were estranged, with Domitian exiling his wife the same year. Though he later recalled her, she lived an onerous existence hating life in the imperial palace until Domitian's assassination in AD 96 (Kean and Frey, 2005, 69).

Next, at the same time Agricola had been achieving military greatness in the far north of Britain, Domitian's desire to emulate his father and brother's success on the battlefield was stuttering at best. In AD 83, he claimed a triumph for a major defeat of the Chatti east of the Rhine, these a major Germanic tribal confederation then predating Germania Superior. Although, as a result of the Roman campaign, a 200km stretch of new *limes* fortifications were built through the Main and Neckar valleys, where they joined the northernmost section of Vespasian's *Agri Decumates*, historians today still disagree on whether this was a real campaign or a fabrication by Domitian, who may have simply built the new *limes* fortifications rather than fight a campaign.

At the time, Tacitus certainly believed Domition unworthy of his triumph. Of the emperor's reception of the good news from Britain, he says (*The Agricola*, 39.1):

> The news of the events in Britain, although reported by Agricola in his dispatches in the most exact and modest terms, was received with unease by Domitian, as was his wont, with a smile on his face and unease in his heart. He was aware that his sham triumph over Germania had been treated as a joke – slaves had been bought in the markets whose dress and hair were contrived to make them look like prisoners of war. But here [in Britain] was a genuine victory on a grand scale: the enemy dead were reckoned by thousands, the popular enthusiasm immense. There was nothing Domitian feared

so much as to have the name of a subject raised above that of the prince. In vain had he silenced the eloquence of the courts and the distinctions of civil careers, if another man was to seize his military glory. Other talents could at a pinch be ignored, but that of a good general must belong to the emperor. Such were the worries that vexed him and over which he brooded in secret until he was tired – a sure sign in him of deadly purpose. Finally, he decided to store up his hatred for the present and wait for the first burst of acclaim and the enthusiasm of the army to die down. Agricola, you see, was still in possession of Britannia.

In short, Domitian was jealous, but knew that even a hint of negative response to Agricola's mighty success would play badly for him with the military, Senate and the people of Rome. A canny political operator if nothing else, he therefore played for time, waiting until Agricola had fallen from public attention before reasserting his authority. However, in the short term, he was forced to reward Agricola, with Tacitus detailing that (*The Agricola*, 40.1): 'Domitian therefore gave orders that triumphal decorations, the honour of a splendid statue and all the other substitutes for a triumph should be voted to Agricola in the Senate, augmented by a most flattering address.'

Once more, there is much to unpack here. In reverse order, since the days of Augustus a triumph in Rome had been the sole preserve of the emperor and his close family, unlike during the Republic, when any successful military leader might be awarded a formal celebratory procession through the public spaces of Rome. Instead, by the end of the first century AD, a general might by awarded the 'substitutes' Tacitus details by the Senate, including awards for success and bravery, and a formal statue.

However, it is Tacitus' initial reference to 'triumphal decorations' that make Domitian's response to Agricola's success unique. This is because he ordered the construction of a huge quadrifrons (four-way) monumental arch at Richborough on the east Kent coast to mark the place where the successful Claudian invasion had earlier landed. At 25m in height, this was one of the tallest monumental arches in the entire empire. Further, it was clad in highly expensive Carrera marble imported from Italy, making Richborough the new imperial gateway to the province from that point.

This dazzling white arch was so tall it was visible on the continent on clear days, leading to its later reuse at the onset of the Carausian revolt in the late AD 280s as a watchtower.

With the arch one can see Domitian slowly prizing the trappings of imperial success in Britain away from Agricola, one of the few times he showed any interest in the province (the only other of note was making Lincoln a *colonia* in the later AD 80s). If that was his ambition, then it worked, with the arch greeting each new governor until the time of Carausius. Indeed, it was so monumental in scale its base can still be seen in the centre of the later Saxon Shore fort at Richborough.

Tacitus tells one final story about Domitian's response to Agricola's success, showing him hedging his bets on how far to reward the British governor. He says (40.9):

> Further, the impression was to be conveyed that the province of Syria, then vacant through the death of the consular Atilius Rufus and reserved for men of senior rank, was intended for Agricola. It was widely believed that a freedman [a former imperial slave in the palace] in Domitian's closest confidence was sent with a letter offering Agricola Syria, but with instructions to deliver it only if he were still in Britannia. The freedman, it is said, met Agricola's ship in the very straits of the Ocean [in this case, the English Channel between Boulogne-sur-Mer and the east Kent coast] and without even hailing him returned to Domitian.

The message here is clear. While in Britain, Agricola had a powerbase, whether he wanted it or not, which Domitian was wary of. This was only fourteen years after the civil wars of AD 69, a sanguinous switch in imperial gear from the Julio-Claudians to the Flavians, which showed dramatic change could take place in the running of the empire. In that context, while Agricola was in Britain, Domitian clearly perceived him a threat to be neutered. The easiest way to do so was to offer one of the four top proconsular postings, either in Syria, Achaea, Asia or Africa Proconsularis. However, given Domitian's freedman found Agricola on the open ocean on his return to the continent, he was no longer in Britain, and so outside the territory he had earlier made his own. Therefore, based on the orders Domitian had given his freedman, he was less of a threat, and so the imperial messenger chose to remain incognito. Domitian gambled here that, once out of Britain, Agricola's kudos would diminish with every mile he drew nearer the imperial capital. To be clear, there is no evidence at all that Agricola was planning anything untoward. However, that is not how the increasingly paranoid Domitian perceived things, nor his sycophantic advisors who relied on his ongoing reign for their power and wealth.

An interesting question here is why Agricola was returning at all. The events as described would have taken place in later AD 84 or early AD 85. Unless Agricola had been given a set term in Britain as governor, his recall to Rome for any new assignment would have come from one man only. This was Domitian. If that were the case, then sending of an imperial freedman with the offer of a new and lucrative posting in Syria seems a deliberate attempt by the emperor to placate pro-Agricolan public opinion, but in the full knowledge that his envoy would miss a governor returning on his own orders. Such a scheming move was very much in character with Domitian.

However, one thing was now without doubt. Agricola's term as governor in Roman Britain was over. Soon his great achievements in the far north began to unravel as late Flavian Rome under Domitian gradually lost interest there, mostly through lack of political interest. When the Flavians first came to power, conquest in northern Britain was viewed as a good investment in time, money and political capital to further the martial reputations of Vespasian and, later, Titus. Domitian, having built his triumphal arch in Richborough, was now only interested in his own conquests north of the Danube. Within four years of Agricola's departure, the 44ha marching camps in the far north below the Moray Firth, the Glenblocker forts, and even the incomplete legionary fortress at Inchtuthil had been abandoned. The latter's incumbent *legio* XX *Valeria Victrix* redeployed south to Chester, where it replaced *legio* II *Adiutrix* after the latter was recalled by Domitian for his Danubian campaigns. A writing tablet found at Carlisle dated 7 November AD 83 referencing the XXth legion being there shows it withdrew sooner rather than later. Another tablet, dated around the same time, indicates Agricola himself was there too. This mentions one of his mounted guards, being addressed to a 'trooper of the Ala Sebosiana, guardsman of Agricola'. It is highly unlikely this crack unit would travel without the governor. Similarly, the *Classis Britannica* headed south too. Thus, as the end of the first century AD approached, the fleet found itself principally operating out of Chester on the west coast and South Shields on the east.

Now, from north of the Highland line, the surviving local population began to trickle back to their fertile homelands further south as the Romans withdrew, with the northern frontier finally settling again along the natural isthmus between the Solway Firth and Tyne.

Tacitus has the last word on the fantastical story of Agricola in Britain. In his angry summary at the beginning of *The Histories*, he says that during the Flavian period, 'Britain was completely conquered ... and straightaway let go' (1.2). Thus, the only time the whole main island of Britain fell under complete Roman control, it ended with a sad whimper, not a bang.

Conclusion

Agricola was back in Rome by spring AD 85 after handing over 'a province peaceful and secure' to his successor Lucullus (Tacitus, *The Agricola*, 40.9). However, once in the imperial capital it quickly became clear the rumoured promotion to the governorship of Syria would not be forthcoming. The reason was soon apparent, with Tacitus detailing that (*The Agricola*, 41.1):

> often during this period Agricola was denounced to Domitian behind his back, and as often behind his back acquitted. His danger did not arise from any charge against him or any complaint by an injured party, but from an emperor hostile to merit, his own renown and that deadliest type of enemy, the singer of his praises.

This was double trouble for Agricola: a jealous emperor, and sycophantic advisors keen to ensure their wealth and position. Indeed, from the time he arrived back in Rome he was forced to keep a low profile, with Tacitus saying (*The Agricola*, 41.1):

> By night he entered the city, and by night he went, when instructed, to the palace. He was welcomed with a perfunctory kiss and, without a word, dismissed to join the crowd of courtiers ... In order not the publicise his arrival by the pomp of a crowded welcome, he avoided the attentions of his friends. Anxious to tone down his military renown, irksome to civilians, he displayed his other qualities and drank deep of peace and repose. He was modest in his dress, affable in conversation, never seen with more than one or two friends.

Here, Agricola may have been too successful as Tacitus concludes this part of his narrative by saying (*The Agricola*, 41.1): 'As a result, the majority, who usually measure great men by their self-advertisement, after closely observing Agricola, were left asking why he was famous; few could read his secret outright.'

As a literary health warning, it is worth noting that Tacitus is at his most arch here. Turney says the author's narrative now 'departs from biography and begins an uncomfortable combination of history, name-calling, political statement and eulogy' (2022, 252). This is all true, though Domitian's underlying lack of military success still cuts through the invective as the real reason he turned on Agricola. I have already discussed his AD 83 Chatti campaign, where he claimed a triumph, though with no evidence of a major victory. However, it was north of the Danube where he truly failed to accrue military glory.

There, the three most significant threats he faced were the Germanic Suebi, the Dacians and the Sarmatians. The Germans were the eastern neighbours of the tribes north and east of the Rhine who had destroyed Varus' three legions in AD 9, while the Dacians were closely related to the Thracians. Together with their Carpi and Getae allies, they resided in the Carpathian Mountains and Danubian flood plain.

Meanwhile, the Sarmatians were an Iranian people who inhabited the Pontic Steppe, having migrated west from the fourth century BC onwards. The Romans first encountered them when they invaded Moesia in Nero's reign.

By the early AD 80s, the Dacians were harassing Roman settlements in Pannonia and Moesia on the upper and lower Danube. The Sarmatians soon joined them. Then, in spring AD 85, just as Agricola arrived back in Rome, the Dacian king Decebalus crossed the Danube into Moesia with a large warband seeking plunder and slaves. Disaster followed for the Romans when the Moesian governor Gaius Oppius Sabinus was killed leading a winter fightback against the invaders. This forced Domitian to the front line in person, beginning Domitian's Dacian War, a conflict that lasted three years. Once on the Danube, the emperor joined a large force under the command of his praetorian prefect Cornelius Fuscus, a veteran Flavian general who'd fought with Vespasian in AD 69. A Roman counteroffensive then drove the Dacians and Sarmatians out of imperial

Conclusion 173

territory by spring AD 86, after which Domitian returned to Rome to celebrate a triumph.

However, Fuscus' victory proved short-lived. In mid-summer AD 86, Domitian ordered him north of the Danube on an ill-planned invasion of Dacian territory. His huge force comprised vexillations of the Praetorian Guard, *legio* V *Alaudae* and four other legions, together with a matching number of auxiliaries. Sadly for the Romans, after crossing the Danube on a pontoon bridge and some initial success, Fuscus led them into a trap where Decebalus was able to mount a large-scale ambush near Tapae in modern Romania. This was a key fortified settlement guarding access to Sarmizegetusa, Decebalus' capital city, and one of the few places where invaders could attack the Dacian heartland from the south. Surrounded, Fuscus tried to lead his men in a counter-attack but was killed, with the *aquila* eagle standard of the Praetorians captured by the Dacians and *legio* V *Alaudae* wiped out.

This was a major humiliation for Domitian, who returned to the region that autumn. Once there he divided Moesia on the lower Danube into two provinces, Upper and Lower, and transferred three additional legions to the Danubian frontier, including *legio* II *Adiutrix*, which had been recalled from Britain. In AD 87, he then ordered Tettius Julianus, another leading *legate*, to lead another large-scale invasion north of the Danube into Dacia. This crossed the river near the legionary fortress at *Viminacium*, the new capital of Moesia Superior in eastern Serbia, and then marched to Tibiscum, a major Dacian settlement, which the Romans sacked. They then pushed on to Tapae, scene of Fuscus' earlier demise. There they finally defeated Decebalus in late AD 88, though Domitian was forced to end the campaign before he could besiege Sarmizegetusa when new trouble broke out on the Rhine frontier. Keen to avoid conflicts on both the Danube and Rhine, Domitian agreed a peace treaty with Decebalus, ending his Dacian War. Though he claimed another victory, the details show otherwise. Specifically, in order to gain free access through Dacian territory to flank the Germans on the Rhine frontier from the east, Domitian agreed to pay Decebalus an annual subsidy of 8 million *sesterces*. Contemporary writers were highly critical of this, particularly given the deaths of Sabinus and Fuscus were unavenged.

For the remainder of the emperor's reign Dacia remained a peaceful neighbour, though by the early AD 90s, the Romans became increasingly aware the canny Decebalus was using his annual Roman subsidy to fortify his kingdom against any later Roman incursion. Belatedly, Domitian responded by deploying even more troops to the region, including two auxiliary cavalry *ala* from Syria and five auxiliary foot cohorts from Pannonia to Moesia Superior. However, his assassination ended any plans to invade Dacian a third time, the damage to his reputation from his failure to humiliate Decebalus playing a key role in his demise.

Jarringly missing from any narrative on Domitian's Dacian War is his most successful military leader, Agricola. Tacitus makes clear this was a deliberate act by Domitian and his advisors, saying (*The Agricola*, 41.9):

> One after another came the loss of all those armies in Moesia and Dacia, in Germania and Pannonia, through the rashness or cowardice of their generals; one after another came the defeats of all those experienced officers and the capture of all those cohorts. No longer was it the frontier and the riverbank that were in question, but the legionary headquarters and the maintenance of the empire. So, as loss was piled on loss, and year after year made notable by death and disaster, public opinion began to clamour for Agricola to take command. His energy, resolution and military experience were universally contrasted with the passivity and cowardice of the others. It is clear enough Domitian's own ears were stung by the lash of such talk. The best of his freedmen spoke out of loyal affection, the worst out of malice and spleen, but all alike goaded on an emperor so ready to go wrong.

Tacitus is harsh here regarding Sabinus, Fuscus and Julianus. However, there is no doubt Domitian's grasp on power was growing increasingly precarious. The last thing he wanted was to give Agricola another chance of military glory. Thus the leading Roman general of the age idled away his time, awaiting another call to imperial service that never came. Tacitus continues (*The Agricola*, 42.1):

> At last the year arrived in which Agricola was due to draw for the proconsulship of Africa Proconsularis or Asia, and, with the execution

of Civica Cerealis [a governor of one of the Moesian provinces executed by Domitian for treason in AD 88] still fresh in memory, Agricola did not lack warning nor Domitian precedent. Some of the emperor's confidants approached Agricola in order to ask whether he really intended to take a province. They began somewhat slyly by praising the life of peaceful retirement, went on to promise their own assistance should Agricola care to decline, and at last with open threats and exhortations dragged him off to Domitian. The emperor, his hypocrite's part prepared, had assumed a majestic air; he listened to Agricola's request to be excused and, granting it, allowed himself to be thanked, with never a blush at such odious a favour.

The inference here is that Agricola's reputation was still such that he was expected to be assigned a key proconsular governorship, but Domitian was loath to appoint him. The emperor therefore coerced Agricola to publicly announce he had retired from public service, and instead sought a simple, quiet life at home. As a salacious afterthought, Tacitus adds Domitian then refused to award Agricola the proconsular salary usually awarded to those at senior levels if they chose not to take a consular governorship.

The above could simply be taken at face value, with the paranoid Domitian removing Agricola as a perceived threat in return for his life. However, two other theories are worth briefly considering. In the 1960s, T.A. Dorey suggested that, if one cuts through Tacitus' biased narrative, here we have Agricola truly worn out by years of hard campaigning, perhaps with a debilitating illness (1960, 95). Meanwhile, Turney considers whether Domitian's plans for Agricola were even more Machiavellian than Tacitus implies. He suggests the emperor deliberately wanted to appoint Agricola to govern Africa Proconsularis or Asia so that he could then accuse him of corruption and put him on trial to destroy his reputation. Turney says (2022, 262): 'The temptations for embezzlement and treason when in charge of Rome's most critical provinces had led to plenty of trouble in the past.' If that were the case, the wily Agricola dodged this imperial blow by declining any further public office and retiring to continue his quiet life in Rome. In reality, we have no way of knowing whether any of these interpretations are correct. What we can say with certainty is that he definitely retired, and never returned to public life.

Agricola passed away on 23 August AD 93, three years before the Flavian dynasty ended. He was only 53. By this time, Tacitus had left the imperial capital with his wife, likely in AD 89, to command a legion on the frontiers of the empire. However, despite not being present, he does allude to Agricola being poisoned, saying (*The Agricola*, 43.1):

> The end of Agricola's life was a bitter blow to us and a sorrow to his friends; to those outside his circle and even to complete strangers it was a matter of some concern. The general public as well, those mobs so busy with their own affairs, flocked to his house and discussed the news in the markets and clubs. When his death was announced no one exulted, no one forgot too readily. The sense of pity was increased by the persistent rumours that he had been poisoned. We have no definite evidence, that is all I can say for certain. I would note, however, that throughout the whole illness there were more visits from prominent [imperial] freedmen and court physicians than is usual with an emperor making calls by proxy; perhaps this was real concern, perhaps mere prying. It was generally agreed that on the day of his death the key stages in his decline were reported by relays of runners, and no one could believe that tidings brought so quickly would be unwelcome.

Clearly, Domitian was paying very close attention to Agricola's demise. Later, Tacitus posthumously addresses his father-in-law directly as he closes *The Agricola*, full of sorrow that he and his wife weren't at Agricola's side when he passed. He says (45.10):

> You were fortunate indeed, Agricola, in your glorious life, but no less in your timely death [in avoiding the debacle of Domitian's final years in power]. Those who were present at your final words attest that you met your death with a cheerful courage, as though doing your best to absolve the emperor of guilt. But your daughter and I have suffered more than the pang of a father's loss, for we grieve that we could not tend your illness, cheer your failing powers and take our fill of your look and embrace. We could not have failed to catch some last commands, some words to be engraved on our hearts forever. This

is our special sorrow, our peculiar hurt, that through the accident of long absence from Rome we lost you four years before you died. All more than all, dear Father, was assuredly done to honour you by the devoted wife at your side; but there were tears due to you that were not shed and, as light failed, there was something for which your darkening eyes looked in vain.

From this passage it is clear Agricola's wife Domitia outlived her husband.

As for Domitian, his end was not so peaceful. The emperor's grip on power had been unravelling for years. Already he'd survived a serious usurpation attempt when Lucius Antonius Saturninus, governor of Germania Superior, had led a rebellion in the winter of AD 89. Motivated by a personal grudge, at first this was a serious affair involving *legio* IV *Gemina*, at that time on the Rhine after its exploits north of the Danube, and *legio* XXI *Rapax*. Both legions were based in Mainz (Roman *Moguntiacum*), the provincial capital. However, fate proved unlucky for Saturninus when the German allies he had bribed to cross the frozen Rhine to support him were prevented by an untimely thaw. The revolt was then quickly put down by two of Domitian's leading generals, Lucius Appius Maximus Norbanus and the later emperor Trajan. Predictably, Domitian had Saturninus and any he believed implicated in the plot executed, with their heads displayed on the *rostra* speaking platform in the *forum Romanum*. Meanwhile, *legio* XXI *Rapax* was sent to Pannonia Superior in disgrace, with the emperor then forcing the Senate to pass a law banning any two legions from sharing the same camp again.

This was the first of a series of major proscriptions by Domitian against his political enemies in Rome, or at least those he perceived to be so. Here Suetonius speaks of his serious persecution of the Roman elites, with over twenty senators executed (*The Twelve Caesars, Domitian*, 10.1). These included Lucius Aelius Lamia Plautius Aelianus, former husband of the estranged empress, and three of Domitian's own family members. These were Marcus Arrecinus Clemens, Titus Flavius Clemens and Titus Flavius Sabinus. The second, a cousin of the emperor, was at one stage close enough for Domitian to name his young sons as his successors, renaming them Vespasian and Domitian. In an act of spite, Domitian then exiled Flavius Clemens' wife Domitilla, his own niece, away from Rome. Now no one at the top of Roman society felt safe from the emperor (Tacitus, *The Agricola*, 45.1).

Increasingly unpopular across all levels of Roman society, Domitian now turned to the key lever at his disposal to ensure his security. This was the military. In the first instance, he increased the salary of his Praetorian Guardsmen, despite the strain this put on the imperial treasury. Then, in a game-changing move, he reformed his intelligence-gathering operation. To that point, the Julio-Claudian and Flavian emperors had eschewed any formal means of internal spying, considering it un-Roman. However, as Domitian strove to accrue more power for his protection, he restructured the *frumentum* grain supply section of the *praetorium* imperial general staff into a brand-new secret service. This proved a very shrewd move, and one that Domitian's successors embraced. The logistics specialists of the *frumentum*, often former soldiers of non-commissioned officer rank, had long travelled far and wide across the empire ensuring grain and other goods reached the troops wherever needed. Many were now retasked to gather intelligence at the same time, keeping the name by which they had earlier been known, *frumentarii*. In effect, they became Rome's first official secret agents. As Sinnigen explains, Rome's first secret service 'was staffed by supply sergeants whose original functions had been the purchase for and distribution to the troops of grain' (1961, 66).

Domitian also created a headquarters for his new secret service, which he opened in AD 94. This was located at the Castra Peregrina (camp of strangers), an old Republican military barracks on the Caelian Hill, situated between the Temple of Claudius and Nero's Macellum Magnum market. This was a very fashionable district in Rome and home to many of its wealthiest families, and only a short walk from the Palatine Hill and *forum Romanum*. It was thus ideally placed to help the *frumentarii* keep track of the activities of Rome's leading citizens. Domitian also created a new post to command his secret service, the *Princeps Peregrinorum*, who reported to the *Praefectus Urbi*, head of the *cohortes urbanae*.

A surprising amount is known about Domitian's new *frumentarii*, despite the fact they were a secret service, this largely from inscriptions on tombstones and commentary from contemporary historians. For example, at Domitian's instigation they wore an official uniform when not operating covertly, this to ensure good behaviour from all in their view.

Sadly for Domitian, his obsession with security was to no avail. On 18 September AD 96, he was assassinated in a court-led conspiracy. Here, Suetonius says Domitian's court chamberlain Parthenius played the leading role, likely because the emperor had recently executed his close friend Epaphroditus, Nero's former personal secretary (*The Twelve Caesars, Domitian,* 10.1). Parthenius convinced the new praetorian prefect Petronius Secundus to join him, with Domitian's estranged wife Domitia soon agreeing to assist them. Together they convinced a steward of the exiled Domitilla called Stephanus to do the deed using a dagger hidden in the bandages of an ostensibly injured arm. Suetonius provides the detail, saying (17.1):

> Stephanus pretended that he had discovered a plot, and was for that reason granted an audience: whereupon, as the amazed Domitian perused a document he had handed him, Stephanus stabbed him in the groin. The wounded emperor put up a fight, but succumbed to seven further stabs [from others at court who joined in], his assailants being a subaltern named Clodianus, Parthenius's freedman Maximus, a chamberlain called Satur and one of the imperial gladiators.

Domitian was dead at the age of 44, though the assault cost Stephanus his life too, given he was stabbed in a final act of defiance by Domitian as he fell (Kean and Frey, 2005, 73). The emperor's body was transported out of the palace on a common bier on the orders of an old nurse of the emperor's called Phyllis. It was later cremated without ceremony and the ashes mixed with those of Domitian's niece in the Temple of the *gens Flavia* on the Quirinal Hill. Given Domitian had no son to succeed him, and with the sons of the executed Flavius Clemens dropped from imperial succession, thus ended the Flavian dynasty.

The Senate now moved quickly to achieve political stability in Rome. The *Fasti Ostienses*, a chronological calendar of major events in Roman history including the dates of magisterial appointments from 49 BC to AD 175, details that on the same day as Domitian's assassination the Senate declared the veteran Senator Marcus Cocceius Nerva emperor. So began the Nervo-Trajanic dynasty, later to peak with the conquests of Trajan.

By that time, Agricola's conquests in the far of north of Britain had unravelled, despite Tacitus' attempts to immortalise them in his *Agricola*. This new, post-Agricolan reality left a legacy of enormous consequence in Britain that still impacts our world. Domitian's short-sighted and ill-fated decision to withdraw Agricola from Britain after his mighty victory, and the Roman troops from the far north after the whole main island of Britain had been conquered, set in place the chain of events leading to today's political landscape on the main island of Britain, with the often contentious relationship between Scotland and England. If the Romans had remained in the far north to extend the province of Britannia into the region, then certainly the Scottish Borders, Fife and the upper Midland Valley would have seen a Mediterranean-style stone-built urban environment appear no different to that in the north of England, with an integrated transport system by road, river and sea to match. However, the Romans didn't remain, and so the region went its own way from that point, for better or worse. This was a true sliding-door moment in British history that changed things forever.

It also changed the nature of Roman Britain from that point too. From that moment, the abandoned far north was always a source of endemic trouble to the province in the south. To counter this, a huge military presence was required in Britain, which I estimate to be 12 per cent of the entire military establishment of Rome in what was only 4 per cent of the empire's geographic area. This completely changed the nature of Britannia, with the whole economy in the north and west bent on maintaining this enormous military presence. The building by Hadrian of his immense and costly fortified frontier along the Solway Firth–Tyne line is the true embodiment of this. From that point, Britain was a place of difference in the Roman Empire, the troublesome, hard to conquer province in the far-off northwest.

Yet another of Domitian's decisions regarding Agricola in Britain also has major implications today. This is his decision in AD 81 to deny Agricola's request to invade Ireland, the second main island of the British archipelago in terms of size. Though one can take with a pinch of salt Tacitus' conviction that his father-in-law believed a single legion was enough for this new invasion, if the Romans had invested in such a venture and succeeded, again our world might be different. Modern

Ireland would have spent at least a period as part of the Roman world, which may have had major implications for all that followed.

In conclusion, what we can say definitively is that Agricola was truly one of the great figures of British and Roman history. He was certainly the only Roman who could claim to have conquered the whole of the main island of Britain, only to be undermined by the pettiness of an insecure and spiteful emperor. However, through Tacitus, we come as near as possible to knowing his true story through classical narrative. I leave my final words on the story of Roman Britain's greatest warrior governor to Tacitus himself, who concludes his *Agricola* by saying (46.1):

Agricola's story has been told to posterity and, so handed down, he will live on.

Bibliography

Ancient Sources
Apuleius, *The Golden Ass*, trans. P.G. Walsh (Oxford: Oxford World Classics, 2008).
Aurelius, Marcus, *Meditations*, trans. M. Staniforth (London: Penguin, 1964).
Caesar, Julius, *The Conquest of Gaul*, trans. S.A Handford (London: Penguin, 1951).
Cato, Marcus, *De Agri Cultura*, trans. H.B Ash and W.D. Hooper (Harvard: Loeb Classical Library, 1934).
Dio, Cassius, *Roman History*, trans. E. Cary (Harvard: Loeb Classical Library, 1925).
Eusebius, *Ecclesiastical History: Complete and Unabridged*, trans. C.F. Crusé (Seaside, Oregon: Merchant Books, 2011).
Eutropius, Flavius, *Historiae Romanae Breviarium*, trans. H.W. Bird (Liverpool: Liverpool University Press, 1993).
Flaccus, Quintus Horatius (Horace), *The Complete Odes and Epodes*, trans. D. West (Oxford: Oxford Paperbacks, 2008).
Frontinus, Sextus Julius, *Strategemata*, trans. C.E. Bennett (Portsmouth, New Hampshire: Heinemann, 1969).
Gaius, *Institutiones*, trans. F. De Zulueta (Oxford: Oxford University Press, 1946).
Herodian, *History of the Roman Empire*, trans. C.R. Whittaker (Harvard: Loeb Classical Library, 1989).
Historia Augusta, trans. D. Maggie (Harvard, Loeb Classical Library, 1921).
Homer, *The Iliad*, trans. E.V. Rieu (London: Penguin, 1950).
Jordanes, *Getica* (Morrisville, North Carolina: Lulu Press, 2014).
Justinian, *The Digest of Justinian*, trans. A. Watson (Philadelphia: University of Pennsylvania, 1997).
Livy, *The History of Rome*, trans. B.O. Foster (Cambridge, MA: Harvard University Press/Loeb Classical Library, 1989).
Pausanias, *Guide to Greece: Central Greece*, trans. P. Levi (London: Penguin, 1979).
Pliny the Elder, *Natural History*, trans. H. Rackham (Harvard: Harvard University Press, 1940).
Pliny the Younger, *Epistularum Libri Decem*, ed. R.A.B. Mynors (Oxford: Oxford Classical Texts/Clarendon Press, 1963).
Plutarch, *Lives of the Noble Greeks and Romans*, ed. A.H. Clough (Oxford: Benediction Classics, 2013).
Plutarch, *Obsolescence of Oracles*, trans. F.C. Babbitt (Harvard: Loeb Classical Library, 1989).
Polybius, *The Rise of the Roman Empire*, trans. I. Scott-Kilvert (London: Penguin, 1979).
Ptolemy, *Geography*, trans. J. Lennart Berggren and Alexander Jones (Princeton, New Jersey: Princeton University Press, 2001).
Quintilian, *Institutes of Oratory*, trans. J. Selby Watson (Scotts Valley, California: Create Space Independent Publishing Platform, 2015).
Suetonius, *The Twelve Caesars*, trans. R. Graves (London: Penguin, 1957).

Tacitus, Cornelius, *The Agricola*, trans. H. Mattingly (London: Penguin, 1970).
Tacitus, Cornelius, *The Annals*, trans. M. Grant (London: Penguin, 2003).
Tacitus, Cornelius, *The Histories*, trans. W.H. Fyfe (Oxford: Oxford Paperbacks, 2008).
Seneca, *Dialogues and Essays*, trans. J. Davie (Oxford: Oxford University Press, 2008).
Siculus, Diodorus, *Library of History*, Vol. 3, trans. C.H. Oldfather (Harvard: Loeb Classical Library, 1939).
Strabo, *The Geography of Strabo*, trans. D.W. Roller (Cambridge: Cambridge University Press, 2014).
Statius, *Silvae*, trans. and ed. D.R. Shackleton Bailey (Harvard: Loeb Classical Library, 2003).
Vegetius, *De Re Militari*, trans. N.P. Milner (Liverpool: Liverpool University Press, 1993).
Victor, Aurelius, *De Caesaribus*, trans. H.W. Bird (Liverpool: Liverpool University Press, 1994).

Modern Sources
Allen, S., *Celtic Warrior 300 BC –AD 100* (Oxford: Osprey Publishing, 2001).
Avery, A., *The Story of York* (Pickering: Blackthorn Press, 2007).
Barker, P., *The Armies and Enemies of Imperial Rome* (Cambridge: Wargames Research Group, 1981).
de la Bédoyère, G., *Praetorian: The Rise and Fall of Rome's Imperial Bodyguard* (New Haven: Yale University Press, 2017).
de la Bédoyère, G., 'The Emperors' Fatal Servants', *History Today*, March 2017, pp. 58–62.
Bentley, P., 'A Recently Identified Valley in the City', *London Archaeologist*, Vol. 5, No. 1 (1984), pp. 13–16.
Bidwell, P., *Roman Forts in Britain* (Stroud: Tempus, 2007).
Birely, A.R., *The Fasti of Roman Britain* (Oxford: Clarendon Press, 1981).
Birley, A.R., *The Roman Government of Britain* (Oxford: Oxford University Press, 2005).
Birley, A.R., 'The Frontier Zone in Britain: Hadrian to Caracalla' in L. de Blois and E. Lo Cascio (eds.), *The Impact of the Roman Army (200 BC–AD 476)* (Leiden: Brill, 2007), pp. 355–370.
Birley, E., 'The Fate of the Ninth Legion' in R.M. Butler (ed.), *Soldier and Civilian in Roman Yorkshire* (Leicester: Leicester University, 1971), pp. 71–80.
Bishop, M.C., *The Secret History of the Roman Roads of Britain* (Barnsley: Pen & Sword, 2014).
Bishop, M.C., *The Gladius* (Oxford: Osprey Publishing Ltd, 2016).
Breeze, D.J., *Roman Scotland* (London: Batsford Ltd/Historic Scotland, 2000).
Breeze, D.J. and Dobson, B., *Hadrian's Wall* (London: Penguin, 2000).
Brodribb, G., 'A Survey of Tile at the Roman Bath House at Beauport Park, Battle, East Sussex', *Britannia*, Vol. 10 (1979), pp. 139–156.
Burgess, R.W., '*Principes cum Tyrannis*: Two Studies on the *Kaisergeschichte* and its Tradition', *The Classical Quarterly*, Vol.43 (1993), pp. 491–500.
Campbell, D.B., 'The Fate of the Ninth', *Ancient Warfare*, Vol. 4 No. 5 (2011), pp. 48–53.
Campbell, D.B., *The Fate of the Ninth* (Glasgow: Bocca dela Verita Publishing, 2018).
Connolly, P., *Greece and Rome at War* (London: Macdonald & Co., 1988).
Cornell, T.J., 'The End of Roman Imperial Expansion' in J. Rich and G. Shipley (eds.), *War and Society in the Roman World* (London: Routledge, 1993), pp. 139–170.
Cornell, T.J. and Matthews, J., *Atlas of the Roman World* (Oxford: Phaidon Press Ltd, 2006).
Cotton, J., 'A Miniature Chalk Head from the Thames at Battersea and the "Cult of the Head" in Roman London' in J. Bird, M. Hassall and H. Sheldon (eds.), *Interpreting Roman London: Papers in Memory of Hugh Chapman* (Oxford: Oxbow Books, 1996), pp. 85–96.
Cowan, R., *Roman Legionary, 58 BC –AD 69* (Oxford: Osprey Publishing, 2003a).

Cowan, R., *Imperial Roman Legionary, AD 161–284* (Oxford: Osprey Publishing, 2003b).
Cowan, R., *Roman Battle Tactics, 109 BC –AD 313* (Oxford: Osprey Publishing, 2007).
Cunliffe, B., *Greeks, Romans and Barbarians: Spheres of Interaction* (London: Batsford Ltd, 1988).
Cunliffe, B., *Britain Begins* (Oxford: Oxford University Press, 2013).
D'Amato, R. and Sumner, G., *Arms and Armour of the Imperial Roman Soldier* (Barnsley: Frontline Books, 2009).
D'Amato, R., *Imperial Roman Naval Forces 31 BC–AD 500* (Oxford: Osprey Publishing, 2009).
D'Amato, R., *Roman Army Units in the Western Provinces (1)* (Oxford: Osprey Publishing, 2016).
D'Amato, R., *Roman Heavy Cavalry (1)* (Oxford: Osprey Publishing, 2018).
Davies, M., 'The Evidence of Settlement at Plaxtol in the Late Iron Age and Romano-British Periods', *Archaeologia Cantiana*, Vol. 129 (2009), pp. 257–278.
Dorey, T.A., 'Agricola and Domitian', *Greece & Rome*, Vol. 7, No. 1 (1960), (Cambridge: Cambridge University Press).
Elliott, P., *Legions in Crisis* (Stroud: Fonthill Media Ltd, 2014).
Elliott, S., *Sea Eagles of Empire: The Classis Britannica and the Battles for Britain* (Stroud: The History Press, 2016).
Elliott, S., *Empire State: How the Roman Military Built an Empire* (Oxford: Oxbow Books, 2017).
Elliott, S., *Septimius Severus in Scotland: The Northern Campaigns of the First Hammer of the Scots* (Barnsley: Greenhill Books, 2018a).
Elliott, S., *Roman Legionaries* (Oxford: Casemate Publishers, 2018b).
Elliott, S., 'Clash of the Titans: The Battle of Lugdunum, AD 197', *Ancient Warfare*, Vol. 13, No. 3 (2020), pp. 27–35.
Ellis Jones, J., *The Maritime Landscape of Roman Britain* (Oxford: BAR/Archaeological and Historical Associates Ltd, 2012).
Erdkamp, P. (ed.), *The Cambridge Companion to Ancient Rome* (Cambridge: Cambridge University Press, 2013).
Fernández-Götz, M. and Roymans, N., *Archaeology of the Roman Conquest* (Cambridge: Cambridge University Press, 2024).
Fields, N., 'Headhunters of the Roman Army', *Minerva* (Nov/Dec 2006), pp. 9–12.
Frere, S., *Britannia: A History of Roman Britain* (3rd edn.) (London: Routledge, 1974).
Frere, S., 'M. Maenius Agrippa, the Expeditio Britannica and Maryport', *Britannia*, Vol. 31 (2000), pp. 23–28.
Gaffney, V., Fitch, S. and Smith, D., *Europe's Lost World: The Rediscovery of Doggerland* (York: Council for British Archaeology, 2009).
Garrison, E.G., *History of Engineering and Technology: Artful Methods* (Boca Raton, Florida: CRC Press, 1998).
Goldsworthy, A., *Roman Warfare* (London: Cassell, 2000).
Goldsworthy, A., *The Complete Roman Army* (London: Thames & Hudson, 2003).
Graafstaal, E., 'What Happened in the Summer of AD 122: Hadrian on the British Frontier – Archaeology, Epigraphy and Historical Agency', *Britannia*, Vol. 48, pp. 76–111.
Grainge, G., *The Roman Invasions of Britain* (Stroud: Tempus, 2005).
Hingley, R., 'Roman Britain: The structure of Roman imperialism and the consequences of imperialism on the development of a peripheral province' in D. Miles, (ed.), *The Romano-British Countryside: Studies in Rural Settlement and Economy* (Oxford: BAR/Archaeological and Historical Associates Ltd, 1982), pp. 17–52.
Haywood, J., *The Historical Atlas of the Celtic World* (London: Thames & Hudson, 2009).

Hingley, R., *Globalizing Roman Culture – Unity, Diversity and Empire* (London: Routledge, 2005).
Hingley, R., *Londinium: A Biography* (London: Bloomsbury Academic, 2018).
Holder, P., 'Auxiliary Deployment in the Reign of Hadrian' in J.J. Wilkes (ed.), *Documenting the Roman Army: Essays in Honour of Margaret Roxan*, Bulletin of the Institute of Classical studies Supplements (London, 2003), pp. 101–146.
Holland, T., *Dominion* (London: Little, Brown, 2019).
Hornblower, S. and Spawforth, A., *The Oxford Classical Dictionary* (Oxford: Oxford University Press, 1996).
James, S., *Rome and the Sword* (London: Thames & Hudson, 2011).
Jones, B. and Mattingly, D., *An Atlas of Roman Britain* (Oxford: Oxbow Books, 1990).
Jones, R., *Roman Camps in Scotland* (Edinburgh: Society of Antiquaries Scotland, 2013).
Kamm, A., *The Last Frontier: The Roman Invasions of Scotland* (Glasgow: Tempus, 2011).
Kaye, S., 2015, 'The Roman Invasion of Britain AD 43: Riverine, Wading and Tidal Studies Place Limits on the Location of the Two-Day River Battle and Beachead', *Archaeologia Cantiana*, Vol. 136, pp. 227–240.
Kean, R.M. and Frey, O., *The Complete Chronicle of the Emperors of Rome* (Ludlow: Thalamus Publishing, 2005).
Keppie, L., *The Making of the Roman Army, from Republic to Empire* (London: Batsford, 1984).
Keppie, L., 'The Fate of the Ninth Legion: A Problem for the Eastern Provinces?' in L. Keppie (ed.), *Legions and Veterans: Roman Army Papers 1971–2000* (Stuttgart: Franz Steiner Verlag Wiesbaden GmbH, 2000), p. 247.
Keppie, L., *The Legacy of Rome: Scotland's Roman Remains* (Edinburgh: Berlin, 2015).
Kiley, K.F., *The Uniforms of the Roman World* (Wigston: Lorenz Books, 2012).
Knüsel, C.J. and Carr, G.C., 'On the significance of the crania from the river Thames and its tributaries', *Antiquity*, Vol. 69 (1995), pp. 162–169.
Kolb, A., 'The Cursus Publicus' in C. Adams and R. Laurence (eds.), *Travel and Geography in the Roman Empire* (London: Routledge, 2001), pp. 95–106.
Kulikowski, M., *Imperial Triumph: The Roman World from Hadrian to Constantine* (London: Profile Books, 2016).
Lambert, M., *Christians and Pagans* (New Haven: Yale University Press, 2010).
Le Bohec, Y., *The Imperial Roman Army* (London: Routledge, 2000).
McWhirr, A. and Viner, D., 'The Production and Distribution of Tiles in Roman Britain with Particular Reference to the Cirencester Region', *Britannia*, Vol. 9 (1978), pp. 359–377.
Manley, J., *AD 43: The Roman Invasion of Britain* (Stroud: Tempus, 2002).
Marsh, G. and West, B., 'Skullduggery in Roman London', *Transactions of the London and Middlesex Archaeological Society*, Vol. 32 (1981), pp. 86–102.
Mason, D.J.P., *Roman Chester* (Stroud: The History Press, 2001).
Mason, D.J.P., *Roman Britain and the Roman Navy* (Stroud: The History Press, 2003).
Mattingly, D., *An Imperial Possession, Britain in the Roman Empire* (London: Penguin, 2006).
Mattingly, D., *Imperialism, Power and Identity: Experiencing the Roman Empire* (Princeton: Princeton University Press, 2011).
Matyszak, P., *Roman Conquests: Macedonia and Greece* (Barnsley: Pen & Sword, 2009).
Merrifield, R., *The Roman City of London* (London, Ernest Benn, 1965).
Millett, M., *The Romanization of Britain* (Cambridge: Cambridge University Press, 1990a).
Millett, M., *Roman Britain* (London: Batsford, 1995).
Milne, G. and Richardson, B., 'Ships and Barges' in G. Milne (ed.), *The Port of Roman London* (London: B.T. Batsford, 1985), pp. 96–102.

Moffat, B., 'A Marvellous Plant: The Place of the Heath Pea in Scottish Botanical Tradition', *Folio*, Issue 1 (2000), pp 13–15.
Moody, G., *The Isle of Thanet: From Prehistory to the Norman Conquest* (Stroud: Tempus, 2008).
Moorhead, S. and Stuttard, D., *The Romans Who Shaped Britain* (London: Thames & Hudson, 2012).
Myers, S.D., 'The River Walbrook and Roman London', PhD thesis (Unpublished: University of Reading, 2016).
Oleson, J.P., *The Oxford Handbook of Engineering and Technology in the Classical World* (Oxford: Oxford University Press, 2009).
Oman, C., *England Before the Norman Conquest* (London: Methuen, 1938).
Ottaway, P., *Roman Yorkshire* (Pickering: Blackthorn Press, 2013).
Oosthuizen, S., *The Emergence of the English* (Leeds: ARC Humanities Press, 2019).
Parfitt, K., 'Folkestone during the Roman Period', in I. Coulson (ed.), *Folkestone to 1500: A Town Unearthed* (Canterbury: Canterbury Archaeological Trust, 2013), pp. 31–54.
Parker, A., *The Archaeology of Roman York* (Stroud: Amberley Books, 2019).
Parker, P., *The Empire Stops Here* (London: Jonathan Cape, 2009).
Pausche, D., 'Unreliable narration in the *Historia Augusta*', *Ancient Narrative*, Vol. 8 (2010), pp. 115–135.
Perring, D., 'London's Hadrianic War', *Britannia*, Vol. 41, pp. 127–147.
Pitassi, M., *The Roman Navy* (Barnsley: Seaforth, 2012).
Pollard, N. and Berry, J., *The Complete Roman Legions* (London: Thames & Hudson, 2012).
Potter, D., *Rome in the Ancient World: From Romulus to Justinian* (London: Thames & Hudson, 2009).
Redfern, R. and Bonney, H., 'Headhunting and amphitheatre combat in Roman London, England: new evidence from the Walbrook valley', *Journal of Archaeological Science*, No. 43 (2014), pp. 214–226.
Reid, R., 'Bullets, Ballistas and Burnswark: A Roman Assault on a Hillfort in Scotland', *Current Archaeology*, Issue 316, Vol. 27 (2016), pp. 20–26.
Rodgers, N. and Dodge, H., *The History and Conquests of Ancient Rome* (London: Hermes House, 2009).
Ross, S. and Ross, C., 'Recent Roman Discoveries during the A1 Upgrade in North Yorkshire', *Current Archaeology*, Issue 359, Vol. 30 (2020), pp. 18–22.
Rowsome, P., 'Mapping Roman London: Identifying its Urban Patterns and Interpreting Their Meaning' in J. Clark, J. Cotton, J. Hall, R. Sherris and H. Swain (eds.), *Londinium and Beyond: Essays on Roman London and its Hinterland for Harvey Sheldon*, Council for British Archaeology Research Report, Vol. 156 (York, 2008), pp. 25–32.
Russell, M., 'What Happened to Britain's Lost Roman Legion?', *BBC History Magazine* (May 2011), pp. 40–45.
Salway, P., *Roman Britain* (Oxford: Oxford University Press, 1981).
Scarre, C., *The Penguin Historical Atlas of Ancient Rome* (London: Penguin, 1995).
Scarre, C., *Chronicle of the Roman Emperors* (London: Thames & Hudson, 1995).
Sinnigen, W.G., 'Two Branches of the Late Roman Secret Service', *The American Journal of Philology*, Vol. 80.3 (1959), pp. 238–254.
Southern, P., *Roman Britain* (Stroud: Amberley Publishing, 2013).
Southern, P., *Hadrian's Wall: Everyday Life on a Roman Frontier* (Stroud: Amberley Publishing, 2016).
Starr, C.G., *The Roman Imperial Navy 31 BC–AD 324* (New York: Cornell University Press, 1941).

Tibbs, A., *Beyond the Empire* (Marlborough: Hale, 2019).
Todd, M., *Roman Britain 55 BC–AD 400: The Province Beyond the Ocean* (Glasgow: Fontana Press, 1981).
Tomlin, R.S.O., *Roman London's First Voices* (London: Museum of London Archaeology, 2016).
Turney, S., *Agricola: Architect of Roman Britain* (Stroud: Amberley Publishing, 2022).
Wallace-Hadrill, A. (ed.), *Patronage in the Ancient World* (Routledge: London, 1989).
Watson, G.R., *The Roman Soldier: Aspects of Greek and Roman Life* (Ithaca, New York: Cornell University Press, 1969).
Weber, W., *Untersuchungen zur Geschichte des Kaisers Hadrianus* (Leipzig: B.G. Teubner, 1907).
Wheeler, R.E.M., *London: Volume 3: Roman London* (London: Royal Commission on Historical Monuments of England, 1928).
Wilcox, P., *Rome's Enemies (3): Parthians and Sassanid Persians* (Oxford: Osprey Publishing, 1986).
Wilkes, J.J., 2005, 'Provinces and Frontiers' in A.K. Bowman, P. Garnsey and A. Cameron (eds.), *The Cambridge Ancient History, Vol. XII, The Crisis of Empire, AD 193–33* (Cambridge: Cambridge University Press, 2005), pp. 212–268.
Windrow, M. and McBride, A., *Imperial Rome at War* (Hong Kong: Concord Publications, 1996).
Wolff, C., 'Units: Principate' in Y. le Bohec (ed.), *The Encyclopedia of the Roman Army Vol. 3* (Hoboken, New Jersey: Wiley-Blackwell, 2015), pp. 1037–1049.

Index

Africa Proconsularis, 83, 85, 168, 174–5
Agricola, Gnaeus Julius, xi, xiv, 2, 25, 36, 97, 120–1
   birth, 65
   marriage, 80
   death, 176
Alba Longa, 2, 62
Alban Hills, 16, 62, 165
Antonine Wall, 38, 117, 124, 130
Antoninus Pius, 117
Antony, Mark, 12, 18
Apennine Mountains, 3, 4, 13
aquila, 23, 90, 173
aquilifer, 23, 27, 46
Atrebates, 37, 47, 53, 54, 80
Auchinhove, 125, 149–50
Augustus, xiv, xvii, 18–20, 24, 28, 30, 47, 62–3, 97, 165, 167
Auxilia, xvii, 21, 28–30, 33–4, 40, 50–1, 54, 56, 59, 70, 75–7, 87–9, 93–4, 95, 148–9, 156

Balearic Islands, 8
Bay of Naples, 13, 63, 127
Binchester, 110
Bolanus, Marcus Vettius, 93, 95–7, 99–100, 124
Boudicca, xi, xii, 40, 60, 61, 70–6, 78, 96, 99, 100, 106–108, 154, 157
Brigantes, xii–xiii, 37, 53, 56–7, 97, 99, 101–102, 107, 110, 113–14, 118, 128, 137, 154
Britannia, xii, xv, 20, 36, 43, 47, 54, 58, 69–70, 80, 105–106, 109, 115, 130, 132, 135, 147, 161, 167, 168, 180
Broch, 114–15

Caerleon, 80, 103, 163
Caesar, Gaius Julius, xii, 1, 12, 15–18, 28–9, 35–7, 40–1, 44–8, 54, 62–3, 122, 157
Caledonii, 29, 38–42, 118, 141, 144, 148, 152
Calgacus, xii–xiii, 151–3, 155, 157–9
Camulodunum, 40, 52–3, 75
Caracalla, xvi
Caratacus, 47, 49, 52, 56–8
Carrhae, Battle of, 17
Carthage, 7–10, 30
Cartimandua, 57–8, 99, 102
Catuvellauni, 37, 40, 47, 49, 52, 57, 73
Centurion, 23, 25, 27, 29, 33, 57, 70, 77, 90, 129, 145
Cerialis, Quintus Petillius, xiii, 72, 93, 100–103, 107–109, 111, 114, 127, 139
Chester, 80, 101–103, 132, 139–40, 143, 163, 169–70
Cimbrian Wars, 10–12, 14, 22
cives Romani, xvi
civitas capital, xv, 54, 78, 110
Clades Variana, 93
Classis Britannica, xvii, 30–3, 101, 103, 106, 121, 125, 128, 131–2, 134, 139, 143–6, 148, 161–3, 170
Classis Misenensis, 31, 63, 84
Claudian invasion, 40, 47
Claudius, xii, 31, 35–6, 47–8, 52, 57, 59, 71, 80
Cohort, xv, 11, 22–3, 28–30, 85, 145, 158–9, 174
coloniae, xv
Column of Marcus Aurelius, 26
Commodus, 38, 118
constitutio Antoniniana, xvi

Index

Corieltauvi, 38, 53, 80
Corsica, 8
Crannog, 115, 137
Crassus, Marcus Licinius, 12, 17
Crisis of the Third Century, xiv, 19
Cunobelinus, 47
cursus honorum, xi, xiv, 68–9, 80, 97, 104

Dacia, 116, 172–4
Danube, river, 20, 87, 98, 169, 172–3, 177
Decidiana, Domitia, xii, 80
Dee, river, 56, 59, 80, 94, 101–102, 139
Denmark, 10, 44
Dere Street, 110–12
dilectus, 23
Diocletian, xiv
Dominate, xiv
Domitian, xiii, 19, 91–2, 113, 138–41, 147, 152, 162, 164–9, 171–80
Dumfries and Galloway, 115, 132–5
Dumnonii, 37–8, 42, 53–4, 118, 128, 141
Dundee, 145

Egypt, 9, 17
equites, 21, 29, 158–9
Etruria, 3, 5–6, 165

Firth of Forth, 110
Flavian dynasty, 19, 91, 101, 113, 176, 179
Fort, xii, xv, 26, 33, 40, 43, 48, 53–6, 58–9, 72, 79, 101–103, 106, 108, 110–11, 114, 122, 125–6, 129, 131, 133, 137, 139, 141–4, 155, 163–4, 168–9
Fortlet, xv
Fortress, xv, 22, 43, 53–4, 58, 94, 98–9, 101–103, 106, 111, 125, 139–40, 162–4, 169, 173
Forum Julii, 61, 63–5, 91, 134
Frontinus, Sextus Julius, 93, 102–103, 108, 127, 139–40

Galba, Servius Suplicius, 81, 83–6, 88, 95
Gallia Narbonensis, 63, 104
gladius Hispaniensis, 24
Glenblocker forts, 125, 141–4, 163, 169
Graecinus, Lucius Julius, 61, 64–6

Graecinus, Marcus Julius, 64–5
Governor, xi–xv, 19–20, 32, 35, 47, 52, 55–60, 69, 72, 74, 79, 81, 83–5, 88–9, 91–3, 95–6, 98–107, 113, 117, 133–4, 138–40, 142, 147, 160–2, 164, 168–72, 175, 177, 181
Greece, 8, 14, 17–18, 20
Guerrilla warfare, xvii, 42, 57, 119

Hadrian, xii, 12, 111, 180
Hadrian's Wall, 111, 124
Highland line, 42–3, 115–16, 124–6, 131, 140–2, 144, 148–9, 170
Hill fort, 40, 54, 114, 133, 137, 144

Iceni, 38, 53–5, 60, 70, 72–4, 78, 80, 154
Imaginifer, 23
Inchtuthil, 125, 131, 163, 169
Ireland, xiii, 38, 43, 115, 132, 135–40, 163, 180–1

Julii, 61–3
Julio-Claudian dynasty, xii–xiii, 1–2, 18, 62, 81, 83–4, 168, 178

Lancaster, 101
lancea, 30, 77, 158
Latin League, 3–6
Lanterne d'Auguste, 64
legate, 11, 23, 48, 53, 72, 85, 97, 104, 162, 173
legati Augusti pro praetor, xv
legio II *Adiutrix*, 89, 92, 101, 103, 110, 121, 139, 148, 169, 173
legio II *Augusta*, 48, 53, 58, 69, 73–4, 96, 99, 103, 110, 121, 148
legio III *Augusta*, 83
legio IV *Gemina*, 95, 177
legio VII *Gemina Galbiana*, 88–90
legio IX *Hispana*, 48, 53, 58, 72–3, 78, 94, 99–101, 110, 121, 142, 148, 162
legio XIII *Gemina*, 17, 88
legio XIV *Gemina*, 48, 53, 56, 58–9, 72, 79, 96, 99, 101
legio XX *Valeria Victrix*, xiii, 48, 53, 56, 58–9, 72, 91–5, 97–8, 100–101, 105, 107, 110, 121, 125, 139, 148, 163, 169

Legion, xi, xv, 5, 7–9, 11–15, 18, 21–4, 26, 28–9, 45–6, 48, 51, 53–4, 56, 58, 69–70, 72–3, 78, 83, 85, 88–9, 92–102, 104, 106–107, 110, 119, 121, 132, 135, 140, 142–3, 148, 153, 155–7, 169, 172–3, 176–7, 180
Legionary, xv, xvii, 5, 7, 15, 21–6, 28–30, 40, 45–6, 48, 51, 53–4, 56–9, 63, 70, 72–8, 84, 87–90, 94, 97–8, 101–103, 106–107, 112, 121, 125, 127, 130–1, 139–41, 143–4, 148–50, 156–7, 159, 162–4, 169, 173–4
limes, 20, 166
London, 72–4, 79, 106, 108
lorica hamata, 26, 29–30
lorica segmentata, 21, 26–7
lorica squamata, 27, 30

Maeatae, 38–9, 116–19
Magna Graecia, 3
Marching camps, 24, 27, 48, 52, 57, 73, 76, 79, 90, 113, 121–6, 128, 131, 140–2, 144, 149–50, 159, 163, 169
Marcus Aurelius, 26
Marius, Gaius, 1, 10–16, 22, 28, 69
Marseille, 44, 63, 134
Medway, river, 30, 49–51
milliary alae, 29
Miseno, 63
Mons Graupius, Battle of, xii–xiv, 29, 40, 42, 132, 147–51, 161, 164
Moray Firth, 38, 118, 124–6, 144, 148–9, 152, 161, 169
muli mariani, 28
municipia, xv, 79

Narbonne, 63
Nero, 1, 18, 59, 61, 70–1, 78–86, 88, 93, 95, 166, 172, 178–9
Newstead, 26, 126, 129, 131
North Africa, 3, 8–10, 17, 20, 82, 85, 116
Numidia, 8, 11

oppida, 40, 53, 56, 144
optimates, 13–15, 17
Otho, Marcus Salvius, 80, 85–8, 91, 95–6

Pannonia, 20, 47, 87, 94, 98, 172, 174, 177
Parthia, 17, 21, 96
Paulinus, Suetonius, xi–xii, 59, 69–70, 72–80, 103, 106–108, 133, 157
peregrini, xvi, 28
pilum, 24
Plautius, Aulus, 30, 47–54, 72, 98, 157
populares, 13, 15, 17
Pompeii, 13, 127
Pompey, Gnaeus, 12, 15–17
praefectus alae, 29
praefectus castrorum, 23, 57, 73
praefectus classis, 31–2, 89, 162
praefectus praetorio, 82, 84
praefectus urbi, 178
Praetorian Guard, 20, 85, 87, 173, 178
Prasutagus, 70
primus pilus, 23
Princeps, xiv, 18, 23, 178
Principate, xiv, xvi–xvii, 1, 18–19, 21–7, 29, 31, 33, 38, 40
Procilla, Julia, 61, 67, 86
Procurator, xv, 19, 32, 61, 64, 71, 73, 78, 104–105
Publius Cornelius Scipio Africanus, 8
Pyrrhus of Epirus, 7, 22, 121

quingenary alae, 29

Ravenglass, 101
Regional fleets, xvii, 21, 30–4, 54, 59, 63, 79, 84, 89, 101, 103, 162
Rhine, river, 20, 31, 33, 50, 85, 93, 98, 100, 145, 158, 166, 172–3, 177
Rochester, 50
Rome, xii, 1–18, 22, 24, 26–7, 35, 37–8, 43, 45–7, 50, 52–9, 61–2, 65, 67–8, 72, 79–93, 95, 97, 99–100, 102–106, 108, 115, 117, 119, 129–30, 137, 139, 141, 147, 152–3, 164–5, 167, 169, 171–3, 175, 177–80

Sarmatians, 172
Scotland, xii, 38, 42, 44, 56, 102, 110, 114–17, 121–4, 128, 132, 136–7, 143, 146, 149, 162–3, 180

Scottish Borders, 26, 38, 43, 99, 112–13, 116–18, 124, 126, 128, 131–2, 141, 164, 180
scutum, 21, 25
Seleucid-Roman War, 8
Selgovae, 38, 118, 128, 141
Septimius Severus, xi, 42, 116–17, 119, 124, 128, 149
Severan Dynasty, xiv, 19
Sicily, 3, 7–9
Silures, 37, 52, 56–9, 103
Solway Firth, 100, 108, 111, 130, 132–3, 170, 180
St Albans, xv, 72, 74
Stanegate, 111, 114, 128, 130, 163
Sulla, Lucius Cornelius, 15

Tacitus, Publius Cornelius, xi–xiii, 28–9, 31, 41, 57–8, 60–1, 63–6, 68–71, 73, 75, 77–8, 80–1, 84, 86, 88, 91–2, 94–7, 100–103, 105–10, 118, 121, 127–33, 135–6, 138, 141–8, 150–3, 155–68, 170–2, 174–6, 178, 180–1
Tay, river, 38, 118, 126–8, 131, 150, 161, 163–4
Teutoburg Forest, 18, 70, 94, 153
Tiber, river, 2–4, 91
Titus, xiii, 78, 92, 113, 117, 127, 129–30, 132, 138–9, 165, 169

Trajan, 26, 116, 177, 179
Trajan's Column, 26–7
tribunus angusticlavia, 23, 106
tribunus laticlavius, 23

Vacomagi, 38, 118, 141, 144, 148, 152
Varus, Publius Quinctilius, 18, 22, 70, 94, 153, 156, 172
Venicones, 38, 118, 128, 141
Venutius, 58, 99–102
Vespasian, xiii, 19, 42, 47, 53–4, 59, 78, 88–9, 91–3, 96–7, 100, 102–105, 109, 113, 117, 127, 133, 138–9, 165–6, 169, 172, 177
Vexillation fort, xv, 26, 30, 53–6, 58, 72, 89, 99, 102–103, 110–11, 121, 139, 173
Via Domitia, 63
Via Julia Augusta, 63, 91
Vindolanda, 110–11
Vitellius, Aulus, 85, 87–91, 95–6
Votadini, 38, 118, 128, 141

Watling Street, 72–5, 78, 80, 106–107, 157

Year of the Five Emperors, 19
Year of the Four Emperors, xii, 19, 23, 61, 81–2, 91, 94–5, 100
York, 44, 101, 109–12, 117, 142, 162–4

Dear Reader,

We hope you have enjoyed this book, but why not share your views on social media? You can also follow our pages to see more about our other products: facebook.com/penandswordbooks or follow us on X @penswordbooks

You can also view our products at www.pen-and-sword.co.uk (UK and ROW) or www.penandswordbooks.com (North America).

To keep up to date with our latest releases and online catalogues, please sign up to our newsletter at: www.pen-and-sword.co.uk/newsletter

If you would like a printed catalogue with our latest books, then please email: enquiries@pen-and-sword.co.uk or telephone: 01226 734555 (UK and ROW) or email: uspen-and-sword@casematepublishers.com or telephone: (610) 853-9131 (North America).

We respect your privacy and we will only use personal information to send you information about our products.

Thank you!